The
EVERYTHING
Craps Strategy Book

Dear Reader:

Back in 1992 my wife Andrea and I were stuck in a Reno hotel during a huge snowstorm. We were there for a nongambling convention and the roads were closed, so we couldn't leave. We went walking around and noticed a gal who put her credit card in a slot machine. I knew we would never do that, and we struck up a conversation with this older woman.

She informed us this wasn't a credit card, but a player's card, and we could get free rooms, free food, and free shows ("comps") with it. She then told us more about comps than we ever wanted to know. Afterward, Andrea and I both signed up for our first players cards, and a germ of an idea entered my mind. What if we could find a casino game with a 50-50 chance of winning, and then make money just on the comps?

We did find such a game in craps. Not only is the casino edge only 1 percent or so on some bets, but it is a really fun game to play as well! So, we started playing and then started the *Crapshooter Newsletter,* which is still being published today. It has always been our belief that the low edge, plus comps, can make craps a profitable and fun game for anyone to play and win on a consistent basis.

This book is a direct result of fifteen years of research and play at the craps tables of the world. We won't guarantee that you'll win every time you play, but at least you'll understand why you lost. This way you can turn the game of craps into a game of learning, and learn something new each time you play. And when you add in comps, friendly people, and most of all, fun, you get a perfect indoor "sport" that you can play in any casino in the world!

And, as always, good luck at the tables!

Larry Edell

The EVERYTHING® Series

Editorial

Publishing Director	Gary M. Krebs
Associate Managing Editor	Laura M. Daly
Associate Copy Chief	Brett Palana-Shanahan
Acquisitions Editor	Gina Chaimanis
Development Editors	Karen Johnson Jacot Jessica LaPointe
Associate Production Editor	Casey Ebert

Production

Director of Manufacturing	Susan Beale
Associate Director of Production	Michelle Roy Kelly
Cover Design	Paul Beatrice Erick DaCosta Matt LeBlanc
Design and Layout	Colleen Cunningham Holly Curtis Sorae Lee
Series Cover Artist	Barry Littmann

Visit the entire Everything® Series at *www.everything.com*

THE
EVERYTHING®
CRAPS
STRATEGY
BOOK

Win big every time!

Larry Edell

Adams Media
Avon, Massachusetts

To my wife Andrea, the best friend I ever had!

An Everything® Series Book.
Everything® and everything.com® are registered trademarks of F+W Publications, Inc.

Published by Adams Media, an F+W Publications Company
57 Littlefield Street, Avon, MA 02322 U.S.A.
www.adamsmedia.com

ISBN: 1-59337-435-6
Printed in the United States of America.

J   I   H   G   F   E   D   C   B   A

Library of Congress Cataloging-in-Publication Data
Edell, Larry.
The everything craps strategy book : win big every time! / Larry Edell.
    p.   cm. — (The Everything series)
ISBN 1-59337-435-6
1. Craps (Game) 2. Dice games. I. Title. II. Series.
GV1303.E44 2005
795.1'2—dc22
2005026452

This publication is designed to provide accurate and authoritative information with regard to the subject matter covered. It is sold with the understanding that the publisher is not engaged in rendering legal, accounting, or other professional advice. If legal advice or other expert assistance is required, the services of a competent professional person should be sought.

—From a *Declaration of Principles* jointly adopted by a Committee of the American Bar Association and a Committee of Publishers and Associations

Many of the designations used by manufacturers and sellers to distinguish their products are claimed as trademarks. Where those designations appear in this book and Adams Media was aware of a trademark claim, the designations have been printed with initial capital letters.

This book is available at quantity discounts for bulk purchases.
For information, please call 1-800-872-5627.

Contents

Progression Methods: Increasing Your Bets on Wins / 123

Combination Systems / 135

Other Methods and Systems / 145

Things You Need to Know / 155

Craps Stats: Calculating the Edges / 165

Dice Control: The Set, Grip, and Throw / 177

Acknowledgments

This book could not have been completed if it were not for the assistance and understanding of my agent, editor, helpmate, and wife, Andrea Foote. The people at Adams Media had something to do with it also, especially Gina. And finally I'd like to thank my Mom and Dad, who are hopefully looking down upon us and smiling, thinking that their renegade son finally got something right.

Top Ten Ways to
Win More at Craps!

1. Have a definite win goal and loss limit.

2. Make bets with less than a 2 percent casino edge.

3. Maximize your comps.

4. Minimize your flat bets and take maximum odds.

5. Always "push the house" whenever possible.

6. Qualify your shooters and chart your tables.

7. Choose the best casino, table, and shooter for your needs.

8. Keep a notebook detailing your wins, losses, and thoughts.

9. Tip the dealers and call them by name.

10. Have fun, talk to the other players, and make some friends!

Introduction

▶ When you walk into your favorite casino and hear lots of enthusiastic yelling, just follow those sounds and chances are, you'll end up at a craps table. Craps is a people game, with a great deal of player participation and interaction.

If you've ever watched a craps game, you may have smiled at the enthusiasm of the players but when you looked down at the craps table you were stumped. Where are the instructions? How do you play this strange game anyway? Well, this book will teach you how the game is played—and a lot more!

There are many ways you personally can influence this game, like becoming the shooter, garnering comps, or even learning how to control the dice. There are many methods you can learn, not only to play this game, but to win.

Even if you don't play every time you go to a casino, you'll know what the craps players are talking about. When you pass a table and someone yells "Yo!" or "Dollar any," you'll just smile, because you'll know as much, and probably more, than they do. If you do play, you'll be knowledgeable enough to make the best bets at the right time, and most important, have fun. Having fun is what craps is all about!

Chapter 1

The Basics: What Craps Is All About

Okay, go ahead and admit it. You've always wanted to be part of that raucous and rowdy crowd gathered round the craps table. Trouble was, everything looked so fast and complicated. The speed of the bets, all the yelling, and the strange language just made it too intimidating, so you've never played. Now you can learn everything you always wanted to know about craps—and you'll have fun, because craps is a very friendly game!

Why You Should Play Craps

Craps is suddenly enjoying a newfound popularity in casinos due to a number of different factors—the main one being the crackdown on blackjack professionals.

A lot of gamblers are now turning to the craps tables, and finding that their wins there, plus the easy availability of comps, make craps the perfect game to play. Here are some reasons why craps should be *your* best play.

The player controls the game. You can ask for the same (or different) dice, set them in any way you want to before shooting, bargain with the dealers for better odds than advertised, ask for the table limit to be suspended, and make unadvertised bets. Where else can you have this much fun?

Many of the bets have a low casino edge of under 2 percent. Some of the more popular bets are pass line with maximum odds, don't pass with maximum odds, come bet with maximum odds, and don't come bet with maximum odds. If you play at a 100× odds table, the casino advantage here is only .02 percent or less. Where can you find a better deal than that?

QUESTION?

Where did the game of craps come from? Why is it called craps?
Dice games were started by the ancient Greeks over 2,000 years ago, as a fortunetelling method. Eventually they evolved into a parlor game called Hazard, which was brought to the United States from France in the early 1800s. The twos, threes, and twelves were called "crabs," but in New Orleans (where it first became commercial) people started calling the new game craps.

You can increase your money by 900 percent in just two rolls. Try it—bet just one lowly dollar on the two or twelve. If it wins you get $30. Let the $30 ride and if it wins you get $900. You've turned $1 into $900 in less than a minute. Sure, it's highly unlikely. But where else do you even have a chance of winning this kind of money in such a short amount of time?

You can make money just by riding along with a good shooter. Look for someone who makes small $5 bets while other people are shooting, but increases his bets to $25 (or more) when he is the shooter. Maybe he has a craps table at home and practices, or maybe he is a psychic, who knows. But when he bets, you should bet the same way he does. When he wins, you will also. Where else can you make money using someone else's talents?

You get a lot of comps playing craps. Buy in with a large amount and make a big first bet. Also, play at a casino that gives you credit for your spread instead of your individual bets. You can end up with a free room, a free show, and free meals. Where else can you get so much free stuff?

There are long, profitable streaks in craps. A shooter can hold the dice for an hour, and everyone at the table cleans up. Once you learn how to recognize these streaks by charting the tables, you can hang on and be betting black chips before you know it. Where else can you get this mix of pure excitement plus constantly increasing profits?

Craps is a people game, too. You can talk to the gamblers next to you, and the dealers as well. Ask them how the table is going. Talk to everyone. Ask if they're good shooters. Try to notice if there are any don't bettors and how they're doing, especially if you're a don't bettor yourself. Where else can you make friends and money at the same time?

Craps is a wonderful, exciting, profitable game for any casinogoer. Are you are tired of the hassles and changing rules at the blackjack tables? Are you tired of getting no profits and no comps at roulette? Maybe you should give craps a try. It gives you real player control, the possibility of very high profits, a very low casino edge, the ability to ride along with someone else's skills, lots of comps, occasional long money-making streaks, and the ability to determine how the table is going by talking to the other players. Where else can you find a better game than that?

Overview

A game of craps is played with a pair of identical dice. The opposing faces of each die always add up to 7. For example, the 1 is always opposite the 6, the 2 opposite the 5, and the 3 is opposite the 4. And that's it—there are only three combinations totaling 7 on each die.

FACT

The opposing numbers on a set of dice are called "sister numbers," so the 5 (2 on one die, 3 on the other) is a sister number to the 9 (5 on one die, 4 on the other). The 6 and 8 are also sister numbers, as are the 4 and 10.

There are six numbers on each die (1–6), so a pair of dice will give you thirty-six different combinations. The game of craps is based on how often these different combinations appear when someone rolls the dice. **TABLE 1.1** is a diagram of all thirty-six dice combinations.

TABLE 1.1	36 Dice Combinations	
Number	**Combinations**	**Ways to Make**
2	1 + 1	1
3	2 + 1, 1 + 2	2
4	3 + 1, 1 + 3, 2 + 2	3
5	4 + 1, 1 + 4, 3 + 2, 2 + 3	4
6	5 + 1, 1 + 5, 4 + 2, 2 + 4, 3 + 3	5
7	6 + 1, 1 + 6, 5 + 2, 2 + 5, 4 + 3, 3 + 4	6
8	6 + 2, 2 + 6, 3 + 5, 5 + 3, 4 + 4	5
9	6 + 3, 3 + 6, 5 + 4, 4 + 5	4
10	6 + 4, 4 + 6, 5 + 5	3
11	6 + 5, 5 + 6	2
12	6 + 6	1

As you can see, in thirty-six possible combinations, the 7 will appear the most—six times. The 6 and 8 will appear five times each, and the 5 or 9 will appear four times each.

The game of craps is based on the most popular number, 7, and how the other numbers compare to it. For example if a 7 rolls six times (out of thirty-six rolls) and the 6 rolls five times, the odds of the 6 rolling before the 7 are 6:5. In practical terms, this means that if you bet $5 on the 6, and it rolls before the 7 does, you win $6 for your $5 bet, at 6:5 odds. The actual payoffs of your bets are based on similar odds, but you don't have to memorize anything—just ask one of the friendly dealers and they will tell you what the payoff is for each bet. You are allowed to use a sheet of paper (or a card) that lists all of the odds. You can also bring a notebook to keep track of all of your rolls. You can even ask a drink person for a napkin and a dealer for a pen.

FACT

The numbers 4, 5, 6, 8, 9, and 10 are referred to as "point" numbers, because the shooter will try to make one of these particular points to win his bet. If he makes his "point," number, then everyone else who bets with him will win also.

Now let's look at the "pass line" wager—the most popular (and one of the most profitable) bets on the craps table. When a "shooter" tosses the dice, three things can roll—a "natural" (7 or 11), a "point" (4, 5, 6, 8, 9, or 10) or a "craps" (2, 3, or 12). This is all that can occur before the point is established. If the shooter rolls a 7 or 11 before the point is established, all of the pass line bettors win. If he rolls a "craps" (2, 3, or 12), all the pass line bettors lose. If he rolls a "point" number (4, 5, 6, 8, 9, or 10), he must repeat that number again before the 7 rolls in order to win.

The shooters are chosen consecutively, with the dice going around the table in a clockwise formation. If you become the shooter, you must place a bet down on either the "pass" or the "don't pass" line before shooting. When it gets to your turn and you don't want to shoot, just say "pass" and the dice will go to the person next in line. Some people really like to shoot, so if you are nervous about it, there is no disgrace in letting someone else shoot while you get used to the game.

The stickperson pushes three or four pairs of dice to the shooter, who picks up any two and tosses them to the far wall. Here is an example of how it could play out: The shooter's first number is a 7. All the players who have a bet on the pass line win their bet. Her second number is an 11, so everyone wins again. Her third number is a 2 ("craps"), so the pass line bettors lose this time, but she keeps on shooting. The shooter's fourth number is a 6, which becomes the "point." If she repeats the number 6 before the 7 rolls, the pass line bettors win, and she shoots again. However, if the 7 rolls before the 6, the pass line bettors lose and someone else becomes the shooter.

Before you shoot, you might watch some other people shoot and make their bets first. When you are used to the procedure, just wait until the dice come around again and give it a try.

FACT

The "puck" is the plastic disk the dealers use to mark the point. If the white side is up, the game is in play and the puck is on top of the point number. If the black side is up, the point is made or the game is waiting for a new point to be established.

Basic Table Layout

A craps table (**FIGURE 1.1**) may look intimidating, but it isn't once you get used to it. The dealers are always there to answer questions, and your fellow players are usually friendly and eager to help a beginner. The five main bets are the "pass" and "don't pass," "come" and "don't come," and the "place" bets. You will usually start out on the pass line, but watch how everyone bets, and be sure to ask the friendly dealers if you have any questions.

Pass Line

This is the most popular bet on the table. This wins if the come-out roll is 7 or 11 and loses if it is 2, 3, or 12. Once the point (4, 5, 6, 8, 9, or 10) is established, your wager *cannot* be removed but you can add odds to it if desired

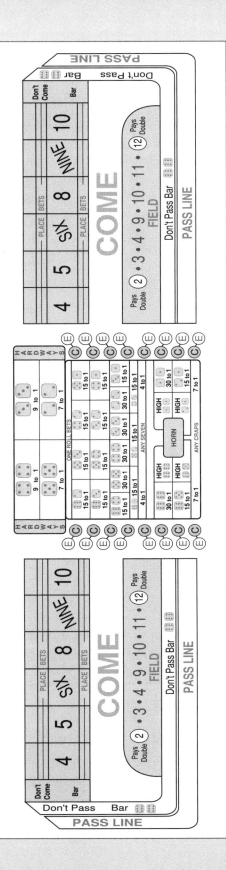

FIGURE 1.1

A typical craps table layout.

(we'll discuss "odds" at the end of this chapter). The shooter must repeat his point again before a 7 rolls for you to win your bet. If the 7 rolls before the point does, you lose your bet.

FACT

The come out roll is the roll made before any point is established. There can be one or more of these for every shooter. If the shooter then makes her point, she shoots again and has another series of one or more come out rolls.

Don't Pass Line

This is the opposite of the pass line, where you were betting that the shooter makes her point. On the don't pass line, you are betting that the shooter will lose and throw a 7 before her point rolls. The don't pass wins before the come-out on the 2 or 3 (it pushes on the 12), and it loses on the 7 or 11. Once the point is established (4, 5, 6, 8, 9, or 10) your wager *can* be removed or you can add odds to it.

Come Bet

Once the point has been established, you can make a come bet, which is similar to a pass line bet. After you put your wager in the come box and the shooter rolls, the dealer will move that bet to the corresponding box for the number rolled. You can then add odds if you desire. It wins if that particular number rolls again before the 7. If the seven rolls before that particular number, you lose.

Don't Come Bet

Once the point is established, you can make a don't come bet, which is similar to a don't pass bet. After you place your wager in the don't come box and the shooter rolls, the dealer will move your bet to the corresponding box for that number. You can then add odds if you desire. Your bet wins if the 7 rolls before that particular number and loses if the number rolls before the 7.

Place and Buy Bets

You do not play craps with money, but exchange it for chips. To do this, drop the money on the table and say, "Change only." The dealer will then give you a combination of whites ($1), reds ($5), and greens ($25). You can also ask for specific denominations, like "all reds please."

You can give money to the dealer and ask it to be placed on one or more of the displayed point numbers (4, 5, 6, 8, 9, 10). If your wager is $20 or more, you can "buy" the number(s) and get a better payoff in return for paying a small commission, or "vig." In either case, you will win if your number(s) roll before the 7 and lose if the 7 rolls before your number(s). Note that with place and buy bets, the number has to hit only once for you to win because you are placing the bet directly on that number. With pass or come bets, the number has to hit twice for you to win; the first time the number hits, it establishes the number you are betting on, and you don't win until that number rolls again. You can make a place or buy bet before or after the come-out roll.

Lay Bets

If you wager $20 or more against a number, you can "lay" it for a small commission, or vig. You will win if the 7 rolls before your number(s) and lose if your number(s) roll before the 7. You can make a lay bet before or after the come-out.

Hardway Bets

A hardway is a "doubles" bet, meaning the number you bet only pays if the dice rolled are a pair. So, you can wager on hard 4 (2 and 2), hard 6 (3 and 3), hard 8 (4 and 4), or hard 10 (5 and 5). If the 4, 6, 8, or 10 roll but the dice are not a pair (called "easy way" rolls), you lose. You also lose if the 7 rolls. For example, if you bet $1 on hard 6 and the 4 and 2 roll, you still lose; the die must roll 3 and 3 (doubles) for you to win.

Horn Bets

This area consists of wagers for the 2, 3, 11, and 12. You can bet them separately or together for several combinations of payoffs. These are one-roll bets, so if the very next roll is not what you wagered, then you lose your bet.

The Field

Although this area is very attractive, it is not a good bet because it is only for one roll. If the very next roll is 2, 3, 4, 9, 10, 11, or 12 you win; otherwise, you lose. You also lose if the 7 rolls. The combination of the 5, 6, 7, and 8 rolls more than the field numbers do.

Any Craps

This is another one-roll bet and wins if the very next roll is a 2, 3, or 12. If anything else rolls, you lose your bet.

Any 7

Another one-roll bet, this has the distinction of being the worst bet, due to its high advantage for the casino. The very next roll must be a 7 for you to win this bet.

C & E Bet

The C & E bet (craps and 11) wins only if the very next roll is a craps (2, 3, or 12) or 11.

Big 6

This bet wins if the 6 rolls before the 7 does. This is similar to a place bet on the 6, but you win less money.

Big 8

Here, the bet wins if the 8 rolls before the 7 does. Again, this is like a place bet on the 8, but you win less money.

Odds Bet

After you make a pass, don't pass, come, or don't come bet, you can add odds to it. These odds pay off higher than the bet does without odds and will be discussed later in this chapter.

QUESTION?

Do I make all the bets myself, or do I give my money to one of the dealers?
You make the pass, don't pass, come, don't come, and field bets yourself. Prop bets and hardway wagers go to the stickman. Buy, lay, come odds, and don't come odds go to one of the dealers. For security purposes, the dealers are not allowed to accept money or chips directly from your hands. Just tell the dealer or stickperson the bet you want and drop the chips on the table.

Basic Theory

Craps is a game anyone can win at any time—if you make the right bet. If the 7 hits at an inopportune time and you lose your bets, some other players may be winning theirs. You can win or lose money on every roll of the dice—you just need to know where to place your bet. Different casinos have different table minimums, so if you are just starting out, you should play at a table with a $1 minimum. These are usually found on weekday mornings. On weekends, you can expect table minimums of $10 or even $25.

As explained previously, this game revolves around the number 7. If you are a "do" bettor, the 7 wins for you before the come-out and loses after the point is established. If you are a "don't" bettor, the 7 loses for you before the come-out and wins after the point is established. Your job then, is to determine whether you play on the pass line (the "do" side) or the don't pass line (the "don't" side). You can do this in four basic ways:

- **Talk to people.** Crapshooters are a friendly lot, and your fellow players are apt to tell you everything they know about the previous shooters and bettors. If the trend is positive, try the pass line. If it's negative, try the don't pass line. If it's choppy, you can find another table, come back later, or try another casino.

- **Let the chips tell a story.** Look at everyone's chips and see how they bet. If those with the most chips bet in a certain manner, just follow their lead and bet in the same manner that they do.
- **Judge the shooters.** Look at the shooter. If she inspires confidence, bet along with her. If you don't like the shooter for any reason, just bet on the don't side.
- **Go with your hunches.** Your own intuition is usually correct. Craps is, after all, a game composed partly of luck. Sometimes your own "first impression" hunches are the best.

Once you get used to determining how to bet, you must now devise a betting method, many of which you'll learn later on in this book. Some are exclusively for the do side and some are for the don't side. Some will work on either side, and you will be able to switch back and forth. Your strategy then, is to adapt your preferred betting method to the table conditions that are occurring at that very minute, keeping in mind the laws of probability on which the odds of craps are based.

ALERT!

If you are watching a good bettor who is making a lot of money, you don't need to match his bets. If he bets $50, for example, you can make the exact same bet with only $5. This way when he wins more money, so will you.

If you are on the do side and the shooter has rolled six times after his come-out roll, you might begin to think that the 7 will roll soon. This is because in the previous section we learned that the 7 rolls (on the average) six times in thirty-six average rolls, or about one in every six rolls. After six rolls, you might start thinking about removing or decreasing your bets. However, if you are the don't side and six rolls have passed, you might start thinking about placing more bets or adding more money to your existing wagers.

There are, of course, many more bets than the pass line or the don't pass. But whatever bet you make, you must always be aware of the possibility of the 7 rolling and attempt to change your bets so that you profit, or at least minimize your losses, from this eventuality. Since the casino bases their payoffs on the odds related to the 7, you should keep them in mind when you are making your bets.

Craps Odds

There are seven different ways to bet on the point numbers when you play craps. They are pass, don't pass, come, don't come, place, buy, and lay. Unfortunately, the odds for any one number are not the same for all of these bets.

For example, the odds for placing the 6 or 8 are 7:6, the "free odds" portion of the come or pass line (for the 6 and 8) are 6:5, and the don't bet odds portion of the 6 and 8 are 5:6

As you can see from **TABLE 1.2**, the 6 and 8 have a 13.88 percent chance of rolling, the highest of any numbers besides the 7, which rolls 16.66 percent of the time. According to this chart, the 2 and 12 roll the least (2.77 percent), so they will have the highest odds. Since the 6 and 8 are the point numbers that roll the most, they have the lowest odds of any point number.

QUESTION?

What is the "casino edge," and is it the same on all craps bets?
The casino edge is a percentage of each bet that is retained by the casino so they make a profit on the game. It is like a small gambling "tax" that you pay for most bets, but varies for each wager. For example, the edge for a "pass line" bet is 1.4 percent, while that of an "any 7" bet is 16 percent. The higher the edge, the more the casino makes, so you will want to make bets with as low an edge as possible.

TABLE 1.2 Dice Combinations		
Number Rolled	**(Dice A/Dice B)**	**Percent Chance**
2	1/1	2.77
3	1/2, 2/1	5.55
4	1/3, 2/2, 3/1	8.33
5	1/4, 2/3, 3/2, 4/1	11.11
6	1/5, 2/4, 3/3, 4/2, 5/1	13.88
7	1/6, 2/5, 3/4, 4/3, 5/2, 6/1	16.66
8	2/6, 3/5, 4/4, 5/3, 6/2	13.88
9	3/6, 4/5, 5/4, 6/3	11.11
10	4/6, 5/5, 6/4	8.33
11	5/6, 6/5	5.55
12	6/6	2.77

Pass Line Bets

If you bet $10 on the pass line you can take "free odds." If you are playing at a table that offers 2× odds (two times odds), and you have a $10 flat bet, you can take up to 2× free odds on the point you are wagering.

The casino calls them free odds because they don't make anything on the odds portion of your bet. Your $10 flat bet on the pass (or don't pass) line really should get the proper odds. For example, if the 6 is the point, you should get 6:5 odds. On a $10 bet you should really get back $12 instead of $10, but you don't. To get true odds, you must make an additional bet behind your bet. Here is how it works.

On a 2× table, you place a $10 bet on the pass line. The point is, say a 5. You place your odds behind the $10 on the pass line, just in back of your main bet.

For example, if you placed $20 (2× $10) behind your $10 pass line bet, and won, you would win $10 for the flat (basic) portion of your bet, and $30 (at 3:2) for your odds bet, winning you a total of $40.

If you bet $10 on the pass line and 6 or 8 is the point, you can take $25 odds behind your bet (more on this later). You would win $30 (at 6:5) on the odds portion, for a total of $40. And, if 4 or 10 is the point and you place $20 odds behind your $10 flat bet, you get 2:1 odds and win $40 on your $20 odds bet and $10 on your flat bet, for a total of $50.

Come Bets

You also get the same true odds on come bets. For example, if you bet $10 on the come line, and the next number rolled is 6, you can place another $10 next to your bet, and get paid $12 on the odds portion and $10 on the flat portion. We'll learn a lot more about come bets later.

Don't Pass and Don't Come Bets

With don't pass and don't come bets the odds scheme is a little different. When you are on the don't side, you have to lay odds instead of place them, basically meaning, you have to bet more to get less. For example, if you bet $10 on don't pass, and the point is 10, you have to lay odds of $20 to win $10 on the odds portion, winning you a total of $20 if the 7 rolls before the 10.

FACT

The odds on the don't side are always the exact opposite from those on the do side. For example if the odds on the do side for 6 or 8 are 6:5 (win $6 on a $5 bet), then the don't side for 6 or 8 odds are 5:6 (win $5 on a $6 bet).

After the point is established, you can bet $10 on don't come and lay odds. If your don't come bet lands on the 10, you have to lay another $20 to win $10. The reason for this is that the casino must make a profit. After the point is established, the odds (on a don't bet) are in your favor, and the chances of a 7 rolling before the point is better.

Lay Bets

You can also lay a number at any time. For example, if the 10 or 4 has just rolled, you can lay $40 that the 7 will roll before the 4 or 10 rolls again. However, this bet pays 1:2, so you win $20 on a $40 bet. In addition, you have to pay a 5 percent vigorish ("vig") to the house, to even up the odds (to ensure that the house wins something).

For example, if seven rolls have gone by and the shooter has rolled two 10s, you can bet that the 7 will roll before another 10 does. It's a pretty good wager, and the casino knows this, so you have to pay a small commission. If you bet $40, you have to immediately pay the house $1. It's only $1 and not $2 because the house generously lets you pay a commission on your winnings ($20) instead of your bet. In addition, whether you win or lose the bet, the house usually keeps the 5 percent vig.

Some of the more progressive casinos only keep the vig if you win. If you are planning to lay bets consistently, you should find out what the vig policy is when you're choosing your casino.

Buy Bets

You can buy a number at any time and get the true odds. For example, if a 4 hasn't rolled in a long time, you might think it is due. If you "place" bet the 4 for $40, and win, you will get 9:5 odds, or $72. But if you "buy" the 4 for $40, you'll get true 2:1 odds and win $80 instead of $72. But, you'll have to pay a 5 percent vig on your winnings, or $4, to buy the 4.

ALERT!

You should play at a casino that only collects the vigs on buy or lay bets when you win. Some places collect on both your winning and losing bets. Even if it's only $1 or $2, isn't the money better off in your pocket than the casino's?

The only way to get true odds is to bet the free odds portion of a flat bet, or pay a percentage (vig). You can do this with six of the seven bets we already talked about—pass, come, don't pass, don't come, lay, and buy. When you place bet a number, you never get true odds. The 4 and 10 pay

9:5 (instead of 2:1). The 5 and 9 pay 7:5 (instead of 3:2). The 6 and 8 pay 7:6 (instead of 6:5).

Odds Theory

Each die has six numbers on it. When you toss a pair of dice, two different dice combinations of six numbers each appear on the craps table, so there are a total of thirty-six different dice combinations. To get these thirty-six different combinations for each of the eleven different (2–12) numbers, you need to look at both dice.

- **The 7 can be made six ways**
  1 and 6, 2 and 5, 3 and 4, 4 and 3, 5 and 2, 6 and 1
- **The 6 can be made five ways**
  1 and 5, 2 and 4, 3 and 3, 4 and 2, 5 and 1
- **The 8 can also be made five ways**
  2 and 6, 3 and 5, 4 and 4, 5 and 3, 6 and 2
- **The 5 can be made four ways**
  1 and 4, 2 and 3, 3 and 2, 4 and 1
- **The 9 can also be made four ways**
  3 and 6, 4 and 5, 5 and 4, 6 and 3
- **The 4 can be made three ways**
  1 and 3, 2 and 2, 3 and 1
- **The 10 can also be made three ways**
  4 and 6, 5 and 5, 6 and 4
- **The 3 can be made two ways**
  1 and 2, 2 and 1
- **The 11 can also be made two ways**
  5 and 6, 6 and 5
- **The 2 can be made one way**
  1 and 1
- **The 12 can also be made only one way**
  6 and 6

The casino, of course, knows this chart well, and will offer you a much higher payoff if you bet on the 12 or 2 (the numbers that roll the least) rather than the 7 (the number that rolls the most). The reason for this is that the 12s or 2s combination will roll once compared to the 7, which will roll six times.

The 12 or 2

The odds of the 12 or 2 rolling (in thirty-six average rolls) would be one in thirty-six, and this is related as 36:1. This also means the casino should give you $36 for each $1 you bet on the 12 or 2. However, if the casino did this it would not make any money, so it only pays you $30 and keeps the rest. This casino edge is how the casinos make their profit on the craps tables. So, on the 12 or 2 you will get 30:1 odds, instead of 36:1, and this gives the casino a 13 percent edge.

The 3 or 11

In thirty-six average rolls, the 3 or 11 should roll two times, so the true (mathematical) odds of the 3 or 11 are 36:2 or 18:1. The casino pays only 15:1, which gives them an 11 percent edge.

FACT

The odds of the 2, 12, 3, and 11 are related to thirty-six average rolls, because they are one-roll bets. The odds of the 4, 10, 5, 9, 6, and 8 are related to the 7 because these numbers stay up until they win or lose.

The 4 and 10

In thirty-six average rolls, the 4 or 10 should roll three times, compared to six times for the 7. This means that for every one roll of the 4 or 10 you will see an average of two rolls of the 7. So the true odds of the 4 or 10 are 2:1. If you make a place bet on the 4 or 10, you get 9:5 odds, so the casino edge here is 6 percent.

The 5 and 9

In thirty-six average rolls, the 5 or 9 should roll four times, compared to six times for the 7. This means that for every two rolls of the 5 or 9 you will see an average of three rolls of the 7. So the true odds of the 5 or 9 are 3:2. If you make a place bet on the 5 or 9 you get 7:5 odds, so the casino edge here is 4 percent.

The 6 and 8

In thirty-six average rolls, the 6 or 8 should roll five times, compared to six times for the 7. This means that for every five rolls of the 6 or 8, you will see an average of six rolls of the 7. So the true odds of the 6 or 8 are 6:5. If you make a place bet on the 6 or 8 you get 7:6 odds, so the casino edge here is 1.5 percent.

Pass and Come Bets

The pass and come bets only have a 1.4 percent casino edge, and for this reason they are the most popular bets made at the craps table.

Chapter 2

The Do Side: Basic Pass and Come Strategies

Most of the people screaming and shouting at a craps table are betting on the pass line. There is a wonderful camaraderie among crapshooters, and most of them are betting that the shooter will make her point. In order for the shooter to shoot from the pass line, she must make a bet from the pass line. And in order for everyone else to lend confidence and support to the shooter, they all could make a pass line bet as well. There are many other bets to make, but the pass line wager is always the most popular.

Pass Line with No Odds

This betting system is the beginning of your craps adventure. Its goal is for shooters to roll naturals (7s or 11s) and make point numbers. Most players start out on the pass line because it is easy to do, and as most of the bettors are betting with the shooter, you will feel right at home.

The first thing you need to do is notice the minimum table bet, which is always posted on a small sign, or you can ask one of the friendly dealers. You always bet in chips, not money, so take the minimum bet and place it on the pass line. If your bet is $5 you can use a red $5 chip, or five white $1 chips. Then, just leave it there and wait for a decision; that is, wait for the outcome of the shooter's rolls.

ALERT!

If the shooter is holding the dice, do not make a bet or move your hands onto the table. If he tosses the dice and they hit your hands you will become the most unpopular player in the entire casino!

On the pass line, before the point number is established, you win if the shooter throws a 7 or 11 (a natural), and lose if he throws a 2, 3, or 12 (craps numbers). You don't win or lose on point numbers, yet. The combination of 7 and 11 produces 8 wins, while the combination of 2, 3, and 12 produces only 4 losses. So, before the point is established, the pass line bettor is favored to win by an 8:4 (or 2:1) ratio. After the come-out point is established, you will lose if the shooter throws a 7 and win if he repeats his established point.

Sample Roll

You approach the table, get a dealer's attention, and wait for a lull in the action. You drop a $50 bill on the side of the table layout and say, "Change only." He will take the $50 and probably give you eight red chips and ten white ones. You watch the play until a point is made or the shooter 7s out. You take one red chip and place it on the pass line, just like other people at the table are doing. The shooter gets the dice and tosses them. She throws an 11, so you win. The dealer pushes another red chip next to your bet. You take one and put it on your rack and leave the other one on the pass line. Now the shooter throws a 10, which becomes the point. She then throws a 5, 9, 6, 4, 3, 11, 8, 12, and another 5. None of these numbers have any effect on your bet, so you continue to watch and wait. Now she throws a 7 and you lose. So you won $5 and lost $5, with a net gain of zero.

Since the shooter did not make her point, the next person gets the dice and becomes the shooter. You make another $5 pass line bet, and the shooter throws a 6 right away. Since the 6 rolls a lot more than the previous point of 10, you are optimistic about winning, and, sure enough, a few rolls later he does throw a 6, so you win $5. When you're starting out, be happy with small wins in craps. If you "buy in" with $50 and end up with $10 profit (20 percent of buy-in), then you should be happy—you've done well.

FACT

A 1-unit bet on the pass or come line is referred to as a "flat" bet because it has nothing (no odds) added on to it. You can make a flat bet on the do or don't side, depending on whether you want to bet with or against the shooter.

You can keep playing in a similar manner, but you've probably noticed that some of your fellow players have been adding chips next to their pass line bets after the point was established. This is called adding odds.

Pass Line with 2× Odds

When you made a $5 bet on the pass line and won, you won $5. Would you like to win more money than you bet? You can when you add odds to your pass line bet. Then, depending on the point, you can place more money next to your bet so you will win more money if that number hits. Most casinos allow you to add 2× odds to your pass line bet, but some casinos offer 5×, 10×, or other combinations. Table odds are usually posted on a small sign at the table. If you are unsure about the amount of odds you can add to any bet, just ask the friendly dealer. The dealers are there to help you.

If the point is 4 or 10 (at a 2× odds table), you could wager $10 in odds behind your $5 bet and win $20 (at 2:1 odds) for the odds portion and $5 for the flat portion, for a total of $25.

If the point is 5 or 9, you would place $10 behind your $5 bet and win $15 (at 3:2 odds) for the odds portion and $5 for the flat bet, for a total of $20.

Finally, if the point is 6 or 8, you would wager $10 behind your $5 bet and win $12 (at 6:5 odds) for the odds portion and $5 for the flat portion, for a total of $17.

ALERT!

Remember, the numbers that pay the most have the least chance of winning. So if you want to bet conservatively, you should bet on numbers with lower payoffs (and lower odds).

The 6 and the 8 (each with 6:5 odds) are more likely to roll than the 4 or 10 (each with 2:1 odds). It is safer to bet on the 6 or 8, but more profitable to take a chance and wager with the 4 or 10.

TABLE 2.1 lists all of the odds for the six point numbers. Of course, the dealers will know the odds and payoffs, so you don't have to memorize anything.

TABLE 2.1 Odds Chart			
Type of Bet	**4 and 10**	**5 and 9**	**6 and 8**
True Odds	2:1	3:2	6:5
Pass/Come	1:1	1:1	1:1
Don't/Pass/Come	1:1	1:1	1:1
Pass/Come Odds	2:1	3:2	6:5
Don't Bets Odds	1:2	2:3	5:6
Place Bets	9:5	7:5	7:6
Buy Bets	2:1	3:2	6:5
Lay Bets	1:2	2:3	5:6

Sample Roll

First you wait for a new shooter, and put $10 on the pass line. The shooter's very first roll is a 7, so you win $10. Now she throws an 8, so you add $25 in odds behind your flat $10 bet. The casino lets you add $25 instead of $20 (on the 6 or 8 only) to make the payoff easier to handle. The shooter promptly tosses another 8, and you win $10 for the flat potion and $30 for the odds portion (at 6:5) for a total of $40.

Pass and Come Bets with Odds

Now that you know how to make a pass line bet, we'll look at the next logical step—the come bet. A come bet is like your own personal pass line bet. You can make it almost anytime and add odds if you want to. You can make as many come bets as you want, and they can work with or without a pass line wager.

A come bet is similar to a pass line bet in that you win initially with a 7 or 11 and lose on a 2, 3 or 12. After your come bet point is established, you lose on the 7 and win if your come bet point is rolled again. To make a come bet, just place your chips in the come box and the dealer will move them to your point number once it is established.

If you make a come bet and the next roll is the shooter's point, you will win your pass line bet (if you have one) and your come bet will move to that number as your come bet point for the next roll.

ALERT!

If you make a new come bet on the come line and the shooter rolls one of the numbers you already had a come bet for, you will win your first bet and your second come bet will move to that number. The dealer will just leave your bet there and say "off and on," and pay you. In this case, "off and on" means the dealer pays you OFF and puts the same number back ON.

You can add odds to your come bet, just like you can with you pass line bet. Simply give the dealer your odds bet, after your come point has been established. However, you won't get paid on the odds portion of your come bet until the pass line point is established. In craps lingo, you would say that the odds portion of your come bet is "not working" on the pass line come-out roll. If your come point is rolled on the come-out for the next pass line point, you will win your come bet but the odds will be returned to you. Conversely, if you have a come bet up on the next pass line point and a 7 is rolled, you will lose your come bet, but your odds will be returned to you.

Finally, the come bet, like the pass line bet with odds, gives you a better deal if the point is a 6 or an 8. Using $10 units, you are allowed to take $25 (instead of $20) in odds, giving you a payout of $30 (at 6:5) instead of $24.

The come bet and pass line bets are very similar wagers. However, the pass line bet is made before the game's come-out point is established, and the come bet is made after it is established. You have your own personal point with a come bet, but everyone has the same point with a pass line bet.

Sample Roll

You make a $10 pass line bet and 6 quickly becomes the point. You add $25 odds behind your pass line bet and, at the same time, make a come bet for $10. The next roll is an 8, so your come bet is moved to the 8, and you give the dealer $25 in odds. You also make a second come bet. The next roll is a 5, so your come bet goes to the 5, and you add $20 odds.

Now you have three bets working—on the 5, 6, and 8. You could, of course, make additional come bets, but with those three bets you have $100 at risk so you decide just to wait them out.

The next roll is an 8, so you get paid $10 for your flat bet plus $30 for the $25 odds (at 6:5), for a total of $40. You decide to make another $10 come bet and do so, and the next roll is 6, the point. You win your pass line bet on the 6 and get $10 for your flat bet plus $30 for the odds portion (at 6:5 odds), for a total of $40. You add $25 odds to your 6. You now have two come bets, one on the 6 and one on the 5, both with odds.

You can make a new pass line bet now, but if the 7 rolls (winning your pass line bet), you will lose both come bets (although their odds will be returned to you). You decide to wait out the come bets and not make any other bets. The same shooter gets the dice again and rolls a 10, establishing the pass line point. He then rolls a 5, so you win your come bet for $40 ($10 flat plus $30 odds) and then he rolls a 10 and makes his point. You are now left with one bet, the come bet on the 6.

The same shooter gets the dice again and this time rolls a 7 on the come-out, so you lose your last come bet but get your $25 odds returned.

So, you won $40 on the 8, $40 for the pass line 6, and $40 for the 5. You lost only $10 (the flat portion only) for the come 6, so you're $110 ahead!

There is another important bet in craps—the place bet. It doesn't pay as much as the come or pass line bets, but it's still very useful—and profitable.

ESSENTIAL

> You can add free odds to your pass/come bets, but can't make pass/come bets at any time, or take them down until they win or lose. You can make or take down place bets at any time, but you can't add odds to them.

Pass Line with Place and Come Bets

You can make a bet at any time that the 4, 5, 6, 8, 9, or 10 will appear before the 7 does. The easiest way to make this bet is to make a place bet. Actually, though, you don't make a place bet yourself. You put the money on the table and say to the dealer "Place the 6 and 8 for $6 each," or something similar, and the dealer will actually move your chips to your position on that particular number.

If you do place the 6 and 8 for $6 each and either number rolls before the 7, you'll win $7 (at 7:6 odds). The odds for place bets are less than the added odds bets on the pass line and come (6:5 odds). The big advantage for place bets is that they can be placed and removed at any time. Bets on the pass and come lines can't be removed.

So, if you make two place bets (for example, the 6 and 8 for $6 each) and one of them hits, you can take both bets down and ensure yourself a profit without any further risk. The place odds for the 5 and 9 are 7:5, so if you bet $5 you'll win $7. The amount you bet on these must be in multiples of 5, so you can bet $5, $10, $15, etc.

And finally, the place odds for the 4 and 10 are 9:5, so if you bet $5 you'll win $9. The amount of these bets must also be in multiples of 5, so you can bet $5, $10, $15, etc.

ALERT!

You can make a $5 place bet on the 6 or 8, but it will only pay even odds (1:1). Whenever you place bet the 6 or 8, you should always wager in multiples of 6 (like 6, 12, 18, 24, 30) in order to maximize your payouts at 7:6 odds.

When you win a place bet, the dealer will leave the original bet up, and give you your winnings. If you want your original bet back, you must ask for it by saying, "My place bet down, please," or something similar.

If you want to add your winnings to your original bet, just tell the dealer, "Press my bet, please." If your original bet was a $6 place bet on the 6, you will have won $7. The dealer will add $6 to your existing bet so you now have a $12 place bet on the 6, and he will return $1 to you as change.

If you might want to use an existing bet later, you can call it "off" instead of taking it down and putting it back up again. For example, just tell the dealer, "My place 6 off," and he will put an "OFF" marker on it. When you want it back on again, just let the dealer know.

Here are three different methods you can use to combine place, come, and pass line bets. You can use $6 units for the 6 and 8, and $5 units for the 5, 9, 4, and 10.

$26 and $27 Across Bets

The across bet means you want a bet on every place number except for the point. If 6 is the point, you'll have $6 on the 8, and $5 each on the 4, 5, 9, and 10, for a total bet of $26. If 6 or 8 is not the point, you'll be betting $27 across, so you'll have $6 on the 6, $6 on the 8, and $5 each on three of the remaining nonpoint place numbers. "I want $26 across."

You would start out making a $5 pass line bet and then betting $26 (or $27) across. Now start making come bets. Every time a point number shows, you will win your place bet and have it replaced with a come bet. On a long roll this is a terrific way to stay on the table and increase your profits.

Inside Bet

The inside numbers are 5, 6, 8, and 9. When you bet $22 inside, you bet $5 each on the 5 and 9, and $6 each on the 6 and 8. If one of these numbers is the point, you can omit it. For example, if 6 is the point you can bet $16 inside and you'll get $5 on the 5 and 9 and, $6 on the 8.

You would start out making a $5 pass line and make your inside bet. Then make two come bets only and wait for the roll results. If both come bets hit and you still have some place bets up, just take them down and wait for the next come-out.

Outside Bet

The outside numbers are 4, 5, 9, and 10. When you bet $20 outside, you are betting $5 each on all of them. As usual, if one of them is the point you can omit it, and only bet $15 outside. Like the inside method, you would begin with a $5 pass line bet, and then make your outside bet. Follow it up with two come bets only and wait for the roll results. Again, if the two come bets hit and you still have place bets up, you can take them down and wait for the next come-out.

As you can see, place bets are an integral part of the crapshooter's arsenal. Even though they pay less than odds on the pass and come, they can be placed or removed at any time. Of all the place bets, the 6 and 8 are the most popular. We'll see how these bets combine with the pass line bet next.

Pass Line with 6 and 8 Place Bets

The 6 and 8 combined roll ten times in thirty-six sample rolls, while the 7 rolls only six times. So if you place both numbers, you have a 10:6 or 5:3 chance of winning.

Let's start out making a $10 pass line bet and place bets of $12 each on the 6 and 8. After the come-out (after the point has been established), if either number hits you'll win $14 and then take down, or remove, both bets.

If the point is 6 or 8, take maximum odds on the point and place $24 on the other number. For example, let's say you make a $10 pass line bet. The shooter rolls a 6 on the come-out, establishing the point. Now, you place $25 odds on your pass line bet, and you make a $24 bet on the 8. If both numbers hit, you'll win $40 for your pass line bet ($10 + $30) and $28 for your place bet, for a total of $68.

Another way of doing this is to only bet the 6 and 8 when they are not the point. This way, if the 6 or 8 rolls, you win. If the point rolls, you win on your pass line bet

ALERT!

With a place bet, you should always be ready to take it down after just one win. In fact, after five rolls you might want to remove all of your place bets in order to decrease the risk of losing your bet if a 7 rolls.

You do lose, of course, on the 7, but let's look at what is really happening here. You can place a number whether it is the point or not. If the number is the point and you place it, it is not called a put bet. Put bets are pass line bets made after the come-out and are discussed later in the text. Place bets can be removed at any time but pass bets can not.

If the point is 5, for example, you only bet on the pass line and the 6 and 8. In thirty-six sample rolls, you theoretically will win (from the 5, 6, or 8) fourteen times—five each from the 6 and 8 and four times from the 5. You might lose only six times, from a possible 7. This now gives you a 14:6 or 7:3 advantage if the 5 (or 9) is the point.

Even with the 4 (or 10) point you still have a big advantage. In thirty-six sample rolls you theoretically will win (from the 4, 6, or 8) thirteen times— five each from the 6 and 8 and three times from the 4 (or 10). You might lose only six times, from a possible 7. So you now have a big 13:6 advantage if the 4 (or 10) is the point.

Of course, when you bet on the pass line, you can take maximum odds if you want to (after the point has been established). In some casinos this is 2× odds. But other casinos offer what they call "true" odds, which is really 3×, 4×, and 5× odds.

Multiple Odds Strategies

Many casinos are adopting a new odds scheme they call "true odds" or "true table odds." While this does increase the player advantage, the casino's goal is really to make the game simpler, get more money into play, and of course, increase the actual amount of money you use to bet with.

What "true odds" does is increase the odds payoff on added odds bets like the pass line, don't pass, come, and don't come bets. Instead of 2× odds on all the point numbers you will now receive multiple odds—3× on the 4 or 10, 4× on the 5 or 9, and 5× on the 6 and 8. This does make everything a lot easier for the dealers because all the payouts are now equalized.

ALERT!

For true table odds to work you must bet in multiples of $5. If you want to bet some other amount, you can—but you'll only get even odds (1:1). You can bet $15 or $25 odds, but not $12 or $24. Remember, this only applies to true table odds.

- **4 and 10 with $5 units**: On the 4 or 10 you get 3× odds, so on a $5 bet you can add $15 (3 × $5) on odds. The 4 and 10 odds portion pays 2:1, so your $15 odds bet wins $30 (2 × $15).
- **5 and 9 with $5 units**: On the 5 or 9 you get 4× odds, so on a $5 bet you can add $20 (4 × $5) on odds. The 5 and 9 odds portion pays 3:2, so your $20 in odds wins $30 (3/2 of $20).
- **6 and 8 with $5 units**: Finally, on the 6 and 8 you get 5× odds, so on a $5 bet you can add $25 (5 × $5) odds. The 6 and 8 odds portion pays 6:5, so your $25 wins $30 (6/5 of $25).

The dealers know in advance if you bet $5 and take maximum odds all the payouts will be $35 ($30 odds plus $5 flat bet), no matter which point number you bet on. The other flat bets bring similar results. On a $10 bet with true odds, all of the odds payouts will be $60, whether you bet on the 4, 5, 6, 8, 9, or 10. And finally, with a $25 flat bet all of the odds payouts will be $150.

Higher bets are easier to figure also. A $5 flat bet wins a $30 odds payout, and a $25 bet (5× the $5 bet) wins $150 (5× the $30 odds payout). A $100 bet would then win $600 in odds, which is 4× the $25 odds bet winnings, or 20× the $5 odds bet winnings.

While all this is very good for the average crapshooter, you now must have a higher bankroll to afford to bet maximum odds.

You don't have to bet true odds to play at a true odds table. In fact, it may be better to make smaller bets at first and then, if you win, increase your bets. A cardinal rule of craps is to always increase your bets when winning and to decrease them when losing. You could start off at the lowest level you can on the pass/come line, and increase your bets using your winnings. If the table goes sour, you will lose a lot less and have some money left to play again later. But if the table heats up, you will increase your bets to reap the maximum benefit.

To do this you would start off with a $5 pass line bet. If it wins, add 1× odds. If that wins, add 2× odds. Keep adding until you get to the maximum odds for that number. If you start losing, just decrease your odds bet by 1 unit. If you get back to the flat bet you should quit.

Sample Roll

You make a $5 pass line bet. The shooter throws a 6, establishing that number as the point. The shooter makes his point (the 6), so your next bet is $5, which is 1× your starting bet of $5. He makes his point twice more, so you win two more times and are left with a $5 pass line bet with 3× odds ($15). Now he misses, so your next bet is the $5 pass line bet with $10 odds. If the new shooter makes his first point, your next bet would be the $5 pass line bet plus $15 odds again.

Chapter 3

The Don't Side: Basic Don't Pass and Don't Come Strategies

When you are playing craps, time is money. The longer you last with your bankroll, the more you can win. When you play the don't side of the table, you are looking for a streak of 7-outs, meaning that you want 7s to roll after the come-out. Those 7-outs can really kill the do players, especially if they have three or four bets working. But on the don't side, if you bet it right, no one number can clobber your bets. So your money lasts longer on the don't side, you last longer, and you win more cash!

Don't Pass and Don't Come with Odds

When you bet on the don't pass, you are betting that the shooter misses her point. For example, if the point is 5 and a 7 rolls before the 5, you will win your bet. However, if the 5 rolls before the 7, you will lose your bet. Since the don't pass is the opposite of the pass line bet, you will lose your bet on a 7 or 11 before the come-out—that is, before the point is established. You'll win on the 2 or 3, and the 12 is usually a push in most casinos. Crapshooters bet on the don't side if the table is cold, or when they have a hunch that the shooter won't make his point.

On the pass line, crapshooters always root for a 6 and 8 point and groan when a 4 or 10 show. On the don't pass, it's just the reverse. In addition, the pass line players will lose all of their bets when a 7 hits after the point has been established. But if you have one don't pass and two don't come bets up, there is no one number that can defeat you.

FACT

Casinos on the East Coast have a "Bar 2" indicator on the don't pass, while those everywhere else have a "Bar 12." This means that in the East, the 2 is a push on the come-out, while in other casinos, the 12 is the push. The odds are the same for both, though.

You can place the bet yourself in the don't pass box. When you're ready to add odds, just place them next to your flat bet, just like you would do on the pass line. Since you "add" odds on the do side, the correct term on the don't side is "lay." So, for the 4 or 10, you would lay $2 in odds for every $1 you expect to win. For the 5 and 9, you would lay $3 in odds for every $2 you expect to win. And, for the 6 and 8, you would lay $6 in odds for every $5 you expect to win.

When you make an initial don't pass bet you will win your bet if a 2 or 3 rolls, but lose your bet if a 7 or 11 rolls—just the opposite of a bet from the pass line. On the don't pass the 12 is a "push." The don't come bets work in the same manner.

You also make a don't come bet yourself. Just place a chip in the don't come box. If you get past the come-out, the dealer will then physically move your chip to your point. He may glance back at you for a second, and if you want to add odds to your wager, now is the time to do so.

Once you do get past the come-out, you have a mathematical advantage on any point number, even the 6 or 8. However, on the don't side, you always have to bet more to get less, because the odds are reversed from the pass line odds.

For example, on the pass line, when you add odds to the 4 or 10, you can add $10 and win $20 because the odds are 2:1. However, on the don't side, the odds are 1:2, so you have to add $20 in odds to win $10. On the 6 or 8 pass line you add $25 to win $30 (6:5 odds). Here on the don't side, you have to wager $30 to win $25 (5:6 odds). And finally, with the pass line 5 or 9 you usually wager $20 to win $30 (3:2 odds). On the don't you bet $30 to win $20 (2:3 odds).

While this may not seem right, you have to remember that on the don't side you have the advantage, not the house, after the point is established. Another thing that doesn't seem "right" is that the other bettors may taunt you for betting "wrong." While the right bettors can yell and scream when they win, if you are the least bit happy with your don't side wins, your fellow bettors may seek another table elsewhere. Craps etiquette says that don't bettors always stay very low-key.

You can become the shooter with a bet on the don't pass line. You would then be hoping for a 7 to roll, instead of the point after the come-out. Before the come-out, you will lose on the 7, while the right bettors will win.

ALERT!

Betting on the don't pass is not betting with the house. The house bets against both right and wrong bettors. The house wants you to lose, just as it would if you were betting from the pass line.

Don't Pass with One Don't Come Bet

There are several ways to protect both bets from the 7/11 come-out possibility. For an easy hedge bet on the don't pass or don't come, you could try a $2 bet on the hardway number if the point is 4, 6, 8, or 10. Four of the six points on the don't side can be hedged by hardways: the 4, 6, 8, and 10. Only the 5 and 9 do not have hardways. When you are betting on the don't side, you should always be aware of possible hardways when you want to hedge your bets. If the point rolled is 4 or 10, you would lose your $10 don't pass but win $14 ($2 at 7:1). If the point rolled is 6 or 8, you would lose your $10 don't pass but win $18 ($2 at 9:1). If the "easy way" rolls on any of these numbers you will also lose your bet, but this is still a good hedge for the don't side.

Once your minimum don't pass point is established, you can also protect your higher don't come bet by laying odds for one roll only. This way if the 7 rolls you lose your don't come bet but win your don't pass bet.

One thing to always remember is that the odds are reversed on the don't come or don't pass. You have to bet more to get less on the don't side, because you have the advantage over the casino on every bet once you get past the come-out.

If you have a $5 flat don't pass bet, and you lay single odds ($10) on the 4 or 10, you'll win $5 on 1:2 odds. When you lay single odds ($9) on the 5 or 9, you'll win $6 at 2:3 odds. And finally when you lay single odds ($6) on the 6 or 8, you'll win $5 at 5:6 odds.

Sample 4/10 Roll

You make a $10 don't pass bet and the point is 4 or 10. You lay $10 odds and make a don't come bet. If the 7 rolls now you lose your don't come bet ($10) but win your don't pass bet ($10 flat, plus $5 odds).

Sample 5/9 Roll

If you make a $10 don't pass bet and the point is 5 or 9, you can lay $9 odds and make a don't come bet. If the 7 rolls now you lose your don't come bet ($10) but win your don't pass bet ($10 flat, plus $6 odds).

Sample 6/8 Roll

Finally, if you make a $10 don't pass bet and the point is 6 or 8, you can lay $12 odds and make a don't come bet. If the 7 rolls now you lose your don't come bet ($10) but win your don't pass bet ($10 flat, plus $10 odds).

If the 7 doesn't roll after the don't come is established in all of these bets, just remove your don't pass odds bet. You are left with positive advantage bets on both the don't pass and don't come. Of course, if you have sufficient bankroll to support the added odds, you can leave them up.

QUESTION?

How do the dealers keep track of all the bets on a very busy table?
The point number boxes are divided up according to how many people are playing. For example, if twelve people are betting, the top two spaces on the number square could be for the two bettors on either side of the boxperson. The two bottom spaces are for the people on either side of the stickman. And the four remaining spaces on each side of the box would be for the four people remaining on both sides of the table.

Don't Pass with Two Don't Come Bets

If you know in advance that you're going to make a lot of don't pass or don't come bets, be sure to stand at one of table corners so you'll be close to the don't areas. If the casino has a large craps pit, you might want to choose one that has corner players, as that might mean the table is in the middle of a cold streak.

Now that you know how to establish your first don't come bet, the second one is pretty easy. Your second don't come can be placed without a money loss. If the 7 rolls now, you will win your first don't come, lose the second, and win your don't pass.

Sample Roll—Don't Pass Odds

You make a $10 don't pass bet and the point is 6. You lay $12 odds and make a $10 don't come bet. The shooter rolls a 5, so you remove your don't pass odds and make a second don't come bet. Now you're home free. If the 7 rolls now you lose your second don't come bet but you win both your don't pass and your first don't come bet.

If you don't like adding odds to your don't pass bet, you can just reduce your don't come bet. For example, if your don't pass is $10, make your don't come $5.

Sample Roll—Reducing Don't Come

You make a don't pass bet for $10 and the point is 5. Make a don't come bet for $5. Now, if the 7 rolls you lose your don't come bet ($5) but win your don't pass bet ($10). If the 7 doesn't roll, you can make a second don't come bet for $10. Even if the 7 hits now you will lose your second don't come ($10) but win your don't pass ($10) plus your first don't come ($5).

If the point rolls before your don't come bets are decided, you will be left with them for the next come-out. This is one of the rare times that both the do and the don't players will be rooting for a 7.

Not many people play the don't, but they should. You learned in a previous chapter that craps decisions are made 1/3 of the time on the come-out roll, when the pass line player has the advantage. The remaining 2/3 of the time, the decision will be made on the established point. This is when the don't player has the advantage over the house.

Basic Don't Pass with Place Bets

As you now know, you have an advantage over the casino whenever you are on the don't pass line and the point has been established. Of course, you could still lose if the point rolls before the 7 does. Here is a surefire way of winning (or at least breaking even).

If you make a $12 don't pass bet and the point is 6 (or 8), you could also make a $12 place bet on the same number. If the point rolls, you would win $14 (at 6:5 odds) and lose $12 (from the don't pass), for a profit of $2. If the 7 rolls, you would lose $12 (from the don't pass) and win $12 (from the place bet), so you break even.

Now if you really want to stay on the safe side, you can also use this method to hedge your 4/10 or 5/9 bets.

If you make a $12 don't pass bet and the point is 5 (or 9) you could also make a $10 place bet on the same number. If the point rolls you would win $14 (at 7:5 odds) and lose $12 from the don't pass for a total win of $2. If the 7 rolls you win $12 (from the don't pass) and lose $10 (from the place bet), for a $2 win.

Finally, if you make a $12 don't pass bet and the point is 4 (or 10) you could also make a $10 place bet on the same number. If the point rolls you would win $18 (at 9:5 odds) and lose $12 (from the don't pass), for a profit of $6. If the 7 rolls you would lose $10 (place bet) and win $12 (from the don't pass) for a profit of $2.

ALERT!

When you win a don't pass bet, your bet and winnings are left in the don't pass box. It is up to you to take them down and make another bet, if you want one. If you leave your chips on the layout, they will be considered another bet.

Don't Pass and Place Bets

The payoffs and the math are easy for $25 don't pass players. For the 6 and 8, place $24 on the point. If it shows, you win $28 and lose $25, for a profit of $3. If the 7 shows you win $25 and lose $24. For the 5 and 9, place $20 on the point. If it shows you win $28 and lose $20, for a profit of $8. If the 7 rolls you win $25 and lose $20 for a profit of $5. Finally, for the 4 or 10 you also place $20 on the point. If it shows you win $36 and lose $20 for a profit of $16. If the 7 rolls you win $25 and lose $20 for a profit of $5.

QUESTION?

Are there better places to stand at the table than others?
It doesn't matter where you stand if you just want to make place bets or pass line bets. But if you like don't pass, don't come, or come bets, you might want to stand in the upper corners so you can make these bets without asking for help from the dealers.

Advanced Don't Pass with Place and Field Bets

If you plan on betting don't pass, you should find a cold table. You can find a cold table just by looking at the faces of the bettors and the chips in their racks. You are looking for a table with either a lot of don't bettors, or one with a lot of unhappy do bettors. When you've found the best cold table in the casino, wait until a 7 is rolled and make a $30 don't pass bet. Hopefully the fact that a 7 just rolled will mean it will not roll again until you need it to. After your $30 don't pass point is established, place $10 on the 5, $12 each on the 6 and 8, and $5 on the field.

You will now win on almost any number, while you wait patiently for the 7 to show. As soon as the 6, 8, or 5 wins, take them down, one by one. This way you maximize your winnings as you wait for the shooter to 7-out. You will only lose if the point number shows, and hopefully by then, your losses will have been covered by the place bets.

On a very short roll, you will win. If the point is a 6, for example, and the shooter rolls an 8 and a 7, you win $14 for the 8 and $30 for the don't pass, for a total win of $44. You lose your 5, 6, and two $5 field bets (remember, you are betting the field on every roll) for a total of $32, so you're ahead by $12.

The field is a one-roll bet. You're betting that the next roll will be a 2, 3, 4, 9, 10, 11, or 12. If the roll is a 5, 6, or 8 roll, you lose. Also, when you win a field bet, your bet and winnings are left on the field, and it is up to you to remove the winnings and make another bet.

You'll also win on long rolls. Again, after your $30 don't pass point is established, place $10 on the 5, $12 each on the 6 and 8, and $5 on the field. For example, say 6 is still the point and the next rolls are 4, 5, 10, 8, 3, and 7. You'll win $5 on the 4 (field bet), $5 on the 5 ($10 – $5 field), $5 on the 10 (field), $9 on the 8 ($14 – $5 field), $5 on the 3 (field), and $25 on the 7 ($30 – $5 field), for a total win of $54. You'll lose $12 on the 7-out (from the 6), so your net win is $42.

Now, look what happens when the point is made. The same 6 is the point again, and the rolls are almost the same, 4, 5, 10, 8, 3, and, this time, a 6. You win $5 on the 4, $5 on the 5 ($10 – $5), $5 on the 10 ($5 field), $9 on the 8 ($14 – $5 field), $5 on the 3 (field), for a total win of $29. You'll lose $18 on the 6 (don't pass $30 – $12), so you still have a net win of $11.

Multiple Odds Method

Many casinos now offer up to 100× odds to their craps players. Did you know that you can place odds for any amount under 100× as well? For example, you can take 17× odds, or 3× odds if you want to. This can be very profitable if you are betting don't pass as well as don't come bets.

As you will be starting out on the don't side with both don't pass and don't come bets, you need to find a cold table. A choppy one will do, just stay away from tables with lots of happy pass line bettors with lots of chips in their racks. Your flat bet should be $1, $3, or $5 bets at most. You want most of your money to be used for odds, not flat bets, in order to absolutely minimize the casino advantage. Casinos usually have the lowest table limits ($1 to $3) on weekday mornings.

First, make a don't pass bet. When the point is established, take 1-unit odds on the don't pass bet. Place $1, $2, or $5 flat bets in the don't come box for the next two numbers, and take 1-unit odds on both of them. Then, just wait for the outcome.

If you win on any numbers (don't pass or don't come), bet the same way on the next come-out, but this time take 2-units odds on both your bets. One more winning decision and bet 3-units odds, then 4-units odds, then 5-units odds, etc. Notice that you are increasing your odds bets by 1 unit when you are winning, while the flat portion always remains the same.

If you only win on the don't pass but lose your two don't come bets, keep the odds bets the same for the same shooter. If you lose a bet, go down 1 unit on the odds only. If you get down to single odds again and lose, you're finished with this particular wager. And if you get down to single odds on all three bets, take a break for a while or find another table. Or, just switch to the do side and play this system with pass and come bets.

This is a terrific system when you have a cold table. Your profits will multiply due to the increased profits brought on by increasing just your odds bets. These wagers will increase only on a cold or choppy table, which gives you a better chance to catch a long roll.

You'll be in position to win all three initial bets at 1× odds, win all three at 2× odds, etc.

Remember, you always increase your odds bets only while winning and decrease them while losing. You should also have set win/loss limits and adhere to them.

Chapter 4

Do Side Strategies: Betting with the Shooter

Now that you're a little more experienced playing craps, you might come up with one or two or your own surefire strategies. One of these might be a terrific new idea, like doubling your losing bet each time so that you never lose. We'll take a look at that method, why it doesn't work, and how to make it better. We'll also look at a few other methods and the advantages and disadvantages of each.

The Do Martingale

A Martingale system is one that promises winning results, and you will win most of the time. But just one loss can wipe out all of your winnings, and more. A Martingale states that you double your bet upon a loss until you are winning again. So, if you bet $25 on the pass line, for example, and lose, your next bet on the pass line would be $50. Then $100. Then $200, then $400, and eventually you will hit the table limit. Some tables have higher limits than $500, but the end result is the same. If you keep on doubling your bets when you lose, you can hit the table limit and lose all of your money.

Of course, if you start out at only $5 instead of $25, you can go seven full levels—$5, $10, $20, $40, $80, $160, and $320 on a $500 table. But if you happen to lose at the seventh level, you haven't just lost the $320; you've lost all of the other bets as well, for a total of $635!

When you use the Martingale system you are just trying to get even to recoup your losses. So even if you win, you end up just a little bit ahead. Is that really worth the risk? If you lose the first six bets and win the seventh bet you will be ahead by only $5. There are other Martingales besides the system described here, which provide better results for craps players.

ALERT!

Here is one way of looking at a Martingale: You are wagering (at the $5 level) a total of $635 in order to win back a total of only $5. This is not a good bet. You might want to try it by yourself at home with your own dice, or on the Internet to see how it works out.

The Grand Martingale

In the "Grand Martingale," you double your bet and add $1. So, your $5 flat bet progression is now $5, $11, $23, $47, $95, $191, $383. You still end up capping at the seventh level. And you end up losing more if you lose all seven bets in a row—a lot more—your total loss now is $755! However, if you lose the first six bets and win the seventh bet you are ahead by a whole $11—not much, but more than the regular Martingale.

The Short Martingale

The third variation of this system is called the "Short Martingale." You only play for four levels and then if you lose, you quit. So your progression would be $5, $11, $23, and $47. If you lose the first three and win the forth, you will be ahead by $8, and you have less money at risk.

The Rotating Martingale

The fourth and best version is the "Rotating Martingale." You use the same progression as the Short Martingale, but you double your bet and add one to it when you win and decrease it the same way when you lose. This is different from the other three versions and is sometimes referred to as the "Reverse Martingale," because you increase your bets when you win and decrease them when you lose.

For example, you place a $5 bet on the pass line and win, so your next bet is $11. You win again, so your third bet is $23. You lose this one, so go back to the $11 level. When you get to zero, you should quit or switch to the don't pass. Your game ends when you bet at the fourth level ($47) and win.

Martingales are not for everyone, and if you want to try one, you should find a very low-limit table (50 cents or $1) and try it out there before you play with $5 chips. You'll find that one big loss can wipe out all of your smaller wins.

The Odds Only Pass Play

As you might remember from the first chapter, the best bet on the craps table is the unadvertised free odds bet. The free odds bet provides the house with absolutely no commission, or vig, but you usually have to make a pass, don't pass, come, or don't come bet to take advantage of it.

You'll find that by using the following method the payoff is significantly higher than making pass or come bets, and you'll get to meet a lot of people and have a lot of fun.

Many casinos offer 5× odds (or higher) on their tables, but many people do not have the bankroll to take advantage of these higher odds. You'll probably see people placing a pass bet for $10 and then taking $10 odds, instead of the maximum odds that they are allowed. They could be adding 2× odds ($20), 5× odds ($50), or even 10× odds ($100) to their flat bet, but they don't.

Your job, then, is to befriend these people and talk them into letting you add your extra odds to their bet, in a sort of "team effort." It isn't as hard as it seems and, if you befriend just one person at one table, you could end up with many pass or come bets that have absolutely no casino advantage.

With a $10 bet at a 10× table (on the 4 or 10 point), you can add up to $100 in odds, which pays off $200 (at 2:1). If the point is 5 or 9, you can also add up to $100 in odds, which pays off (at 3:2 odds) $150. Finally, if the point is 6 or 8, you can also add up to $100, which pays $120 (at 6:5 odds).

Sample Roll

You are at a 10× table and your new friend has a come bet for $10, which makes it past the come-out and moves to the 5. She only takes 2× odds ($20) on it, so she will win $30 (plus her $10 flat bet) if the 5 shows before the 7. Just ask her if you can add $80 of your odds to her odds bet to total $100 in odds. If the 5 rolls before the 7 you'll win $120. Betting on odds only in this fashion is easy, profitable, and friend-building as well. Give it a try the next time you play.

One way of rewarding your new "team member" is to pay the tips for the cocktail server, or buy her lunch. You might also help her with her bets if she's a beginner. Remember, she has absolutely nothing to lose by letting you add your bets to hers.

The Five Count

Craps is a game of streaks. You will win more money when a positive streak comes along, and lose money if a negative one presents itself. The Five Count lets you risk your money only on shooters who have a chance of a long roll. When you make a craps bet, the most important variable that you can control is the shooter. Some people really are good shooters. They may have a practice table at home, or they learned from one of the many classes available today exactly how to minimize 7s and maximize point numbers. It could mean more profits for you if you can pick which shooters you should bet on and which shooters you should avoid.

The Five Count strategy has five steps: The first step is when the shooter first throws a point number. If he throws a 7, 11, 2, 3, or 12 before the point, it doesn't count. Step two occurs when the shooter throws any number except seven. You now begin betting. Simply place an identical bet on both the come and don't come at the same time.

Step three, four, and five require that you make additional come and don't come bets at the same time, so now you have four sets of come/don't come bets. If one hits, just put another set up, even though you did not make any money, as the two bets will have canceled each other out. On the Five Count, you add full odds to all of your come bets. Then, as each number hits, make another come/don't come bet with full odds just on the come side.

FACT

You will win fewer bets playing the Five Count, but when you do win, you'll win a lot more. You will also lose less money and play longer with the same bankroll. And finally, you'll get more comps than you would without playing the Five Count.

When three rolls go by and none of your numbers hit, call all of your odds off. Wait two rolls, and if the shooter is still going strong, put your odds back up again. Then, continue this procedure for the remainder of the shoot.

The only downside to this, of course, is the 12. When it rolls you lose on the come but push on the don't. But, it is the casino's only edge, and will be more than balanced out from multiple hits on the come odds, which the casino has absolutely no edge on. And, the twelve rolls only once in approximately thirty-six rolls, so this is a pretty safe bet.

By waiting the five rolls before you put any real money at risk, you are testing the shooter. If the shooter throws any five good numbers, you are going to bet by adding odds to all four of your come bets. However, if the shooter throws a lot of nonpoint numbers, or 7s, out you haven't really lost anything. Your money is safe and reserved for a shooter who will win money for you instead of lose it.

As an added bonus, you should receive full comp credit for all of your bets, even the ones that cancel out. So if you are playing at a spread casino and are a $5 bettor at a 2× odds table, you will have eight bets up. This means you are a $120 player, even though only half of your bets will actually be working with odds added to them.

So, not only does the Five Count choose a good shooter for you, but it also doubles your comps and increases your playing time by decreasing your risk.

Darby's Field

As you know, the game of craps is based on how many times the point numbers roll in relation to the 7. The 7 will roll six times in thirty-six sample rolls, so all of the other numbers will roll thirty times. This means the 7 only has a 1 in 6 chance of rolling compared to any other number. The secret to Darby's Field is to minimize the rolls of the 7.

The field is not a good bet by itself. Not only is it a one-roll bet, but it has sixteen chances to win (on the 2, 3, 4, 9, 10, 11, and 12) and twenty chances to lose (on the 5, 6, 7, and 8).

In order to minimize the 7 for this system, you wait for it to roll, and for the shooter to establish a point. Based on the odds distribution, it is rare for the 7 to roll again right away, but it can happen. Those who love to play Darby's Field say it doesn't happen often, but you will have to judge this for yourself.

The system is so simple that it is a one-roll bet. You make this wager, wait for a decision, and then take everything down. You will win this bet many more times than you lose, but one loss can really set you back, so you have to be careful!

Just wait until a point is established and then bet $25 each on the 5 and 9, $30 each on the 6 and 8, and $25 on the field, so you have $135 in play. If the 7 doesn't roll, you will definitely win one of the following:

- If the **9** rolls, you win $50.
- If the **2 or 12** rolls and pays double, you win $50.
- If the **5** rolls, you win $10
  ($35 win on the place, minus $25 loss on the field).
- If the **6 or 8** rolls, you win $10
  ($35 won on the place, minus $25 loss on the field).
- If the **field** rolls, you win $25.

After the roll, you should take down all the other bets and wait for the come-out point to be established before you bet again.

ALERT!

To play Darby's Field, be sure to find a table with lots of successful do bettors and no don't bettors. And, you want a good, experienced shooter that throws lots of point numbers. Ask your fellow players who the best shooters at the table are.

Remember, you are 6 times more likely to win this bet than lose it. So, if you win $50 (on the 2, 12, or 9) six times (6 × $50 = $300) and lose $135 (on the 7) one time you'll be way ahead by $165 ($300 − $135 = $165). Even if you win $25 (on any field number) six times you'll be ahead by $15 ($150 − $135 = $15).

This is why you must wait for the 7 to roll before you start betting, in order to hopefully decrease its appearance. Even if it comes back and hits you right away (which shouldn't happen very often), you'll be able to recoup your losses in two or three shooters.

Still, Darby's Field is very exciting to play—especially when you win.

The Ponzer

If you buy this method from a mail-order dealer you will probably be disappointed because you already know it. This is commonly referred to as a pass/come system, and it's very popular with both beginners and advanced players.

You will always have three bets up per shooter—the pass line and two come bets. If one come bet hits, you put up another come bet and take maximum odds. When the pass line hits, you make another pass line bet with maximum odds.

The only tricky part to the Ponzer occurs when your pass line bet reaches a decision but your come bets stay up for the next shooter, and the dealer wants to know if you want your odds on or off for the come-out.

FACT

If you are playing at a multiple-odds casino, you can play a Ponzer Progression. Keep your flat bets at the minimums and increase your odds bets on both the pass and come bets by 1 unit when winning, and decrease them by 1 unit when losing.

Usually the best thing to do is to call them on if you still have two come bets up, and off if you only have one come bet active. This is because any two points will equal (in the case of 4 or 10) or exceed (5, 9, 6, and 8) the incidences of the 7 on the come-out. Just remember that any two point numbers equals or exceeds the chances of the shooter rolling a seven, so they should be called on.

This leftover come bet decision also goes for the Advanced Ponzer, which is just a little more complicated than the simple Ponzer.

Advanced Ponzer

In the Advanced version, you start out with one pass line bet with maximum odds, and two come bets with maximum odds. However, you also make place bets on the three box numbers not covered by your other bets. And when the come bets hit, you take them down and replace them with place bets. When the place bets are hit you take them down also.

Sample Roll

You make a pass line bet for $10, and the point is 6, so you take $25 in odds. You make a $10 come bet, which goes to the 5, so you take $20 odds and make another come bet. This goes to the 9, so you add $20 in odds to that number. The only box numbers that aren't covered now are the 8, 4, and 10. You make a $12 place bet on the 8, and a $10 place bet each on the 4 and 10.

Now the 5 rolls, so you win your come bet, take it down and replace it with a $10 place bet on the 5. The 5 rolls again, and you just take it down. Now the 9 rolls and you win your second come bet, so you take it down and replace it with a $10 place bet on the 9.

The 5 hits, so you take down your place bet. Now the 6 point rolls, so you start all over with a new come-out. If you have any leftover place bets, you would take those down (just to make your betting simpler) before you would start with a new pass line bet.

Both systems will work very well for hot tables. You might ask your fellow players how things are going and make a decision on the shooter. If he does not set the dice and doesn't bet big on himself you might want to play either the Ponzer or the Advanced Ponzer on the don't side instead of the do side.

The Come Hedge

A lot of people play the come line, because it is very profitable when a long string of hot numbers are hit by the same shooter. But if you leave your come bets up, you might lose them all to the 7. When you bet come and have a short roll, you will lose all your established come bet(s) when the 7 rolls, and only win on your come bet in the come box. So, if you have a $10 come bet established and $10 in the come box, you will push. If you have two or three come bets working and no bet in the come box, and a 7 rolls, you will lose everything.

This hedge system was designed to save your come bets from the 7 by using a don't pass bet. The big advantage of the don't pass bet is that when you lose on the come you will win the don't pass.

Your first bet in this system should be 4 units on the don't pass line. If you are using $5 units, this is for $20. When the point is established, make your come bet for two units ($10). If the 7 rolls now, you win $30 and lose nothing.

If a number rolls, just make a second ($10) come bet and then wait for a decision. If the 7 rolls now, you lose your come bets ($20) but win your don't pass bet ($20), so you again lose nothing.

If only one come bet hits before the 7, you will be ahead because the other come bet ($10) is less than the don't pass ($20). So, you will win $10 for the first come bet and $10 for the don't pass ($20 – $10).

If both come bets hit you can either take down your don't pass (if the point is 6 or 8) or lay odds (if the point is 4 or 10).

ALERT!

You do not want to add any odds to your initial don't pass bet, as they won't pay enough to cover your hedge. For example, on the 4 and 10 you have $30. On the don't pass you have to add $40 to win $20, so you would have a total of $50 ($40 + $10) wagered, when you only need $30.

Let's say you like to add odds to your $10 come bets. You might add $25 if the number is 6 or 8, or $20 if the number is 5/9 or 4/10. So now you have a total of $35 on the 6/8 or $30 on the other numbers. The easiest thing to do is to start off this play with a $30 don't pass bet (6 units) instead of $20. You need to plan your come bets in advance to ensure that you're betting the correct amount on the don't pass.

Chapter 5

Don't Side Strategies: Betting Against the Shooter

More and more people are trying the don't side, but pass line players still rule the table. However, "dark side" players seem to be winning more money, lasting longer, and garnering more comps. Some of the methods they use to do this are presented in this chapter. If you've ever wondered how to profit from the don't side, this chapter will show you how to increase your play time, get better comps, and most important—make more money!

The Don't Martingale

When playing on the don't side with this particular system, it is usually more profitable to make flat bets only. You should also play this method alone and not make any other bets.

You will be playing the don't pass line exclusively and will be increasing your bets by one level when you win and decreasing them by one level when you lose. You will be betting five levels only. One betting unit is $5 and you will be adding $1 to that each time you win, so your progression when winning will be $5, $11 ($10 + $1), $16 ($15 + 1), $21 ($20 + $1), and $26 ($25 + $1). If you win all five bets in a row you will be ahead by $79.

If you lose a bet you will decrease your next bet by 1 unit and $1. Let's say you won the first four bets ($5 + $11 + $16 + $21 = $53). You lose the next bet for $26, so your next bet will be for $19 ($25 − $5 − $1). If you lose that you will bet $14 ($15 − $1), then $9 ($10 − $1), and finally the table minimum at $5.

If you lose your very first $5 bet, your second bet should also be at $5. Before you start betting, however, you should do everything you can to maximize 7s rolling. For example, you should play at a choppy or cold table and avoid tables with lots of cheering, happy players. You do not have to play this system all at once with the same shooter.

> Some people wait for two pass line wins in a row before they play the Don't Martingale. This might increase your chances of a don't pass win, but you'll play a lot less often. At any rate, don't be tempted to make any other bets—just be patient.

ALERT!

Sample Roll

You find a choppy table and the shooter just made the point, so on the new come-out you make a don't pass bet for $5. The point is 5, which the shooter makes. Your next bet should be for $4, but because this is a $5 table you stay at the minimum. The next point is 6, which the shooter doesn't get, so you win $5.

The new shooter puts a black chip on the pass line, and starts setting the dice carefully. You might want to wait this one out, or switch to the pass line. After this roll is finished and a new, less competent shooter appears, and you can resume your betting with $11 ($5 + $5 + $1) on the don't pass.

If you lose any four bets you will be down by $20 ($5 × 4). However, if you win any four bets you will be ahead by $53 ($5 + $11 + $16 + $21). The most important aspect of this method is to bet only on inexperienced shooters. After an hour or so you should be able to get through all five levels and end up with a profit of $79.

The Ricochet

In this system, we are going to make a don't come bet. Both the don't come and the don't pass are terrific bets, but they are liable to lose on the come-out 7 or 11, the exact opposite of the come and pass line bets. In this system we will protect our don't come bet by temporarily making a lay bet.

A lay bet pays true odds, so you will win 1:2 (bet $20, get $10) on the 4 and 10, 2:3 (bet $30, get $20) on the 5 and 9 and 5:6 (bet $30, get $25) on the 6 and 8. Remember, you always have to bet more to get less on the don't side. If, for example, you wanted to lay the 4, you would give the dealer $40 and say, "Lay the 4, please." If the 7 rolls before the 4, you win $20 (at 1:2 odds).

Since the casino doesn't make anything on the lay bet, they have tacked on an additional charge, called vigorish, or "vig," equal to 5 percent of the winning. So, if you won $20 you would owe the casino 5 percent of $20, or $1.

Some casinos charge the lay vig if you win or lose your bet. Some only charge if you win. If you have a choice of casinos, call them on their toll-free numbers and ask if they charge lay vigs only on winning bets. You should try to play at the casinos that only charge on winning bets.

In this system you do not make a don't pass bet. When the point is established you lay the point. For the 6 or 8 you would lay $30 to win $25, at 5:6. If 5 or 9 were the point, you would lay $30 to win $20, at 2:3. And if 4 or 10 were the point, you would lay $40 to win $20, at 1:2.

When you do lay the point, you should also make a $15 don't come bet. When the shooter then throws another point number, you should remove your lay bet. It was just there to protect you from the 7 hitting your don't come bet.

If the 7/11 did hit you in the don't come box, you would have lost $15 on the don't come and made $25 if the point was a 6 or 8, so you would end up $10 ahead. If the point was 5 or 9, you would win $5 ($20 – $15). If the point was 4 or 10, you would have also win $5 ($20 – $15).

After your don't come bet is established and you remove your lay bet, you should make one more don't come bet. You are now home free. Even if the 7 rolls now, your first don't come bet will cancel out your second don't come bet. And if the 7 doesn't roll, you have two good established don't come bets just waiting for the 7. Since these are don't come bets, they pay off the same flat amount that you bet, so if you win both bets (which is probable) you would win $30.

Before you run out and try this system, keep in mind that there is one disadvantage, which the title reflects. If the shooter happens to throw a point and ricochets the very next roll, meaning the same point number rolls, you will lose your lay bet. As a consolation, though, your don't come will move to the point and chances are you'll win some of your money back when the 7 rolls. You can, of course, add maximum odds to your don't come bet (especially if it is a 4 or a 10) and hopefully the 7 will roll before the number rolls a second time.

The 410 Again System

This is another "dark side" method, related to the previous two systems. It's a little more complicated, but once you get used to it, you'll like it a lot. First you wait for a point to be made (not a 7-out) and then, on the next come-out, lay $20 each against the 4 and 10, and make a don't pass bet for $10.

If the 12 rolls, nothing happens. If the 7 rolls, you win the lay bets for a total of $19 ($20 – $1 vig) and lose the don't pass ($10), so you are $9 ahead. If a 2 or 3 rolls, you win $10 and lose nothing.

If the shooter rolls a 5 or 9, you should remove the 4 and 10 lay bets and use $30 of that $40 as odds. So, now you would have a $10 don't pass bet with $30 odds, and will win a total of $30 ($10 + $20) if the 7 shows.

If the shooter rolls a 6 or 8, you should also remove your lay bets and use $30 as odds. So now you would have a $10 don't pass bet also with $30 odds, and you'll win a total of $35 ($10 + $25) if the 7 shows.

If the shooter rolls a 4 or 10, you will have lost that particular lay bet. Remove the other lay bet and use it for odds. You now have a $10 don't pass bet with $20 odds. If the 7 rolls before the point, you'll win your $20 back ($10 + $10), so you'll lose nothing.

As you might know, you are favored to win all of these don't bets after the point is established. This is a way of getting in on the dark side bandwagon with very little risk.

There are, of course, your vigs. On all of the lay bets you could end up paying only $1 for both bets, and pay that only if you win.

FACT

The maximum amount you can lay and still only pay $1 vig is $38 for the 4 or 10, $36 for the 6 or 8, and $39 for the 5 or 9. If you lay any more than these amounts, you will be charged $2 vig instead of $1.

If you want to win more money, you could try betting more. This time you'll start with a $20 bet on the don't pass and lay the 4 and 10 for $38 each. If the shooter rolls a 4 or 10, you will have lost that lay bet. Remove the other lay bet and use it for odds. Now you have a $20 don't pass bet with $38 odds. If the 7 rolls now, you'll win $39 ($20 + $19), and you'll be ahead $1.

If the point becomes 5 or 9, you should remove both lay bets, and use $39 of it for odds. Now you have a $20 don't pass with $39 odds. When the 7 rolls, you'll win $46 ($20 + $26).

If the point becomes 6 or 8, you should remove the lay bets and use $36 for odds, which pays $50 ($20 + $30) when the 7 shows.

The only thing you should watch out for here is a good shooter. (See "Qualifying a Shooter" in Chapter 18.) Aside from when a rhythm roller is shooting, the 410 Again system gives you a chance to make money easily on the don't side—while everyone else is losing on the pass line.

The 31 System

The 31 in the title refers to 31 times the multiple of your unit bet, so if you are a $1 unit bettor, then you need just $31 to play this system. If you are at $5 you need $155 (31 × $5) and if you're a $10 bettor, you'll need $310 (31 × $10).

One of the best things about the 31 System is you can start it on the don't pass, and then switch back and forth (to accommodate good or bad shooters) right in the middle of the system. This progression itself is pretty simple and for $1 units it always adds up to 31: $1, $1, $1, $2, $2, $4, $4, $8, $8 (total $31). If you use $5 units, you need to bet like this: $5, $5, $5, $10, $10, $20, $20, $40, $40 (total $155).

FACT

You might want to find a low-limit table and try this out using $1 units. It's easier to track this way, and you can get used to it before you try it with $5 or $10 units.

The important thing to remember is that when you win a bet, you need to press your winnings to make the next bet and then call the series over and start from the beginning. So, most of the time, you will not be making nine bets. You'll be stopping when you've won any two bets in a row.

Sample Roll

If you are using $1 units and lose the first six bets in a row, you will lose a total of $11 ($1 + $1 + $1 + $2 + $2 + $4). Your next bet, according to the

CHAPTER 5: DON'T SIDE STRATEGIES

progression, is $4. If you bet $4 and win, you now bet $8 and if you win that, you stop. So, you've lost six bets for a $11 loss and won only two bets for a $12 gain ($8 + $4). Even though you lost six bets and won only two, you're still ahead.

If you're betting $10 units and you lose six straight bets in a row—$10, $10, $10, $20, $20, and $40, you're down $110. Now you bet $40 and win, so your next bet is $80. You win this bet also, so you stop because you won two in a row ($40 + $80). You've lost six bets in a row and won only the last two, but you're still ahead by $10 ($120 – $110).

The secret to the 31 System is that you don't have to stay on the don't side. You can watch the shooter and if she bets big on herself or sets the dice, bet with her on the pass or come as long as she holds the dice. Then when the next shooter gets his turn, make the same judgment again. If he bets the table minimum and it doesn't look like he knows what he's doing, just switch back to the don't pass. The object here is not to stay on the pass or the don't pass, it's to make more money.

Remember to stick to this system, and do not make any other bets. Do not go over the 31-unit limit. When you are ahead, put your chips in the back rack and do not touch them!

The 31 System is easy to learn, simple to use, and once you get used to it—very profitable.

The D'Alembert System

The D'Alembert system is unlike many other systems because it advocates something that almost everyone advises against. Still, some people swear by it and use it exclusively in their craps play. When you use this method, you bet 1 unit on the don't pass and increase your bet 1 unit if you lose your bet. You also should decrease your bet by 1 unit if you win your bet.

You will also be starting out on the don't side and possibly switching over to the do side.

The real secret to this system lies in determining when to switch your bet from the don't pass to the pass line, and vice versa.

The easiest way to do this is to wait until three like results come up and then switch. For example, let's say you win three don't pass line decisions in a row. Now it's time to switch to the pass line. If you win three pass decisions in a row, you should go back to the don't pass line.

You could also determine whether to switch just by judging the shooter. If she sets the dice or bets big on herself you should bet on the pass line. If she looks like she shouldn't even be in the casino in the first place, make your bet on the don't pass.

Sample Roll

You color in for $100 just as someone 7s out. The new shooter is a young man who gets asked for his ID by the boxperson. He spends the next few minutes telling his girlfriend how he once turned a $1 bet into $5,000, and then tries to bet $1 on a $5 table. You have no confidence in this shooter, so you place $5 on the don't pass. He rolls a 6 and then promptly 7s out. Since you won, you stay with a $5 bet. Now, his girlfriend shoots. You stay on the don't pass and win again. The third shooter gives you the same bad feelings as the first two, so you bet $5 on don't pass again and you win your third bet in a row. You are tempted to stay on the don't but because you won three in a row, you reluctantly switch over to the pass line.

The new shooter, however, is a "virgin" shooter (see "Craps Superstitions," Chapter 22) and soon gets three passes in a row, so you are way ahead but you are still at your $5 flat bet on the pass line.

FACT

The D'Alembert is one of the few systems where you increase your bets only when losing. In order for this to work properly you must pay very careful attention to the shooter and not make any other wagers.

If you do lose several bets in a row, the D'Alembert can help you get your money back, because you actually make more on higher bets that resulted from a loss, rather than lower bets that resulted from a win. In fact, if you lose more than you win but stop play with a winning bet, you will always be ahead.

If you lose a $5 don't pass bet, your next don't pass bet will be $10. If you lose that one, your next bet will be $15. Win that one and you're even ($15 – $15). Your fourth bet would be at $10, and the next bet would be $5. If you won the last three bets, your next bet would be $5 on the pass line.

Give the D'Alembert a try—it has worked for a lot of crapshooters and might just be the easy system you've been looking for.

The Three-Way 7 Bet

When you make a don't pass or don't come bet, the 7 is your enemy until the point gets established. In the middle of the layout you'll see the "any 7" bet displayed. Why not use that to protect your don't bets?

ESSENTIAL

The any 7 bet has the distinction of being the very worst bet on the entire craps table. It does pay off if three different rolls occur—2 and 5, 3 and 4, and 6 and 1. However, it does not stay up until it wins or loses—it is a one-roll bet. So if a 7 doesn't hit on the very next roll, you lose your bet.

If you figure out the casino advantage to the any 7, it is 16.66 percent—so, it never pays to use this bet in the manner it is presented to the average crapshooter. The any 7 bet only pays off 5:1, while its true odds are 6:1. What if we could boost those odds a little, and instead of 5:1 we could get paid 15:1?

A hop bet is a one-roll verbal bet that's not on the table layout. To win, the shooter must throw the exact combination that you bet. For example, if you toss the dealer $5 and say, "$5 3 and 3 hop," and the 4 and 2 roll, you lose your bet. The good thing about the hop bet, however, is that it pays 15:1. We are going to bet an any 7 hop bet. Most people do not know that you can combine hop bets. For example, you can say, "$1 2 and 2 hop, plus $1 5 and 5 hop." This will give you hop bets on the hard 4 and hard 10 for the next roll only.

Since the any 7 is composed of three numbers, you can bet $1 on each of them. You can ask for a $1 2 and 5 hop, a $1 3 and 4 hop, and a $1 6 and 1 hop. A little-known shortcut for this is to make a $3 any seven hop bet—also called a Three-Way 7 hop. This any 7 hop is becoming more popular due to its higher payoffs, but don't be surprised if you have to explain it to the dealer.

As with all hop bets, it is a one-roll bet. If you bet $3 Three-Way 7 hop, you will win $15 if the next roll is a 7, compared to $12 ($3 × 4) on the any 7 bet. On a three-way hop, the two losing bets are subtracted from the winnings, so the end result is $13 ($15 − $2) for the hop bet and $12 for the any 7.

However, if you bet $15 (3 × $5) Three-Way 7 hop, you will win $65 ($5 × 15 − $10) if the next roll is a 7, compared to only $20 ($5 × 4) for an any 7 bet. On a $30 (3 × $10) wager, you will win $130 ($10 × 15 − $20) compared to only $40 ($10 × 4) for the any 7 bet.

The best way to use the any 7 hop bet is to protect another bet that may lose to a 7 being rolled, like the come-out roll for a don't pass bet. Another use is on the pass line for the come-out. If the shooter sets the dice and is proficient at throwing 7s, you can bet the same way. Some people even start a small any 7 hop progression on the come-out. Just bet $1, $3, $6, $9, $12, $15, etc., on each combination until the point is made. Because of the high payout you can try this on several come-outs before you start to lose money.

On the don't pass or don't come you can bet $10 with a $3 (3 × $1) any 7 hop. If the 7 rolls you win $15 and lose $10. If any other number rolls you lose only $3 and get your bet safely moved to the point, where you now have the advantage.

The next time you play the don't, give the any 7 hop bet a try.

Chapter 6

Buy and Lay Bets: Better Payoffs with Vigs

Buy and lay bets are enjoying an increased popularity, primarily due to casinos that only charge "vigs" on winning bets. You'll learn about this and more—how to lay the same numbers, how to use lay bets for protection, and finally, how to lay outside. Once you master the concept of "pushing the house," you'll be able to maximize your profits on lay and buy bets so you win more money, gain more comps, play longer, and have more fun.

Buying the 4 and 10

Most place bettors seem confident that the best place bet is the 6 or 8. This bet pays 7:6, so when you bet $30, you'll win $35. Some people place bet both numbers together, increasing their chances of winning, but at the same time, exposing their money to more risk. If the 7 rolls, you're out $60 (2 × $30), which means you have to win twice more just to get ahead.

The 7 should roll six times in thirty-six rolls, and the combination of the 6 and 8 should roll ten times (five times each). So, in thirty-six rolls, you should win 10 times (at $35) and lose six times (at $60).

This turns out to be a net loss of $10 ($350 – $360). Not too bad, really, considering all the comps you'll be getting while you're playing the 6s and 8s. But are there any other numbers that we can bet on which could provide even a more profitable win than the 6 and 8?

Let's take a look at the 4 and 10, with its standard 9:5 odds. In thirty-six rolls, the 4 and 10 combination should roll six times (three each), the same amount as the 7. By betting $25 on both the 4 and 10, you should win six times (6 × $45) and lose six times (6 × $50), resulting in a net loss of $30 ($270 – $300). However, there are some special circumstances surrounding these numbers.

FACT

The term "vig," or "vigorish," comes from the 1900s accounting term of "adding vigor to the bottom line." When accountants added the commissions (vigors) together, they became vigorishes, which soon got shortened to vigs.

The 4 and 10 can be bought for a 5 percent commission, or "vig." Some casinos only charge this vig if you win and that 5 percent commission is usually only $1 on a $25 bet (instead of $1.25). With a buy bet instead of a place bet, you get true odds, or 2:1 (instead of 9:5) for your bets. This means that if you buy the 4 and 10 and win either number, you'll get $50 (at 2:1) instead of $45 (at 9:5). That's $5 more for just a $1 investment in vig.

If you buy the 4 and 10, you should win six times when either the 4 or 10 hit, at 2:1 odds (6 × $50 = $300). You might also lose six times if the 7 rolls, losing both of your bets (6 × $50 = $300), resulting in an exactly even proposition, not counting the vigs.

If you play in a casino that only collects the vigs when you win, you'll only lose $6 in vigs for six wins, which is $4 less than you'd lose by placing the 6 or 8. And by buying both the 4 and 10, you'll get higher comps, and have a slightly lower risk.

Now a larger difference between the 4 and 10 and the 6 and 8 becomes evident. If you place the 6 and 8 for $30 each and lose (2 × $30 = $60), you'll need to win twice more just to get ahead (2 × $35 = $70, at 7:6). However, if you buy the 4 and 10 for $25 each and lose (2 × $25 = $50), you'll need to win just once more (2 × $25 = $50, at 2:1) to break even.

More and more crapshooters are trying this play, especially in casinos that only charge the vig on winning bets. The next time you think of placing the 6 and 8, try buying the 4 and 10 instead. Now that you know about buying the 4 and 10, let's look at buying the 5 and 9. Not many people do this, but you can make money at it, if you do it right.

Buying the 5 and 9

Most crapshooters do not buy the 5 or 9, as the 5 percent vig makes it unprofitable to do so. For example, on a $30 bet you would have to pay 5 percent of $30, or $2 (rounded up from $1.50) just to make this buy bet. If you place the 5/9 for $30 you will win $42 at 7:5 odds. If you buy the 5/9 for $30 you will win $45, but you'll have to pay $2 vig. So you win $42 on the place bet and $43 ($45 − $2) on the buy bet. You do get $1 more with the buy bet, but there is a way to make even more.

The 5 percent vig that the casino charges is not a precise figure. On the $30 buy bet, most casinos do charge you $2, even though 5 percent of $30 is $1.50. However, if you ask your friendly dealer before you bet if you can pay $1 vig on a $30 buy bet on the 5/9, he will usually agree—especially if you have a credit line, are friendly, call the dealers by their names, and tip them.

You can also ask to buy *both* the 5 *and* 9 for $30 each and only pay $2 vig for both bets. Usually this bet will cost you $3 (5 percent of $60), but here you can save another dollar. Then, when either number hits, just take both numbers down. You'll be doubling your chances of winning for the same low $2 vig!

ALERT!

You should always tip the dealers. If they get tips they will look out for your bets, let you take longer to shoot, and even bump your comps up a little. In addition, if they have to decide something (like charging you $1 or $2 vig per bet), they will usually make a decision in your favor. Tipping doesn't cost—it pays! (See Chapter 15 for more about tipping the dealers.)

Once you have the dealers trained to accept $1 vigs on the $30 buy bets, see if you can bump them up a little. A $40 buy bet will obviously require a $2 vig (5 percent of $40 is $2), but what about a $38 buy bet (5 percent of $38 is $1.90). Just ask your friendly dealer if you can make a $38 buy bet on the 5/9 and only pay $1 vig. You have absolutely nothing to lose by asking. If you win, you'll get $57. If you place the 5/9 for $35, you'll win only $49. As before, ask if you can buy both the 5 and 9 for $38 each. Then, when either number hits, take them both down.

If you succeed and the table is hot with 5s and 9s, you might want to go up one step. Most dealers will let you buy the 5/9 at $50 for only $2 vig (instead of $2.50). The vig will change to $3 when it hits $60 (5 percent of $60 is $3), so ask to buy the 5 and 9 for $58 each and only pay $2 vig. As before, when the first number hits just take both bets down.

At this level by buying the 5/9 for $58, you will win $87 (at 3:2). If you placed the 5 or 9 for $55 you would win $77. So by spending just $2 more, you will win $10 more. It's well worth asking the friendly dealer if you can do this. By buying two numbers and only paying the vig for one of them, you are doubling your chances to win while still paying a minimum vig to the casino.

You can buy or lay the 5/9 or the 4/10, but there is one thing that the 4/10 has that the 5/9 doesn't have—hardways. Let's see how you can win more money by using a hardway bet when you lay the 4 or 10.

Laying the 4 and 10

If you are primarily a don't bettor, you are probably familiar with using lay bets to bet against numbers without going through the don't come box. However, you have to pay a 5 percent vig on the amount of your winnings. So, if you lay the 4 (or 10) for $40, it has a payoff of $20. The vig is 5 percent of $20, or $1.

Usually, if you lay more than $20, the casino will round up your vig to the next even dollar amount. If you lay $50, for example, you will win $25, and 5 percent of $25 is $1.25, so you will be charged $2 vig.

However, if you ask the dealer before you bet if you can lay the 4 (or 10) for $50 and pay only $1 vig, you will usually get it. You can also ask to lay both the 4 and 10 together, for $25 each, and still only pay the $1 vig. Normally these bets would be two separate bets, requiring vigs of $1 each, but if you ask first, you can save $1.

The 4s and 10s are different from the 5s and 9s, because they have their own corresponding hardways, which pay 7:1. Since the 4 (or 10) appears only three times in thirty-six sample rolls, you can use these hardway bets as insurance to protect your lay bets.

FACT

The hard 4/10 pays 7:1, but the hard 6/8 pays more—9:1. This is because there are two soft 4/10 rolls for every hard 4/10, but there are five soft 6/8 rolls for every hard 6/8 roll. So, the hard 6/8 is more difficult to roll than the hard 4/10, and it pays more.

The three ways that a 4 can roll are 1 and 3 (soft), 3 and 1 (soft), and 2 and 2 (hard). By betting the hard 4 in addition to your lay bet, you reduce your possible loss due to the 4 rolling from 3 in 36 to 2 in 36. If you are laying $50 "no-4," you can also bet $7 hard 4. This way if the 7 rolls you win $18 ($25 – $7), but if the hard 4 rolls you only lose $1 ($50 – $49) instead of $50.

The three ways that a 10 can roll are 4 and 6 (soft), 6 and 4 (soft), and 5 and 5 (hard). Just like with the 4, you can reduce the possible loss on your lay bet due to the 10 rolling from 3 in 36 to 2 in 36 by betting on the hard 10. If you are laying $50 no 10, you can also bet $7 hard 10. This way if the 7 rolls you win $18 ($25 – $7) but if the hard 10 rolls you lose only $1 ($50 – $49) instead of $50.

You do lose your $50 lay bet if the soft 4 or 10 rolls, but this happens only 2 in 36 times, compared to 7 in 36 wins (6 in 36 for the 7 plus 1 in 36 for the hardway).

On a combined wager, you can bet $28 no 4 and $28 no 10 and $4 each on the hard 4 and 10. Of course, you should ask if you can only pay $2 vig for both bets. This way if the 7 rolls you win $24 ($28 – $4) and if one of the hard numbers roll, you break even ($28 – $28). And if a soft number rolls, now you only lose one bet and it is certainly to your advantage to put it back up again.

Laying the 5 and 9

You won't see a lot of bettors laying the 5 or 9, as most of the lay bets go behind the 4s and 10s. Plus, the 5 percent vig (on winnings) charged on lay bets seems to reserve lay bets only for the 4s and 10s. But what if there's a way to profit from the 5s and 9s as well?

ALERT!

The key to making profits at the craps table is to ask the dealers for something that is not normally available. This is called "pushing the house," and you should do it as often as possible. If a dealer says no, just bring your business to another dealer at another table—or casino.

For example, when you lay the 5 or 9 for $45, you win $30 at 2:3 odds, minus the $2 vig, so you only get $28 back. Since 5 percent of $30 is $1.50, you might try asking the dealer if you can pay $1 vig instead of $2 for the same bet. That extra dollar is certainly better off in your pocket than the casino's.

You can also try to lay the 5 and 9 for $56 plus $1 vig. A $56 bet will return $38, which is $2 short of the $40 limit (bet $60, get $40), which starts the $2 vig. Remember, all you have to do is ask the dealer if you can make a lay bet for a certain amount. The worst that can happen is that you'll get a polite "no." The whole purpose of betting this way is to maximize your profits by getting as close to the $2 vig limit while still only paying $1.

To do this, you need to get your lay bet payoff in the $35 to $40 range. And you have to be careful about the way you word your bets. For example, if you lay the 9 for $56 plus $1 vig, you can't say "$57 lay the 9," as they might charge you an extra dollar. Make sure they know that you want the bet to be for $56 plus $1 vig.

You should also be able to split your lay bets. Instead of laying the 9 for $54, for example, ask the friendly dealer if you can lay $27 each against the 5 and 9, and still only pay $1 vig. This will give you an extra chance because you can win both numbers together, but you can't lose them both at the same time.

The next time you lay numbers, try to get a better bet than advertised. You have nothing to lose by trying this. You'll gain extra money, increased comps, and the satisfaction that you are getting the very best bet that you can make.

Sometimes laying a number can act as a hedge. If you place the inside numbers, you can lay the 4 and 10 to protect you from the 7.

Using Lay Bets to Protect Your Place Bets

As you probably know, when you place a bet like $44 inside you are betting $10 each on the 5 and 9 and $12 each on the 6 and 8. Since you are not betting on the 4 or 10, you can use these numbers as lay bets to protect your inside places.

When you make a lay bet, make sure the dealer places a plastic marker on your bet that says "LAY" on it, in order to distinguish it from a don't come bet. If you call your bet "off," he will put an "OFF" marker on top of the "LAY" marker.

When you bet $44 inside you are vulnerable to losing instantly on the 7. An easy way to protect these bets is to lay both the 4 and 10 for $50 each. This way if the 7 hits you lose your $44 inside but win $50 on the lay bets. Since you'll have almost $100 on the table, it might be better to take a very conservative approach in utilizing this method.

There are two ways you can do this. You can leave both the place and lay bets up for five rolls only, and then take down the place bets and hope for a 7 to show soon. An even more conservative approach is to leave all the bets up for any two hits and then take all the bets down and wait for the next shooter.

You can also vary the times when your bets are placed. You can, for example, make both the place and lay bets before the come-out, or make the lay bets only, and then the place bets after the point is established.

If you make the lay bets only before the come–out, you will win on the 7s and not lose your place bet money. However, if you make both the place and lay bets you could profit on the come-out points of 5, 6, 8, or 9 (the most popular points).

One way to decide which method to use is to watch the other players. If there is a lot of money on the pass line, go with lay bets only and hope for 7s on the come-out. If bets are scattered all over the table, go with both the place and lay bets.

And if you are unsure about what to do, don't make any bets. Wait until the point is established and then decide whether to bet the lay/place method. You might wait to leave all your bets up for two hits only and then take everything down. This way, your profit will come from your place bets—the lays were just there for protection. The next time you bet $44 inside, try laying the 4 and 10 at the same time.

Laying Outside

The outside numbers (4, 5, 9, and 10) are very attractive to don't bettors. Usually when a don't come or don't pass bet lands on one of these numbers, the bettor is pretty confident, having a better than even chance of winning. But if these numbers are so popular on the don't side, why aren't more people laying outside instead of using the don't come or don't pass?

The reason why more bettors don't lay outside is that if you lay the 4 or 10 for $80 (for example), you get 1:2 odds. You win $40, but you must pay a 5 percent vig on the $40, or an extra $2.

And, if you lay the 5 or 9 for $60, you get 2:3 odds, so you also win $40 and have to pay another $2. The secret here lies in pushing the house to give you a better deal than advertised. Just ask if you can lay $78 on both the 4 and 10, and $57 on both the 5 and 9. This is the most you can lay on all four outside numbers and still only pay $1 each in vigs. When the 7 hits, you'll collect $39 each from the 4 and 10 (at 1:2), plus $38 each from the 5 and 9, for a total of $154 for all four bets.

ALERT!

Before you lay outside, you might want to chart the table for a shooter or two, and then only lay the numbers that have already rolled. For example, if the 5, 9, and 10 have rolled recently, just lay those three numbers and make no bets on the 4.

Make sure you do this only in a casino that only charges the vigs when you win. Also, wait four or five rolls before you lay these bets, and make sure the shooter is not a rhythm roller (see Chapter 18). And, most importantly, when you win all four bets do not cheer or act happy. If you do, you will lose the support of your fellow players, and most importantly, the dealers. You can laugh later when you exchange your black chips for money at the cashier's cage.

Once you've mastered buy and lay bets you are well on your way to becoming an advanced player. There are some bets that advanced players like, however, that we haven't mentioned yet—proposition bets. These are located in the center of the layout and are commonly referred to as "craps numbers"—the 2, 3, and 12—as well as the Yo (eleven) bet.

Chapter 7

Proposition Bets: High Risk, High Payouts

Proposition bets promise high payouts, but they are also high risk. In this section we're going to look at the horn numbers—2, 3, 11, and 12, as well as the hardway numbers—4, 6, 8, and 10. There are progression methods that experienced crapshooters use to profit from the 3/11 or the 2/12, and we'll look at those first. Then we'll take a look at horn betting systems, hardways, and craps numbers. Finally, we'll finish off with a system for making hardway hop bets.

The 3s and 11s

To use this system you need to count the rolls and know how many rolls have passed since the last 11 (or 3) hit. The 3s and 11s roll only twice in thirty-six rolls, or once in eighteen rolls. The payoff for the 11 (or 3) is 15:1, which means that if you bet $5, and the 11 (or 3) hits on the next roll, you'll win $75.

When you start playing, wait for a first 11 (or 3) and begin counting. After twenty rolls, and no second 11 (or 3) appears, you begin betting. If another 11 (or 3) rolls before you count twenty, you start all over. Counting rolls is easy. Use your chip racks—the top one for 3s, the bottom one for 11s. Start with $1 chips and move them across the rack. When five $1 chips are moved, replace them with one $5 chip. Keep a very careful eye on the rolls and don't lose your concentration.

After twenty rolls have passed, begin betting $1 on the 11 (or 3). Continue adding $1 to your bet on every roll, until the 11 (or 3) finally hits. Remember, the 11 (or 3) pays a whopping 15 to 1, so if you have just $20 on the 11, you will win $300. Of course, you have to subtract the money you've bet from the money you've won to figure out your actual profit.

FACT

The dots on the dice are called "pips." The bowl that the dice are stored in is called a "boat." The round disk used to mark the point is called a "puck." A tip for the dealers is called a "toke." And finally, the entire area where you are playing is called the "pit."

When you start betting, there have already been twenty rolls since the last 11 (or 3), so you are really starting on the twenty-first roll. It is unlikely that an 11 will roll less than once in thirty-six rolls. But, in the improbable event that an 11 (or 3) takes more than forty rolls (twenty rolls plus the first counted twenty), you will need to increase your bets by $2, instead of $1.

Sample Results

If you win on the fourth roll (after the initial twenty rolls, which is actually the twenty-fourth) you will make $60 from your $4 bet. But, you've already bet $10, so your profit is $50 ($60 – $10). On the fifteenth roll (after the initial twenty) where you bet $15, you'll win $225, and have a $105 profit, because you've already bet $120.

Before you start betting, tell the dealer what you are going to do and make sure of the betting limit on the 3 or 11.

Some casinos have different limits than others. A table with a $500 flat bet limit may limit you to a $125 craps bet. Make sure you know the craps number limits before you start betting. The next time you see someone roll a 3 or 11, you might want to start counting and give this method a try.

The 2s and 12s

To use this system you need to count the rolls and know how many rolls have passed since the last 12 (or 2). In the last section, we had to wait twenty rolls before betting on the 3 or 11. Since the 2 or 12 roll half as many times as the 3 or 11, we need to wait for forty rolls without a 12 or a 2 before we start betting.

The 2s and 12s roll only once each in thirty-six rolls, or once for both in eighteen rolls. The payoff for the 12 (or 2) is 30 to 1, which means that if you bet $5, and the 12 (or 2) hits on the next roll, you'll win $150.

When you arrive at the table, wait for a first 12 (or 2) and begin counting. After forty rolls, and no second 12 (or 2), you begin betting. If another 12 (or 2) rolls before you start betting, you start all over. Again, use your chip racks to count rolls—the top one for 2s, the bottom one for 12s. Start with $1 chips and move them across the rack. When five $1 chips are moved, replace them with one $5 chip. Remember to keep a careful eye on the rolls and don't lose your concentration.

After forty rolls have passed with no 2 or 12, begin betting $1 on the 12 (or 2). Continue adding $1 to your bet on every roll, until the 12 (or 2) finally hits. Remember, the 12 (or 2) pays a whopping 30 to 1, so if you have just $20 on the 12, you will win $600. Of course, don't forget that you have to subtract the money you've bet from the money you've won to determine your actual profit.

When you start betting, there have already been forty rolls since the last 12 (or 2), so you are really starting on roll forty-one. It is unlikely that a 12 will roll less than once in sixty rolls. But, in the improbable event that an 12 (or 2) takes more than sixty rolls (twenty rolls plus the first counted forty), you will need to increase your bets by $2, instead of $1.

Let's look at some examples. If you win on the fourth roll (after the initial forty, which is actually the forty-fourth) you will make $120 from your $4 bet. But, you've already bet $10, so your profit is $110 ($120 – $10). On the fifteenth roll (after the initial forty) where you bet $15, you'll win $450, and have a $330 profit, because you've already bet $120.

Before you start betting, tell the dealer what you are going to do and make sure of the betting limit on the 2 or 12. Some casinos have different limits than others. A table with a $500 flat bet limit may limit you to a $125 craps bet. Again, make sure you know the craps number limits before you start betting.

The next time you see someone roll a 2 or 12 you might want to start counting and give this method a try. If you've never bet big on prop bets, there is a method in the next chapter that you can use to test these theories, and it wouldn't cost you any money at all.

FACT

There are actually two different kinds of dice used in casinos—Type A and Type B. If you hold the dice so that the 3s are pointing away from you like an arrow (forming an upside-down V) and see two 6s, you have Type A. If you see two 1s, you have Type B dice.

Horn Betting Systems

The two previous methods (betting on the 2s or 12s and the 3s or 11s) could require you to wager several hundred dollars at a time. If you've never played these systems before you might be a little apprehensive about investing so much money on them.

Let's say you are intrigued by the 3/11 system but are afraid of the possible large outlay of cash if the 3/11 doesn't hit in thirty-five rolls. So you ignore this system and bet your favorite—$44 inside and then take down your bets after any one hit. What you can do now is combine both systems and bet real chips on one and imaginary chips on the other. You can use your chip racks to keep track of your imaginary bets, while the helpful dealers will keep track of your real bets.

Let's say you get to the table and color in for $500 and you ask for twenty-five whites, fifteen reds, and sixteen greens. After the come-out, you bet $44 inside, which you give to the dealer. In your imaginary betting, you move one white chip over in your rack, because you must wait for twenty rolls before you start betting on the 3 or 11. You would keep on betting normally with your place bets until the twentieth roll. Now, move one red chip over to signify a 1-unit bet. Then two, then three, and so forth, and see how long it is before you win.

Let's say you won on the twentieth roll, which would mean you have $20 on the 3 or the 11. Since they each pay 15 to 1, you have won $300 (15 × $20), but you must subtract this from what you've already bet. With a piece of paper, you add up $1 + 2 + 3 + 4 + 5 + 6 + 7 + 8 + 9 + 10 + 11 + 12 + 13 + 14 + 15 + 16 + 17 + 18 + 19 + 20$ and find that it totals $210, so your profit on this bet would be $90 ($300 − $210).

After you've done this a few times and get used to the betting and counting, you can try it with real money.

The same goes for the 2s and 12s. However, you are now waiting for forty rolls instead of twenty before you start betting. Of course, since you are playing on paper only, you can also bet on all four numbers. Just wait twenty rolls before you start on the 3 or 11, and forty rolls for the 2 or 12.

The next time you play craps, try these imaginary bets on the 3/11 or the 2/12? It doesn't cost you anything and you just might learn a new, profitable method of play.

Hardway Bets

Most crapshooters know that the hardways have high payoffs—the 6 and 8 both pay 9:1, and the 4 and 10 both pay 7:1. But hardway numbers (4, 6, 8, and 10) only pay off when two identical numbers are rolled. This means you will only win if 2 and 2, 3 and 3, 4 and 4, or 5 and 5 are rolled. The 1 and 1 or 6 and 6 do not count as a hardway, because that is the only way they can roll.

As you know, if you bet on a hard 6, you only win if the dice combination is 3 and 3. You lose if the combination is 4 and 2, 5 and 1, 2 and 4, or 1 and 5 (soft). On a hard 8, you only win if the roll is 4 and 4. You lose if it is 2 and 6, 3 and 5, 5 and 3, or 6 and 2. So, of the five ways to make a 6 or 8, four are soft ways and only one is hard. The hard 4 must roll 2 and 2 to win. You lose on a 1 and 3 or 3 and 1. The hard 10 must roll 5 and 5. You lose on a 4 and 6 or a 6 and 4. So, of the three ways to make a 4 or 10, two are soft and only one is hard.

FACT

A terrific tip for the dealers is a $5 bet on the hard 6 or 8. It could last for many rolls and get the dealers even more involved with the game. If it hits, instead of $5 they get $45 for the 6 or 8, or $35 for the 4 or 10.

The true odds of the hard 6/8 are 10:1, but the payoff is only 9:1, giving the casino a 9 percent edge. And the true odds on the 4/10 are 8:1, but the payoff is only 7:1, giving the casino a 11 percent edge. But, since the hard 6/8 rolls once and the hard 4/10 also rolls once, why are the odds different? And if each hard number rolls the same amount (one in thirty-six) as the 2 and 12, why aren't the odds identical? The payoff for the 2/12 is 30:1. Why don't the hardways pay higher?

When you place a bet for the 2/12, it is a one-roll bet. If any number other the 2/12 rolls, you lose. Their true odds are 36:1, as they each should appear only once in thirty-six rolls. The hardway bets, however, stay up if anything other than a 7 or an easy way rolls. Even though a hard number should roll once in thirty-six rolls, it stays up more often than the 2/12, which is why the payoff is lower.

Since hardways stay up until they are hit or lose, it is easy to start a progression with them—just bet $1 each on the hard 4, 10, 6, and 8—a total of only $4 to start out.

These hard numbers each should roll once in thirty-six rolls. If there is a long time between 7s you could win $7 + $7 + $9 +$9, or $32, for a $4 investment on all four hardways.

If the 7 (or the soft number) rolls, you would increase your bet by $1 and put it back up. So you might have different bets on different numbers. You should also have a 33 percent win goal and loss limit for this hardway method. If you buy in for $500 you would quit if you win or lose $150.

Some crapshooters try to minimize their losses by calling bets off when eight rolls go by. The hardways are also off on the come-out when everyone is rooting for a 7.

Speaking of the come-out, did you know there is a better bet to protect your pass line than the any craps or the C & E bet?

Craps Numbers

Many people use craps numbers to hedge their pass line bet. For example, if you have a $10 pass line bet you might bet "$1 any craps," which will pay you $7 if a craps number (2, 3, or 12) rolls. If it doesn't, of course, you lose your $1. In thirty-six rolls then, you will pay $36.

In thirty-six rolls, the three craps numbers will roll four times, and four times $7 is only $28, so you lose $8 ($36–$28) on this bet every thirty-six rolls. You will also lose even more money on the C & E bet (craps and 11), which is why dealers always push this bet. In thirty-six rolls you will win $28 and lose $48—a $20 loss every thirty-six rolls.

There is a third, rarely used bet for the craps numbers called a three-way craps bet. It is bet in multiples of $3 and pays off even better than a three-way hop bet. It pays 15:1 on the 3 and 30:1 on the 2 and 12.

You can also add another $1 and call for a "three-way craps bet, high 3." This means you are betting $1 each on the 2 and 12, and $2 on the 3. This is especially useful on the pass line. If you have a $25 pass line bet you would normally bet $3 any craps. If a 3 rolls, you would win $21

($3 × 7) and lose $25. On the three-way craps high 3, you still would lose your $25 pass line bet but you would win $30. So you're investing an extra $1 to win $9 more. Actually, you would win $7 instead of $9 because, as in all multiple prop bets, the losing bets are subtracted from the winnings.

If the 2 or 12 rolls and you have a $3 any craps bet you would lose $25 and win $21. If the 2 or 12 rolls and you have $3 three-way craps you would still lose your $25 but you would win $30. For the same bet amount you would win $9 more.

Next time you need to protect your $25 or higher pass line bet give the three-way craps high 3 bet a try.

Hardway Hops

A hop bet is a little understood one-roll, verbal bet you can make on any combination of numbers. For example, if you have an intuitive notion that the combination 4 and 1 will appear on the very next roll of the dice, you can place a bet for 4 and 1 hopping. If the 4 and 1 do appear, you win. If 3 and 2, or any other combinations come up, you lose.

The payoff for a hop bet is usually 15:1. This means you can bet 2 and 3 hopping, or 4 and 2 hopping, or even 3 and 4 hopping. If you bet $5 on any of these bets and the very next roll is for exactly the numbers you bet, then you'll win $75.

You can also bet on hardways hopping. If you think a hardway 4 is due you can bet, for example, a $5 2 and 2 hop. Now the good thing about hardway hops is that they pay double—instead of 15:1, you get 30:1 on your wagers! So, if you bet $5 hardway 4 hop, and the very next roll is 2 and 2, you'll win $150 (at 30:1) instead of $35 at 7:1—$110 more.

ALERT!

Despite what the dealers say, craps number bets (the 2, 3, and 12) do not make good hedges for the pass line bet. Mathematically you are better off using the money for these bets for extra odds on your pass line bets.

A hardway hop is for one roll only, however, while a regular hardway bet stays up until it wins or loses. Also, make sure your favorite casino pays 30:1 on hardway hops. Some of the older casinos still pay 15:1, so ask first to make sure.

At 30:1 this means you can bet $5 hardway hopping on the 4, 6, 8, or 10 and win $150 as opposed to winning $35 on the 4/10 or $45 on the 6/8.

Many people also use hop bets when someone is setting the dice and has developed his own signature roll. This is usually evident when the shooter bets big on a certain number.

Let's say the point is 6 and he buys the 4 or 10 for $50. Instead of you buying the same number you can hop it and win lots more money!

Chapter 8

Other Craps Bets

There are several other bets that we have not yet examined closely. Some are unadvertised wagers like put bets and don't hop bets. Others are popular but as yet unprofitable wagers like the field and big 6 or 8. We'll also look at the "any" bet—any craps. All of these wagers are unprofitable to the average crapshooter, but there are little-known secrets that you can use to turn the odds in your favor.

Put Bets

When you are playing at a casino offering 10× odds and you make a pass line bet, would you rather have a 4 point or a 6 point to add your odds to? If you'd like to be able to choose your point numbers on a 10× or higher casino, then put bets are for you.

A put bet is a wager that has been all but ignored until just recently, but thanks to the proliferation of casinos offering 10× odds and above, it is becoming more common. A put bet is a pass line bet that you put up after the point is established.

If you have not placed a pass line bet and the shooter rolls a point of 6, you can then put a bet on the pass line, with the appropriate odds. This bet loses the 7/11 advantage a pass line player has before the point is established, so it has gone unused in most craps games. Today, though, we see casinos offering 5×, 10×, and 100× odds on pass line bets. These extra odds offset the player's advantage before the come-out roll for pass line bets if the point is a 6 or 8.

The casino advantage to a pass line bet with single odds is 1.4 percent. Add double odds and their advantage drops to .61 percent. Five times odds brings it down to .33 percent and ten times odds is only .18 percent.

ESSENTIAL

You should make a put bet only if the pass line point is 6 or 8 and only if you can add 10× odds or more. This means that if you have a $5 flat bet and take $50 odds, you can win $60 (at 6:5 odds), plus $5 for your flat bet, for a total of $65.

Some casino personnel do not know what a put bet is, so just ask your friendly dealer if you can make a pass line bet with full odds after the point is established. The more experienced dealers will let you make a put bet, even if you don't ask first. Put bets are most beneficial in establishments that offer 100× or unlimited odds, but you can try them in your favorite casino, even if it only offers 10× odds.

The big advantage to put bets is that you get to choose your own point numbers. The disadvantage is that you miss out on the come-out 7s and 11. But remember, you don't add any odds until the point is established, so on come-out 7s and 11s, all you win is your minimum flat bet, which usually is just $5.

It is much more advantageous if you increase the chances of winning your added odds bets, and you have a better chance of doing this with the 6 or 8 points.

Put bets can be very profitable, and there are more unadvertised betting methods that can make you even more profit.

Don't Hop Bets

A hop bet is a one-roll bet that can pay up to 30:1. You must bet the exact dice combination to win. For example, you can bet a 3 and 3 hop and if the result is 4 and 2 or 5 and 1, you lose. On a place bet 6, if you bet $6 you win $7. On a 3 and 3 hop you bet $6 and win $180—$174 more!

If you like to lay bets, you probably at one time or another thought of hedging your lay bet with a hardway wager. For example, if you have a $80 lay bet on the 10 along with a $12 hard 10 bet, you cut the number of ways you can lose from two (4 and 6, 5 and 5) to one (4 and 6). If the hard 10 rolls, you lose your $80 lay bet but win $84 (at 7:1) from the hardway.

Instead of betting $12 hard 10 you can bet just $2 5 and 5 hopping, which can pay 30:1 instead of 7:1. This way you lose the $80 if the hardway rolls but win $60 on the hard 10. Since you are betting $2 instead of $12, you can do this six times before the regular hardway becomes a better bet.

ALERT!

Four of the six points (4, 6, 8, and 10) can be hardway points. A hardway hop can pay 30:1 while a regular hop bet only pays 15:1. So a $5 4 and 4 hop can pay $150 while a $5 5 and 3 hop only pays $75, even though the same numbers were rolled.

Hop bets are even better bets when they just have to be made once or twice, like protecting your bet on the come-out. Let's say you have a $40 don't pass bet, which you are protecting by laying both the 4 and 10 for $40 each.

If no 4, 10, or 7 roll, you would remove your lay bets after the point becomes established. If a 7 rolls you lose your don't pass bet but win both lay bets. If the 4 or 10 rolls, however, you lose those bets and have to put them back up to protect your don't pass bet.

You can protect the lays by betting $5 hard 4 and $5 hard 10. If the hard 4 or 10 rolls, you lose $40 and win $35 for the hardway. But you only need them up until the point is established, so a hop bet might be a better way to go.

You only have to bet $1 2 and 2 hop and/or $1 5 and 5 hop. A $2 hedge bet is easier on the wallet than a $10 one. This way if the hard number rolls you still lose your $40 but win $30. If a soft number rolls with a regular hardway hedge you'll lose $5 compared to losing $1 on the hop bet.

"Any" Craps Bets

Many dealers will encourage you to make additional hedge bets on craps numbers (2, 3, and 12) to protect your pass line bet. You'll always hear any craps bets called whenever a new shooter is coming out.

Let's look at the math for any craps bets. At the end of thirty-six rolls, you've invested $36 (36 × $1) in these hedge bets. The 2, 3, or 12 will theoretically roll four times (once each for the 2 and 12, and twice for the 3) in thirty-six rolls. So, if you win these craps bets four times, you've won $28 (4 × $7), and spent $36 (36 × $1) giving you an $8 ($36 − $28) loss.

You can also bet $2 ($1 each) craps and 11 (C & E). Here, you are betting the 2, 3, 12, and 11. Craps (2, 3, or 12) pays 7:1, while the 11 pays 15:1. If the 11 rolls, you win $24 ($10 pass line + $15 11 − $1 any craps). The 7 will win you $8 ($10 pass line − $2 C & E). If the 2, 3, or 12 roll, you'll lose $4 ($7 craps − $1 11 − $10 pass line) instead of $10.

This time, though, in thirty-six decisions, you've invested $72 (2 × $36) in hedge bets. The 2 and 12 will have each rolled once, and the 3 and 11 twice. You would make $7 on the 2 ($1 × 7), $14 on the 3 ($2 × 7), $7 on the 12 ($1 × 7), and $30 on the 11 ($2 × 15). This totals $58 ($7 + $14 + $7 + $30), but you've already invested $72, so you have a $14 ($72 – $58) loss. Another winner for the house!

Finally, you can make a three-way craps bet (on the 2, 3, and 12) for $3. This is different from the any craps bet because the odds are higher—30:1 for the 2 and 12, and 15:1 for the 3. So if the 2 or 12 roll you win $18 ($30 – $10 – $2) instead of losing $10, and if the 3 rolls, you win $3 ($15 – $10 – $2) instead of losing $10. This bet also means that you will win on the 7 and 11 (from your pass line bet) and on the 2, 3, and 12 (from the 3-way craps bet).

In thirty-six rolls, however, this time you've invested $108 ($3 × 36). The 2 and 12 will roll once, and the 3 twice. At 30 to 1, the 2 and 12 pay $30 each, for a total of $60. At 15 to 1, the 3 pays $30 ($2 × 15). You made $90 ($30 + $60) but spent $108 for a loss of $18.

Unfortunately, as you can see, you cannot profitably protect a $10 pass line bet by hedging it with craps bets.

Any craps is the most common hedge bet and pays 7:1. This means that if you have a $10 pass line bet and a $1 any craps bet, you'll win $9 ($10 – $1) if the 7 (or 11) rolls, and lose only $3 ($10 pass line – $7 any craps) instead of $10 if the 2, 3, or 12 rolls.

Some craps writers have maintained that a craps hedge bet is only profitable with a pass line bet of $25 or more, with a $4 any craps bet. Let's look at the math. If you bet $4 any craps you'll win $112, which comes from $4 (bet) × 4 (number of times 2, 3, or 12 rolls) × 7 (payoff). You'll lose $144 ($4 × 36), resulting in a $32 loss. So, it's still not a good bet. In fact, it's worse than a $10 pass line bet with a $1 any craps bet!

Now, let's look at the same $25 pass line bet with a C & E hedge for $4. If the 11 rolls, you'll win $83 ($25 pass line + $60 11 – $2 any). The 7 will win you $21 ($25 pass line – $4 C & E). If the 2 or 3 rolls, you win $1 ($28 – $25 – $2). In thirty-six rolls you've invested $144 ($4 × 36). The 2 and 12 will each have rolled once, and the 3 and 11 twice each. You would make $14 on the 2 ($2 × 7), $28 on the 3 ($2 × 14), $14 on the

12 ($2 × 7) and $60 on the 11 ($2 × 30). This totals $116. So you've lost $28 ($144 − $116).

Finally, let's look at a $6 three-way craps bet with a $25 pass line bet. If the 2 or 12 rolls you win $31 ($60 − $25 − $4). If the three rolls you win $1 ($30 − $25 − $4). In thirty-six rolls on this bet you've invested $216 ($6 × 36). At 30:1, the 2 and 12 pay $60 each (30 × $2) for a total of $120 ($60 + $60). At 15:1, the 3 pays $60 ($2 × 15 × 2). You made $180 ($120 + $60) but spent $216, giving you a $36 loss.

Craps is a math game, and, as you can see, there is no way you can protect a pass line bet with craps hedge bets—whether your unit is $5, $10, or $25.

So—the secret of protecting your pass line bet is to save all the money you would normally use for hedge bets and use that money to make more free odds bets. If you want insurance, go to your agent—not your craps bet.

The Big 6 and the Big 8

As you might know, the big 6 and 8 are even money bets. This means that if you bet $12 and win, you win $12. If you placed $12 on the regular 6 or 8, you would win $14, at 7:6 odds. The casino gives a lot of space to the big 6 and 8, so beginners who are afraid to give the dealer a place bet can bet directly on the big numbers in the corner. In most cases these bets should be avoided.

The casino advantage for the big 6 or 8 is 9.09 percent, while the exact same bets are available as place bets with a casino advantage of only 1.5 percent. Usually only beginners bet the big numbers, because they are too shy to give their money to the dealers for a bet.

There are two good uses for the big 6 and 8. The first involves those match play coupons so common in the casino fun books. Most of these coupons state they are for flat bets only, and are usually used for pass or don't pass bets, with no odds. If you put a match play coupon for $5 along with $5 on the pass line, you take a chance on getting stuck with a 4 or 10.

But if you put your $5 coupon along with $5 on the big 6 or 8, you are getting the best bet you can get, under the circumstances. If the 6 or 8 hits, you'll get back $10 in real money. It's not as good as placing the numbers, but you can't use a match play coupon with place numbers.

The other good use of the big 6 or 8 involves table limits. If you happen to hit a really hot table and have progressed your bets on the place 6 and 8 up to the table limit, then the dealers will not let you increase your place bets. However, they will always let you make additional flat bets on the big numbers in addition to your place bets. So instead of a $1,000 table limit, you now have a $2,000 limit on the 6 and 8. This becomes especially useful in tournament play.

In a tournament, the winning crapshooters are usually decided in the last few moments of a game. It is not uncommon to see someone place $480 on the place 6 and 8, as well as on the big 6 and 8, hoping for a 6 or 8 on the last few rolls of the dice. If the 6 or 8 does roll, they'll receive $480 for the big number bet, and $560 for the place bet—a total of $1,040 for one roll of the dice!

Of course, if you don't play tournaments, use match play coupons, or approach the table limits, you probably won't use the big 6 and 8. There is another bet that everyone knows is a bad bet—the field. But sometimes, betting on the field will bring profits instead of disappointments.

The Field

The field bet, when used by itself, is not a good bet. It must be used with other bets or in a progression to make it profitable for the experienced crapshooter. These seven different field numbers (2, 3, 4, 9, 10, 11, and 12) can be made a total of only sixteen times, leaving twenty for the other numbers. If a 5, 6, 7, or 8 rolls you lose. So, if you place a field bet by itself, you'll win sixteen times and lose twenty times (in thirty-six theoretical rolls). And, most of the field only pays off 1:1—that is, if you bet $5, you win $5.

If you bet $5 on the field and the 4 rolls, you'll win just $5 (at 1:1) instead of the $9 (at 9:5) you would win if you placed the 4.

The seven field numbers can be made a total of sixteen times. The 6 and 8 can be rolled ten times, the 5 four times, and the 7 six times. So if you bet on the 5, 6, and 8 in addition to the field, you can win thirty times (16 + 10 + 4) and lose only to the 7, which rolls six times.

The 2 and 12 on the field each pay 2:1, but the vig on the field bet is still a hefty 5.6 percent. You should look for casinos that pay 3:1 on the 2 or 12. This brings the casino vig down to only 2.8 percent, a much more acceptable level.

You can place $25 on the 5, $30 on the 6 and 8, and $20 on the field. If the 5, 6, or 8 roll, you win $35 and lose $20, giving you a $15 profit. If the 2 or 12 roll, you win $40 (the field pays double on 2 and 12). And if the 3, 4, 9, 10, or 11 roll, you win $20.

The trick to this, of course, is not leaving everything up so it can get whacked by the 7. You should wait for a come-out 7 before you make this bet, leave all your bets up for one roll only, and take everything down. Then wait for another come-out 7 before you start betting again.

For smaller bankrolls, try placing the 5 for $5, the 6 and 8 for $6 each, and $2 on the field. Again, wait for a come-out 7 first, and leave your bets up for one roll only. You'll win $2 on the 3, 4, 9, 10, and 11, $5 ($7 – $2) on the 5, 6, or 8, and, $4 on the 2 or 12.

The next time you want to bet inside, try betting the field also—but just for one roll.

Chapter 9
The Do Side Systems

The pass and come bets are the most popular in an average game of craps. Not only do you get to root for the shooter, but you can add odds to your bets, which have no casino advantage. The first method we will examine, however, adds no odds to your pass and come bets, but you still could make a good profit. We'll also look at two do side progressive systems and two famous mail-order methods.

The Come Balance

As you know by now, a come bet is similar to a pass line bet in that you win on the come-out 7 or 11 but lose on the 2, 3, or 12. This complicates matters because when you have a pass line bet and a come bet, sometimes they will cancel each other out.

Let's say you have a $10 pass line bet and the point is 6. You make a come bet and the 7 rolls. You will win your come bet and lose your pass line bet. This new method takes advantage of that quality, and "balances out" the come bets with pass line bets on the next come-out. You will make money on repeating numbers and you'll never lose to a 7-out.

In order for the Come Balance to work, you must balance your new come bets with any existing bets on the layout, and keep them balanced. Since there are only six point numbers, you will probably get some repeats before a 7 rolls. Let's take a close look at this method.

Start out with a $5 pass line bet. When the point is established, make a come bet. So now you have a $5 pass line bet and a $5 come bet, for a total of $10. Your third wager should be for $10, so that if the 7 rolls now you wouldn't lose anything. You would win $10 on the come and lose $5 on your established come and $5 on the pass line, so the bets would cancel out.

Your fourth bet would be the total of your three previous bets, which is $20. By now you should get a few repeat numbers, and that will be your profit.

Sample Roll

You bet $5 on the pass line and the point is 6. You make a $5 come bet, and the shooter rolls an 8, so you now have $10 in play. Make a $10 come bet. The shooter rolls a 5, so you now have $5 on the pass line (the point is 6), $5 on the come 8, and $10 on the come 5. This totals $20, so you now make a $20 come bet.

The shooter tosses an 8, so you win your first come bet for $5 and your $20 moves to the 8. You now have $20 on the 8, $10 on the 5, and $5 on the pass line, for a total of $35, which is your next come bet. Now the shooter throws another 8, so you win $20 and your $35 goes to the 8. You now have

$35 on the 8, $10 on the 5, and $5 on the pass line, for a total of $50, which is your next come bet. The next roll is a 7, so you win $50 and lose $50 for a push, but you've already won $20, so you're ahead.

FACT

The easy way to bet the Come Balance system is to add up all of your chips on the table (come plus pass line) and that would be your next bet on the come. And make sure you concentrate only on this system and do not make any other bets.

The only disadvantage to this method is that you are very vulnerable to losing your new come bets to the 2, 3, or 12. The best way to hedge your come-out is with a 3-way craps bet, which pays 15:1 on the 3 or 30:1 on the 2 or 12. You can also bet $1 any craps, which pays 7:1 if any craps numbers roll. Both of these are one-roll bets, so they will need to be replenished on each new come bet.

But whether you hedge your bets or not, give the Come Balance a try. You have eliminated the threat of the 7, and by the time it rolls, hopefully you will have three or four repeat numbers. You can make money on every shooter with this system, and, at the same time increase your comps as well.

The Fibonacci

This is a somewhat advanced system but once you get used to it, you'll see that it almost always wins—just as long as you stick to the rules and don't make any other bets.

Fibonacci is a mathematical term signifying that you have a number series where the total of each two consecutive numbers is larger than all of the preceding numbers. For example, a simple Fibonacci series would be 1, 1, 2, 3, 5, 8, 13. As you can see, 13 + 8 (21) is more than 1 + 1 + 2 + 3 + 5 (12). Also 5 + 8 (13) is more than 1 + 1 + 2 + 3 (7). Another attribute to this series is that the next number would be the sum of the two previous numbers. For example, 13 is the sum of 8 + 5. Also, the next number after 13 would be 13 + 8, or 21.

This mathematical series can be very profitable to a crapshooter! You can bet flat bets on the pass, don't pass, come or don't come. If you win any two consecutive bets, no matter where you are on the progression you will make money. And, if you win any two out of three bets, you will also have a profit if you stick to the system.

The progression you must bet is, of course, the Fibonacci series. You will bet multiples of 1, 1, 2, 3, 5, 8, 13, 21, 34, 55, 89, 144, etc. With the exception of the first two bets, your new wager is always the sum of your prior two bets, so you don't have to memorize anything.

Sample Roll with $1 Units

You start betting, first $1 on the pass line, lose, and bet another $1. Now once the first two bets are established, the next bet is always the total of the two previous bets, so you bet $2, which you lose also. The next bet is $3 ($2 + $1), which you lose. You fifth bet is $5 ($3 + $2), but you lose that one also. Now your sixth bet is $5 plus $3, or $8, which you win. Your seventh bet is $8 + $5, or $13, which you win also. Now let's see what happened.

You lost the first five bets—$1 + $1 + $2 + $3 + $5, for a total of $12. You win the next two bets for $8 and $13, so you've won $21 and lost $12. You have a $9 profit.

Let's say you lose the first eleven bets. You would lose $1 + $1 + $2 + $3 + $5 + $8 + $13 + $21 + $34 + $55 + $89 or a total of $232. If you win only the next two bets at $144 and $233, you would win $377 and be ahead by $144.

You will also profit if you win any two out of three bets. If you won the eleventh bet of $89, lost the twelfth bet of $144, but won the thirteenth bet of $233, you would still be ahead by $178!

Your goal in this system is to make a profit. Once you win any two out of three bets, you pocket the profit and start over again at bet 1. You should quit when you win 50 percent of your buy-in, so if you buy in for $500, you should stop when you win $250.

In the highly unlikely event that you lose fourteen straight bets in a row, you'll be in trouble, because you'll be down almost $1,000 and at the same time up against the casino's $500 bet limit. The secret of avoiding this improbable but remotely possible fate is simply to qualify your shooter before you bet. Take a look at the section on qualifying the shooter in Chapter 18, and then give the Fibonacci a try!

FACT

With the Fibonacci, you don't have to bet on every shooter. If you see someone you don't like, just remember where you are (bring a pad and paper) and start up at the same place in the progression when a new shooter gets the dice.

The Rotating Field

As you probably know, the field bet is a one-roll bet. So if any number other than 2, 3, 4, 9, 10, 11, or 12 rolls, you lose. The other numbers, 5, 6, 7, and 8, roll a total of twenty-six times while the field numbers roll only twenty times. On the surface, it looks like the field is a bad bet.

Craps professionals know that their winning depends on streaks. When a positive streak occurs, they bet more. When a negative one appears, they bet less. When you play the field, you can determine whether to increase or decrease your bets by using a rotating field progression.

In order to accomplish this efficiently, you will need a win goal and a loss limit. Let's say your buy-in is $500, so your starting unit on the field should be $5. You should not make any other bets and you should quit when you've won or lost the same amount—30 percent of your buy-in, or $150. You need to keep betting on the field without missing any bets. This means you have to bet before the come-out as well, and be completely sure the dealers know your bet is on. If you make a bet and the dealer thinks it is off, then you won't get paid.

To bet, just take a red chip and place it on the field. If you win, increase your bet by 1 unit ($5). If you win again, increase it by 1 unit again. So now you have $15 on the field. If you lose, just go down 1 unit.

You are not doubling your bet on a win, even if you hit a 2 or 12. You are going up 1 unit when you win and going down 1 unit when you lose. If you have $50 on the field and the 12 (or 2) hits and you win $100, just increase your next bet by $5 to $55 and pocket the rest. Your win goal of $150 means the money in your pocket plus your money on the table. So if you started out with $500 and now have a combination of $150 on the table plus on your rack, it's time to stop and take a break.

ALERT!

When you win a field bet, the dealer will add the winnings to your bet and return everything to you. You must then make a new bet on the field at the proper level. You must do this quickly, before the next roll, so you should always have your next bet ready!

If the shooter happens to hit a string of nonfield numbers, you are limited in your losses, because you are decreasing your bet by 1 unit on a loss until you hit zero. Then you'll start betting 1 unit ($5) again. At zero, if you lose four bets in a row you are down $20 (4 × $5). If you then win the next four bets in a row you are up $50 ($5 + $10 + $15 + $20).

The most important part of this method is to make sure your field bet is always on, even before the come-out. Once you tell the dealers what you are doing, they will help you with this, but when you first start out betting, make sure that they know your bet is on. You don't want to lose money even though you made the correct bet!

The Paroli

The Paroli is an aggressive play and, although most people use it on the pass line, you can use it on the don't pass as well. The Paroli states that when you win your bet you increase the next one, but when you lose your bet you stay at the same level. When you increase your bet you do it by doubling it plus adding 1 unit. Your goal is to win four straight decisions in a row.

Sample Roll with $5 Units

You bet $5 pass, and win. Instead of betting $10, you add 1 unit and bet $15, or 3 units. You win this second bet, so you double it and add 1 unit, at seven units, or $35. You win this third bet, too, and now bet 15 units, or $75, for your fourth bet.

At this fourth level, you will win a total of twenty-six units, or $130. However, if you lose this fourth-level bet, you will only lose 4 units ($75 – $55 = $20).

The secret to this play is to latch onto a small streak of at least four consecutive wins on either the pass or don't pass. In order for you to profit from the Paroli you must be ready to switch from do to don't or vice versa. You can chart the table, of course, but the easiest way is to watch the shooters.

If the shooter looks confident and bets big on himself, bet on the do side—just follow his lead. If you don't like the shooter for any reason, just bet the don't pass.

The mindset of many crapshooters is to stay on the pass line for their entire life. Don't do this. It is no crime to switch to the don't side. You are not betting with the casino. Both the do and don't players are betting against the casino and it is no crime to play the back line.

Sample Roll Paroli Switching

You notice the shooter is not well dressed, but he looks sixty or so and has a players card. He has lots of green chips in his rack, so on that basis alone you pop a red chip on the pass line. Soon the point is made, so your next bet on the pass is for $15. He makes it again. Your third bet, for $35, misses, and you get a new shooter. This time you just look at this guy and don't like him for some reason. Since you've learned to go with your hunches, you start all over (because you lost the last play) at $5 on the don't pass.

As you expected, he 7s out so your next bet (still on the don't pass) is $15, even though you're not sure of the shooter—a middle-aged gal with lots of white chips. She just bets one on herself, and sure enough she soon 7s out. Your next bet is $35 and an old guy wearing overalls takes the dice. In your years of experienced shooting, you've discovered that old guys with overalls really know how to play, so you switch back to the do side. He makes the point, so now you're at $75 and your last (fourth) bet, and he makes that too.

Next time you play, give the Paroli a try—especially if the shooter is wearing overalls!

The La Bouchere

The La Bouchere is also known as the Cancellation system and works fairly well, but you need to come up with your own set of four different "lucky" numbers in order to play. Some mail-order operators sell this (along with their own "exclusive" lucky numbers) for $20 or more.

ALERT!

For your "lucky" numbers, you might try the year of your spouse's birth, your birthday, or your anniversary. When you find a sequence that works for you, then those will become your "lucky" numbers!

First, you'll need four random one-digit, nonzero numbers. In this scenario we'll use the numbers 1, 2, 3, and 4. You might want to use the La Bouchere with a pen and pad until you get used to it, but if you've played it once or twice you can do the math in your head.

To get the first bet you're going to make, you just add the two outside numbers. In this case, you would add 1 and 4 to get your first bet of $5. If you win this first bet, you cross out the numbers that made the bet, and you are left with 2 and 3. So, your next bet is 2 + 3, or $5.

If you happen to lose your first bet, you simply add the number lost to the progression, so it is now 1, 2, 3, 4, 5. Your next bet would be the sum of 1 and 5, or $6. If you lose that bet, add $6 to the progression, so it is now 1, 2, 3, 4, 5, 6 and your next bet would be $7.

Let's say you now win the $7 bet, so you cross out 1 and 6 and are left with 2, 3, 4, and 5. The sum of the two outside numbers is 7, so you bet $7. You win this, cross out the 2 and 5, and the next numbers are 3 and 4, so you bet $7 again.

Your series ends when all the numbers are crossed out.

As you've probably noticed, you are crossing out two numbers with every win and adding only one number with every loss. This means you can lose more bets than you win and still come out ahead.

You can play this system, maintaining the same progression from the do or the don't side—either pass/come or don't pass/don't come. You should use a 30 percent win goal or loss limit, so if you buy in with $500, you should stop when you've won or lost $150.

The big disadvantage to this unique system is that a long string of loses on either the do or don't side will eventually bump you into the table limit. It won't happen as often as with the Martingale, but it might happen. The secret to winning the La Bouchere lies in knowing exactly when to switch sides. You must get used to switching your bets. You can stay on the do for good shooters and switch to the don't for bad shooters. Or, you can switch on every three consecutive decisions. For example, if you win any three decisions in a row, keep the same progression and switch to the other side.

Sample Roll

Let's use the 1, 2, 3, 4 progression and start off with a $5 bet (4 + 1) on the pass line. You lose, so you add 5 to the progression and get 1, 2, 3, 4, 5. You lose your next $6 bet, so you are now at 1, 2, 3, 4, 5, 6. You lose the $7 bet, so you are now at 1, 2, 3, 4, 5, 6, 7.

You've lost three bets in a row, so you switch to the don't pass with a $8 bet. You win, so you cross out the 7 and 1 and are left with 2, 3, 4, 5, 6. Your next bet is also $8, which you win, and now you are at 3, 4, 5. You win your third $8 bet and are left with only one number (4), but since you won three in a row you switch to the pass line. You bet $4 and win, so your series is over. You lost $5 + $6 + $7 ($18) and won $8 + $8 + $8 + $4 ($28), so you're $10 ahead.

Chapter 10

The Don't Side Systems

As much as people like betting with the shooter, sometimes they find out that more profits lie on the don't side. Many people will judge the shooter's looks and mannerisms and, if they don't measure up, the don't pass suddenly gets a lot of bets. In this chapter we'll first look at the Don't Pass Parlay—one that's easy to use and simple to remember! You'll also learn about a few other don't systems. If you like the dark side, then you'll love this section!

Don't Pass Parlay

Don't betting is becoming more popular now, thanks to methods such as charting the tables and qualifying the shooters. A lot of bettors will start out on the pass line, but if a less than stellar shooter comes up to bat, many bettors will switch to the don't side.

You will begin betting this system after a shooter has made two points in a row. Then, make a don't pass bet for 2 units. If you win this bet, make another don't pass for 4 units. When you win this second bet, make another 4-unit don't pass along with a don't come bet for 2 units and take 2× odds.

If these are won, make a fourth don't pass bet of 4 units, along with two don't come bets, both with 2× odds. If you win all of these bets, you are finished, and you need to wait for another two pass line wins to begin again.

Now, a lot can happen to the bets you have on the layout, as you can win some and lose others. You must keep track of your bets, and four bets are pretty easy to track, once you get used to it. You might want to start out using a pen and paper to keep track. The four bets in this Don't Pass Parlay are as follows:

- Don't pass bet (2 units)
- Don't pass bet (4 units)
- Don't pass bet (4 units), plus don't come bet (2 units with 2× odds)
- Don't pass bet (4 units), plus two don't come bets (each 2 units with 2× odds)

If you lose any don't pass bet, you must go down 1 unit and bet again. So if you are at 2 units and lose, go down to 1 unit. If you are at 4 units and lose, go down to 3 units.

FACT

In the Don't Pass Parlay, you should never add odds to your don't pass bet. You will only be adding odds to the don't come bets. If you are at 2 units with double odds and lose, go down to single odds. If you are at single odds and lose, go down to 2 units with no odds.

When you win either your don't pass or don't come bets, go up 1 unit. So, if you have one 4-unit don't pass and two don't come bets with double odds and you win the don't pass but lose both don't comes, you would bet 5 units on the don't pass and two don't come bets (2 units each) with no odds. Your game is over when you win the entire series of don't pass and two don't comes with double odds.

If you are on the don't pass and the shooter rolls a 2 or 3, it is a win, so you increase your next bet by 1 unit. If you are in the don't come and the shooter throws a natural, you lose and should decrease your next don't come bet. If you lose two don't pass bets in a row you should start over because it means that the shooter won the pass line two times in a row.

You need to be mindful of the shooter. This system is used primarily as an alternative to the pass line when the shooter is obviously unqualified. If a new, qualified shooter gets the dice you should immediately get your bets back on the pass line. But if there are lots of don't bettors at the table, playing in this manner could ensure a quick and easy profit on the dark side.

The Crossout

This system goes under a variety of names, and sells mainly through mail order. It is similar to the La Bouchere on the do side, but starts out with three "lucky" numbers of your choice on the don't side instead of four numbers on the do. It also changes the numbers to units. In the La Bouchere, if you end up with the number 10, you bet $10. In the Crossout, you bet 10 units, or $50.

Sellers of this system advertise that you will win more times than you lose, because Crossout also asks you to choose your own three personal "lucky numbers." This may be, but it has nothing to do with the numbers that you choose. It is called the Crossout Craps system because you literally cross out the first and last numbers in your series, as you do in the La Bouchere system.

First, you choose your three "lucky" numbers. These need to be all one-digit numbers, so if your anniversary is May 28, your lucky numbers are 5, 2, and 8. You need to put them in numerical order, so they end up being 2, 5, and 8.

The amount bet is always the sum of the two outside numbers, in this case 10 units (2 + 8). So, if you are playing $5 units, your very first bet should be $50.

When you win, the two outside numbers are scratched off. So, if you bet $50 on the don't pass line and win, you scratch off the numbers you just bet, which are 2 and 8. You're only left with one bet, the 5. So on your next bet, you would bet 5 units, or $25. If you win that one, your series is over and you won $75.

If you happened to have lost your very first bet (for 10 units), it is added to the sequence. In this case your progression now becomes 2, 5, 8, 10. Your next bet would be 12 units (10 + 2). If you win, scratch off the 2 and 10, and your bet would then be 13 units (5 + 8). Remember, your series is finished when all of the numbers have been scratched off.

ALERT!

What Crossout Craps really does is have you bet less when you're losing and more when you're winning. You can actually lose more decisions than you win and still make a profit! Just stick to the system and don't make any other bets.

Sample Roll Using 2, 5, 8 as the Lucky Sequence

You bet 10 units ($50) on the don't pass and lose, so you are now at 2, 5, 8, 10. You bet 12 units ($60) and lose again, so now you're at 2, 5, 8, 10, 12. You bet $14 units ($70), lose, and now bet 16 units ($80). You lose again and bet 18 units ($90). Finally, on this $90 bet you win, and your progression is 2, 5, 8, 10, 14, 16, 18. Since you won, you cross out the 18 and 2, so you bet 16 + 5, or 21 units for $105. If you win that, you cross out the 16 and 5, and bet 8 and 14 (22 units, or $110). You win that and have only one number left, so you bet 10 units, or $50, and win. Now your series is over.

You started out by losing the first four bets in a row—$50 + $60 + $70 + $80, for a total of $260. However, you won the next three bets in a row—

$105 + $110 + $50, for a total of $265. So you lost four bets and won only three and you still came out ahead.

Why not try this at home with your own set of lucky numbers!

Oscar's Grind

Oscar's Grind is a very basic system that seems to work well if you adhere to a strict win goal and a loss limit. With this system, your win goal should be 50 percent of your buy-in. So if you color in for $500, you should stop when you've won $250. Your loss limit is 10 betting units, so if your unit bet is $5, you should stop betting when you are down $50. This is a flat bet don't pass system, so you must not add odds or make any other bets.

You start out on the don't pass. If you lose, your next bet stays the same. If you win, increase your bet by 1 unit. Each time you win, increase your bet by 1 unit until you make a profit. Then continue betting the same amount until you reach your goal.

Sample Roll

You color in for $500 and have a unit bet of $5. You bet one red chip on the don't pass line and win your first bet. Your next bet is $10, which loses. You stay at $10 and lose again, so you are now down a total of $15. You bet $10 and win, so you are still down by $5. You increase your bet 1 unit to $15 and win, so you are now ahead by $10. Even though you won, you stay at the $15 level because you are ahead. Even if you win the next five rolls, you stay at the $15 level.

Now let's say you lose your first six $5 bets on the don't pass, so you're down $30. Your next bet would be $5, of course. You win this seventh bet, so you're now down $25. Your eighth bet is for $10 and you win, so now you're down only $15. Your ninth bet is $15 and you win, so you are even, but not profitable yet. Your tenth bet is $20 and you win, so you now have a profit and will stay at that $20 level until you reach your win goal.

The secret to Oscar's Grind is the shooter, so judge your shooters accordingly. You don't have to bet on every one, and a good way to determine skill is just to watch the shooter. Does the shooter bet big on herself and small on everyone else? Does she carefully set and throw the dice? If you have any positive feelings at all about the shooter, you should just wait for the next one. But remember where you were in the progression and take off from there.

ALERT!

Bring a pad and paper and make notes on all the people at your table before they become shooters. Sometimes first impressions turn out to be true impressions. This way you can decide in advance whether to bet on them or not.

A simple offshoot of this system is to indeed bet on every shooter but determine by looking at him and how he bets whether to bet on the pass or don't pass. If you do this, you will be switching back and forth between shooters but keeping the same progression.

Sample Roll

The new shooter is young and keeps talking to his girlfriend all the time while he's at the table, explaining to her the bets he should have made on the last shooter but didn't. Then he puts a white chip down instead of a red one. You put a red chip on the don't pass. He 7s out right away, so you are ahead by $5. The next shooter watches the way the stickperson returns the dice to her and starts to set them right away. You smile and pop $10 on the pass line. You win but now you are ahead, so you stay at the $10 level until you either reach your win goal or have a loss, in which case you drop down to $5 again.

Oscar's Grind is an easy system to play, and it's fun to look at and judge the shooters just before they shoot. You won't get them right all the time, but as you become more experienced, you'll get them right most of the time.

Four Times Four

This system is very popular because it starts out with a low $5 don't pass bet and almost never loses. It is especially good on a choppy table, and even better on a cold table. Before you play, ask the others around you how the table is going. If there are no don't bettors you might want to switch to the do side or find another table.

The Four Times Four is primarily a don't side system but if you have a hot shooter you can play it on the pass line as well. Then, when the table cools down, switch back to the don't side and continue to follow the same system.

What this system supposes is that it is unlikely for four shooters in a row to make their points. To make sure this does not happen, pay careful attention to the shooter. If he bets big on himself or he carefully sets the dice, do not bet on this shooter; just wait for the next one.

You start out on the don't pass with just a $5 bet. You will not place any odds in this system. It is for flat bets only. If you lose this first $5 bet, your next bet on the don't pass will double to $10. If this second bet is lost, you double to $20 and then to $40. If you lose all four don't pass bets, this series (number 1) is over and you go the next series (number 2) and start your bet at $10 instead of $5. Don't be tempted to start out at $80 in order to chase your losses—stick to the system or it will not work!

Sample Roll

You bet $5 on the don't pass and lose, and then bet $10 and lose. So you're now down $15. The third shooter 7s out on your $20 bet, so you've won $20, lost $15, and now you're ahead by $5. You lost two bets and won only one bet but you're still ahead. And whenever you win a bet, just start all over with the original $5 don't pass bet.

Now let's look at all four series:

1. 5, 10, 20, 40
2. 10, 20, 40, 80
3. 20, 40, 80, 160
4. 40, 80, 160, 320

You will note that in any progression you will always come out ahead if any one shooter in four does not make his point. For example, in series number 2, $40 is more than $20 + $10 and, $80 is more than $40 + $20 + $10.

This is a pretty good system, especially if the shooter is not a dice setter or rhythm roller. You must pay very careful attention to the shooter before you make your bet. If she sets the dice, do not bet. If she bets big on herself, do not bet. There are plenty of bad shooters, so don't end up betting on a good one!

The Progressive Don't

This is a good, steady system for people who have a lot of time at the tables. You would play entirely on the don't pass line, and you should wait for two pass line wins before you start betting. If you have some patience with this system you can make a lot of money.

After two passes, you begin by making a 1-unit bet on the don't pass line. Then, you'll follow a very slow progression on losing bets only. It is easy to remember because the number of units you bet is the same as the number of the progression in the series. For example, when you get to 5 units, you would bet it five times. So, the entire progression would look like this:

1, 2, 2, 3, 3, 3, 4, 4, 4, 4, 5, 5, 5, 5, 5, 6, 6, 6, 6, 6, 6, 7, 7, 7, 7, 7, 7, 7

If your betting unit is $5 you would be betting (on a loss only) the following:

$5, $10, $10, $15, $15, $15, $20, $20, $20, $20, $25, $25, $25, $25, $25, $30, $30, $30, $30, $30, $30, $35, $35, $35, $35, $35, $35, $35

When you win two bets in a row, just go back to the beginning (1 unit). If you win one bet and lose the next one, just stay with the progression. When you do win two don't pass bets in a row, remember to wait until there are two corresponding pass line wins before you start betting again.

If the shooter throws a craps it counts as a win. If he throws a 7/11, it counts as a loss. If he throws a 12, just stay where you are.

In this and most other don't betting systems, you should leave the shooting to others. It is difficult enough to qualify shooters, keep track of your bets, and pay careful attention to the system you are using.

Sample Roll

You wait until there are two consecutive pass line wins and you bet $5 (1 unit) on the don't pass. You lose, so you bet $10 (2 units) and lose that also. Now you bet $10 again and lose. You win your fourth bet for $15 (3 units) but lose the fifth ($15) and sixth ($15). You win your seventh bet ($20), so you bet it again ($20) and win, so you go back to the beginning and start again. You've lost five bets ($5 + $10 + $10 + $15 + $15) for a total of $55. You've only won three bets ($15 + $20 + $20) but even though you had terrible luck and lost two more than you won, you still ended up breaking even.

Now let's look at a slightly better scenario with $10 units. You wait until there are two consecutive pass line wins and bet $10 on the don't pass. You lose your first $10 bet, so you bet $20 and lose that one also. Your third bet is also $20 (still 2 units), which you win. You lose your fourth bet (3 units) for $30. You win your fifth bet for $30 (3 units) but lose your sixth bet (also 3 units). You win your seventh (4 units) and eighth bets for $40 each. Since you won two in a row, you go back to the beginning and wait for two passes again. This time, you lost four bets ($10, $20, $30, $30) and won four bets ($20, $30, $40, $40) so you lost $90 and won $130.

The most important aspect of this system is to wait for two pass line wins before you start betting. You should also make no other bets and stick to the progression.

Chapter 11

Regression Systems: Decreasing Your Bets on Wins

The theory behind regression systems is that the longer you have bets on the table, the more vulnerable you become to the 7. In order to win more, you should start off with larger bets and after 5 or 6 rolls have only a very minimum (if anything) left on the table. If the 7 hits now you won't lose much as you've already made your profit from the earlier rolls. In this chapter we'll look at five good regression systems.

6 and 8 Regression

You probably know that the 6 and 8 are the most common point numbers. There are some people who bet on these numbers exclusively—but what do you do when the 7 rolls? If your bets have been pressed up to $60 each or so, all of your winnings will be wiped out.

The theory behind regression betting is that the longer the roll, the more likely it is for a 7 to roll. One of the most popular regression plays is on the 6 and 8. Just place $30 on both numbers and when either number hits, regress them each by $6. So your regression would be $30, $24, $18, $12, and $6 on each number. If any combination of five 6s or 8s is rolled after the point, you could win up to $105 ($35 + $28 + $21 + $14 + $7).

The beauty of this system lies in betting a small amount to win a larger amount. After the first hit you win $35 and bet $24 on both numbers ($48 total). You are risking only $13 ($48 – $35) to win $28 ($24 at 7:6). After the second hit, you win $28 and bet $18 on each number (for a total of $36), so you're risking nothing ($36 – $36) to win $21.

After this second hit you've won $63 ($35 + $28), so even if the 7 rolls now, you still have a small profit and, the third, fourth, and fifth hits are all profit with absolutely no risk.

FACT

The 6 and 8 together will roll an average of ten times, compared to only about six times for the 7 in thirty-six sample rolls. This means you have a 10 to 6 (or 5 to 3) positive advantage that the 6 or the 8 will roll before the 7 does!

Of course, if you start out at a higher bet level you can eliminate the risk after the very first roll. When you bet $60 6 and 8, you'll win $70 if either number hits. You can regress both numbers down to $30 each and keep the $10 profit. Then regress to $24, $18, $12, and $6 as before. You'll win $175 if any five 6s or 8s hit. You can eliminate risk on the $30 6 and 8 also. On the first hit (a win of $35), just regress to $12 each and keep the $11. This way the 7 cannot hurt you.

There are many other regression techniques you can come up with yourself. After you win any place bet, just regress it to a lower level. Then keep regressing until you get to the minimum table bet and just let it sit. This way you'll stay active during a hot roll and have minimum risk on the table.

5 and 9 Regression

The 5/9 Regression starts out with a buy bet and then regresses to smaller place bets. This is a five-level regression, and if you win the fifth level you remove you last bet(s) and wait for a 7 to roll before you begin again.

You begin by buying both the 5 and 9 for $38 each. You should be able to do this for $1 each, as 5 percent of $40 is $2 and $39 is $1 less. Ask the dealer first and make sure you can do this. If you win either bet it pays off at 3:2 ($57 minus vig) instead of 7:5 (about $55).

Once you have both bets working, just wait for a hit and collect your $57. On the number that hit, regress your bet to the second level, which is $35.

You can buy this bet for $34 and get a payoff of $51 (minus $1 vig) at 3:2 odds. This only ends up being about $1 more than the place bet, so our next bet will be placed, not bought.

The third-level bet is $25. When you place this bet at 7:5 odds you win $35. The fourth level is $10, which at 7:5 pays $14. The fifth and final level is $5, which pays $7.

So if you would win all five levels of either the 5 or the 9, you would win $57 + $51 + $35 + $14 + $7, for a total of $164.

Of course, you will be betting on two numbers at once, so both numbers might be at different levels. For example, the 5 might be at $25 while the 9 is still at $38.

If you lose track of your bets, ask a cocktail server for some napkins and a dealer for a pen. They will always want to help you because they think that you will tip them (and you should) if you win big!

Sample Roll

The shooter looks prosperous, acts prosperous, and puts two green chips on the pass line. You think this crapshooter will do well and you decide to play the 5/9 Regression. She starts out with a point of 6 and you politely ask the dealer if you can buy both the 5 and 9 for $38 each and pay $1 each vig. The dealer recognizes a potential big tip and he agrees. You give him $76 and he makes the bets for you.

The shooter's second roll is a 5, so you win $57 and regress your five to $35, which you also buy. The third roll is an 8, so nothing happens. The fourth roll is another 5, so you win $51 and regress your 5 to $25. The dealer will probably ask you if you want to buy that also, but just tell him no. You want to make a regular place bet.

Her fifth roll is a 9, so you've won another $57 and ask the dealer to buy the 9 for $35 and give you the change. So now you have a 5 with $25 on it and a 9 with $35 on it. The shooter's sixth roll is a 6, so she made the point and gets ready for the new come-out. The friendly dealer may ask if you want your bets "working," and you politely tell him no. The shooter rolls a come-out 7, a 3, and then another point of 6. She now tosses a 9, so you've won $51 and you regress your 9 down to $25. Her eleventh roll is another 9, so you win another $37 and regress the 9 down to $15. Unfortunately she now throws a 7, so you lose your two bets before the regression is finished. However, you won $57 + $51 on the 5 and $57 + $51 + $37 on the 9. You lost $40 ($25 on the 5 and $15 on the 9) and won $253, so your net gain is $213!

For many people betting on the 5s and 9s is the perfect compromise. They pay more than the 6 and 8 and roll more than the 4 and 10. Why not give the 5/9 Regression a try the next time you play!

4 and 10 Regression

A lot of crapshooters like to bet the 4s and 10s because they pay more than any other place or buy number. In addition, you can also bet on the hard 4 or 10, which lends a little extra spice to your game.

The 4/10 pay 2:1 on a buy bet and 9:5 on a place bet. So, on a $40 buy bet you would win $80 and on a $40 place bet you would win $72—an $8 difference.

If you buy both the 4 and 10 for $40 each, you will end up paying $4 in vigs, so you should ask the friendly dealer if you can buy both numbers for $39 each and only pay $1 each in vigs.

This regression system is similar to the 5/9 Regression, in that it is five levels and the first two levels are bought and the last three are placed.

You would start out buying the 4 and 10 for $39 each. The second level you buy them for $34, which pays $68 (less vig) at 2:1.

The third level you place for $25. This pays 9:5, or $45. The fourth level is placed for $15, which pays $27, and the fifth level is $5, which pays $9.

As an optional side bet, you might want to bet a hardway or two. Some crapshooters wait until a "soft" 4 or 10 rolls and then start betting on the corresponding hard number. A simple progression of $1, $2, $3, $4, $5, and $6 is all you need. If you lose your first five bets and win the sixth, you've lost $5, won $7, and had a little fun doing it.

FACT

A hardway progression is especially good to reward friendly dealers. Not only will it keep them interested in the game, but a hard 6 or 8 pays off at 9:1. So if you bet a $5 hard 6 "for the dealers," it will pay off $45 when it wins!

Sample Roll

You get to the table, color in, and wait for a new shooter. When the shooter gets the dice you just don't like him. You don't know why, but you decide not to bet now, and instead wait for the next shooter. He throws a 4. But what if you are mistaken and he throws a lots of 4s?

You should never let this worry you. Your own first impression is always the most valuable. You should always rely on yourself, not other people. Just let him shoot and wait. Now he throws a 5 and then 7s out. You were right.

The next shooter looks good and bets $25 on herself. She confidently throws a come-out 7 and then a point 5. You ask the friendly dealer if you can buy both the 4 and 10 for $39 each and only pay $1 each in vigs. He of course agrees and you make your bets. The very next roll is a soft 4, so you win $78 on your $39 bet. You regress your 4 down to a $34 buy bet. Since a soft 4 was rolled, you now also bet $6 hard 4.

The shooter's next three rolls are 3, 6, and 12, so nothing happens. Her sixth roll is a hard 4, so you win $68 on your $34 buy bet and $42 on your $6 hard 4 bet (7:1 payoff on the hard 4). You now regress your 4 down to a $25 place bet. Now the shooter tosses the dice off the table and your very first thought is "uh-oh." Several other bettors take down their bets and you decide to do the same. The shooter asks for the same dice and throws a 9 and everyone breathes a sigh of relief. However, her next roll is a 7, so you remind yourself that you are glad you went with your first impression, because your own first impression is usually correct.

So you won $78 + $68 + $36, a total of $180—and that was just on the four! If the shooter didn't toss the dice off the table you might have won even more money on the 10.

Next time you play, give the 4 and 10 regression a try—you'll be surprised how easy it is to play—and how much money you'll make!

Inside Bet Regression

The inside numbers are 5, 6, 8, and 9, which are the most popular numbers on the layout. Betting on this combination gives you twenty-four chances to win and only six chances to lose (on the 7), giving you a big 4 to 1 advantage!

If you bet $44 inside you'll have $10 each on the 5 and 9, and $12 each on the 6 and 8. You can regress each bet when it hits, and then take them all down when you get any three hits. It doesn't matter if any of these numbers are the point when you start betting.

If your $10 5 hits, you'll win $14. Keep $9 and regress it down to $5. Then, if your $12 8 hits, you'll win $14. Keep $8 and regress it down to $6. If the 8 hits again, you'll win another $7 and then take down all the bets. You've just won $35!

If you're at a hot table you can leave all the regressed bets up after any three hits. In the previous example, you would have $5 on the 5, $10 on the 9, $12 on the 6, and $6 on the 8. If the 9 hits, regress it down to $5 and if the 6, hits regress it to $6. You now have $56 in profit and $22 on the table, so you're ahead no matter what happens.

A slight variation of this method is to bet $22 inside and leave everything up for any two hits and then take all of the bets down. If the table is really hot, instead of taking the bets down you can press up the 6 and 8 to $12 each and when you get any third hit, take everything down. Next time you place any bets, try this inside regression. It will minimize your losses when the 7 shows, and give you profits with very little risk!

FACT

When you bet regression systems, you should have a strict win goal and loss limit. If your average bet is $10 and you buy in with $500, you should quit when you win or lose about $150. If you buy in with $1,000, you should quit when you win or lose $300.

Outside Bet Regression

When you bet outside, you are betting the 4, 5, 9, and 10. If you give the dealer $40 outside, he will place $10 bets on each of the four numbers. The 5/9 pay $14 (at 7:5) and the 4/10 pay $18 (at 9:5). The combination of the four numbers will roll fourteen times (in thirty-six) compared to six times for the 7, giving you more than a 2:1 advantage!

If you continue to place the outside numbers for thirty-six sample rolls, you'll win $220 (6 × $18 + 8 × $14). In the worst case you'll lose all $40 six times (from the 7), or $240—resulting in a net loss of $20. It's highly unlikely to happen but still, you won't lose too much money betting in this manner.

To turn these outside numbers into profit makers you need to buy all of them instead of placing them. You can buy the 4 and 10 in many casinos for $39 and only pay $1 vig each. You should also be able to buy the 5 and 9 for $38 with $1 vig for each number.

So, now you have $38 on the 5/9, and $39 on the 4/10. In thirty-six theoretical rolls, you should win on these numbers fourteen times—three times each on the 4 and 10, and four times each on the 5 and 9.

On the 4 and 10 you'll win $78 (at 2:1). The 4 and 10 roll three times each (a total of six times), so you win a total of $468 (6 × $78). On the 5 and

9, you'll win $57 (at 3:2). The 5 and 9 roll four times each (a total of eight times), so you win a total of $456 (8 × $57). The total possible win (if you win all fourteen of your bets) is $468 plus $456, or $924.

The 7, however, should roll six times, and if you have all four bets up when it rolls you'll lose all of them for a total of $154 ($38 × 2 + $39 × 2). In this worst-case scenario, though, you won't lose much. If the 7 rolls six times, you'll lose $924 ($154 × 6), so theoretically you will break even (minus the vigs).

Practically, you can buy all four numbers and then take each down as they hit. This will decrease your exposure and increase your odds of winning more money. If you're unsure about the shooter, take all your bets down after any one hit.

If the shooter is a proven one, take each bet down as it hits, and when you win all four bets (for a total of $270), either wait for another qualified shooter or until this shooter throws a 7 (hopefully on the next come-out) before you buy all four bets again.

Regression-Progression

This method combines a regression on the do side with a progression on the don't side. This means you will be increasing your don't side bets and, at the same time, decreasing your bets on the do side.

The idea behind this system is to make as much money on the do side at the beginning of the shooter's rolls and then move your profits to the don't side while you wait for the 7-out. Ideally, you will win all of your bets on the do side and then win all of your bets on the don't side. In addition, the don't side bets will partially protect your do side bets. In case of an early 7, you will not lose much money.

On the do side we will be placing the 6 and 8, the most popular point numbers. We will start at $30 each. These numbers pay 7:6, so when either one hits you will win $35. This will be a three-level regression, so after either number hits, your next bets in the series will be $24 and $12.

At the same time, we will be laying the 4 and 10, the least popular point numbers. This is also a three–level bet, but we will be increasing these bets as the 6 and 8 bets are decreased. We'll start at $20 each, and then go to $30 each, and then $40 each. Lay bets pay 1:2, so if you bet $20 you will win $10. A $30 lay will win $15, and a $40 lay will win $20.

Every time the 6 or 8 hits, you will regress both of those bets and increase both the 4 and 10 lay bets to the next level. If no 6 or 8 hits within five rolls, take both place bets down and increase your lay bets to $30 each.

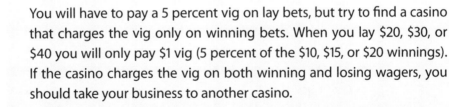

You will have to pay a 5 percent vig on lay bets, but try to find a casino that charges the vig only on winning bets. When you lay $20, $30, or $40 you will only pay $1 vig (5 percent of the $10, $15, or $20 winnings). If the casino charges the vig on both winning and losing wagers, you should take your business to another casino.

Let's look at an example. The point is 5 and you place the 6 and 8 for $30 each (a total of $60) and lay the 4 and 10 for $20 each (for a total of $40). The next roll is a 6, so you win $35. You ask the friendly dealer to regress both place bets down to $24 each. The dealer gives you your $35 winnings plus $12 ($30 – $24 × 2), for a total of $47. Take $20 of that and ask to increase your don't bets up to $30 each.

Now you have $24 each on the 6 and 8, and $30 each on the 4 and 10. Several rolls go by that don't affect your bets, and then another 6 rolls. You win $28, and you ask for your place bets to be regressed down to $12 each. You get $24 back ($24 – $12 × 2), for a total of $52 ($24 + $28). You use $20 of this to increase your lay bets up to $40 each.

Now an 8 rolls, so you win your final regression. You've won $14, so you ask to take down both place bets, but leave both $40 lay bets up and wait for the 7 to roll. When it does, you win $20 on each number for a total of $40. So you've won $35 + $28 + $14 from the place bets and $40 from the lay bets, for a total of $117.

Here are the basic Regression-Progression rules:

- Regress the 6 and 8 $30, $24, $12 on each 6 and 8 hit.
- Progress the lay 4 and 10 $20, $30, $40 on each 6 and 8 hit.
- Remove 6 and 8 place bets after the third hit.
- If no 6/8 hit after five rolls, take down the place bets and increase the lay bets.

You will still lose with the 7s, but not as much as you would with regular place betting. You'll be susceptible to lose more in the early rolls and less in the later rolls, due to the canceling out effect.

When you first start out and have $30 each on the 6 and 8 and $20 each on the no-4 and no-10, you are protected from the 7. On this first level if the 7 rolls you will lose $60 and win $20, but on the second level ($24 each on the 6 and 8 plus $30 lay bets), you lose $48 and win $30. On the third level you have $12 each on the 6 and 8 and $40 lay bets, so you lose $24 and win $20. If you get only one win in any of these levels, however, you will turn your slight loss into a good profit.

FACT

Since the 4 and 10 are even point numbers, you can insure these lay bets by betting on the hard 4 or 10. This pays 7:1, so a $3 bet will return $21 (close to your $20 bet), $4 will return $28 (close to your $30 bet), and $5 will return $35 (close to your $40 bet).

Let's look at an example of what happens if the shooter 7s-out before this progression-regression is complete.

You start out with $30 each on the 6 and 8, and lay the 4 and 10 for $20 each. The first roll is an 8, so you win $35 and regress both place bets down to $24. You also increase both lay bets to $30 each. Now a 7 rolls. You lose both place bets for a total of $48, but win both lay bets for a total of $30. You already won $35, so you've won that plus $30 (from the lay bets), for a total of $65. You lost only $48 so you're still $17 ahead (minus the vigs).

You would win even more if the shooter 7s out after the second level.

You start out with a place bet of $30 each on the 6 and 8, and lay the 4 and 10 for $20 each. The first roll is an 8, so you win $35 and regress both place bets down to $24. You also increase both lay bets to $30 each. Now a 6 rolls so you win $28 and increase your 4 and 10 to $40 each. You regress your 6 and 8 to $12 each. A 7 rolls, so you lose your place bets for $24 but win the lay bets for $40. You already won $63 ($35 + $28), so your total win is $103. You've lost $24, so you're ahead by $79 (again, minus the vigs).

This Regression-Progression is designed for choppy or cold tables, so give it a try the next time you run across one.

Chapter 12

Progression Methods: Increasing Your Bets on Wins

When a hot shooter comes along, many crapshooters like to increase their bets so they end up playing with the casino's money. Often a long roll will produce hundreds of dollars in extra earnings if their bets are pressed and left working. In these five progression systems, you will increase your bets on a win, and decrease them on a loss. Using the casino's money to pile up your profits can be easy to do—and profitable too!

6 and 8 Progression

The 6 and 8 are the most popular numbers that right bettors wager on in almost any craps game. The 6 or 8 place bet pays off at 7:6, so if you bet $6 you will win $7. If you bet $30 you'll win $35.

Some people bet the 6 and 8 and if one hits, they take down both bets and wait for a new shooter. But what if the shooter throws plenty of 6s and 8s?

This is a simple four-level progression system that will give you some profit for very little risk. Don't make any bets until a 7 rolls and a point is established. It doesn't matter if the point is 6 or 8.

- **Level 1**   Place both the 6 and 8 for $6 each. If either one hits, you will win $7.
- **Level 2**   Add $5 to that and increase both of your bets to $12. Now you have $12 on both the 6 and 8. If either one hits, you will win $14.
- **Level 3**   Keep $2 and increase both of your bets to $18 each. Now if either one hits you win $21.
- **Level 4**   Stay at the $18 level until you get one more hit, then take down both bets.

You've won $7 + $14 + $21 + $21, for a total of $63. And the beauty of it is you started out with only a $6 bet on both numbers.

FACT

The 6 and 8 will roll five times each, for a total of ten times in thirty-six sample rolls. The 7 rolls only six times, so you have a 10:6 chance of winning these place bets!

There are some people who like to be in a stronger betting position and win more money. These crapshooters will play the same four-level progression but start off with an initial bet of $30 instead of $6. Let's look at an example.

- **Level 1** Place both the 6 and 8 for $30 each. If either one hits, you win $35.
- **Level 2** Keep $11 and add $12 each to both bets, so you now have $42 on both the 6 and 8. If either one hits, you will win $49.
- **Level 3** Keep $31 and increase both bets to $60 each. Now if either one hits you will win $70.
- **Level 4** Stay at the $60 level for one more hit and then take down both bets.

So in the same four levels you've now won $35 + $49 + $70 + $70, for a total of $224! Of course, you should make sure the shooter is qualified before making any progression bet. If the shooter is unknown you may want to try the $6 progression, but if he is a proven winner, give the $30 progression a try!

5 and 9 Progression

A lot of people bet on the 5 and 9 because they pay more than the 6 and 8, and roll more than the 4 and 10. We are going to look at two simple four-stage progression systems designed to maximize your profits and minimize your risk. The 5 or 9 place bet pays off at 7:5, so if you bet $5 you will win $7. If you bet $25 you will win $35. To play the basic 5 and 9 Progression, just wait until a 7 rolls and a point is established. It doesn't matter if the point is 5 or 9.

- **Level 1** Place bet both the 5 and 9 for $5 each. If either one hits, you will win $7.
- **Level 2** Add $3 to the $7 and increase both bets, so you now have $10 each on the 5 and 9. Now if either one hits you will win $14.
- **Level 3** Keep $4 and increase your bets on both numbers to $15 each. Now if either hits you will win $21.
- **Level 4** Stay at the $15 level for one more hit and then take down both numbers.

So, in four levels you won $7 + $14 + $21 + $21, for a total of $63!

FACT

The 5 and 9 each roll four times in thirty-six sample rolls, for a total of eight rolls. The 7 rolls an average of six times. So, you have an 8:6 (or 4 to 3) advantage of winning either the 5 or 9 before the 7 rolls in this progression!

If you want to win more money, you could bet more on the progression. This time let's start out with a $25 bet on both the 5 and 9.

- **Level 1**   Place both the 5 and 9 for $25. If either one hits you will win $35.
- **Level 2**   Keep $5 and add $15 to each bet, so now you have $40 on both the 5 and 9. If you win either bet now, you'll win $56.
- **Level 3**   Keep $16 and add $20 to each bet, so you now have a $60 5 and 9. If you win either bet now, you'll win $84.
- **Level 4**   Stay at the $60 level for one more hit, then take down both bets.

So in four levels you've won $35 + $56 + $84 + $84, or a total of $279.

When you get to level 2, you can buy both the 5 and 9 for $38 each. This buy bet will usually cost you $1 in vig, but it will pay off at 3:2 instead of 7:5. So you will end up betting $1 less ($38 + $1) and winning $1 more ($57). When you get to level 3, you can buy both the 5 and 9 for $60 each. This buy bet will usually cost $2 in vig. So you will end up betting $2 more ($60 + $2) and winning $6 more ($90, at 3:2).

4 and 10 Progression

The 4 and 10 pay more than any other point number and if you find a shooter proficient in tossing these outside numbers, you can make a good profit with this simple progression. The 4 and 10 place bets pay 9:5, so if you bet $5 you'll win $9. If you make a $25 place bet, you can win $45.

We're going to look at a four-level progression similar to those we explored with the 6s and 8s and the 5s and 9. In the previous sections there was not a whole lot of difference between place and buy bets, and if you placed or bought the 6/8 or the 5/9, the results were similar. Here, however, there is a large difference, so after the first two initial bets we will be using buy bets only.

- **Level 1**   Place bet the 4 and 10 for $5 each. If you win you get $9.
- **Level 2**   Add $1 to your bets and place both the 4 and 10 for $10 each. If you win you will get $18.
- **Level 3**   Add $10 and buy the 4 and 10 for $19 each (a total of $38). This should cost you $1 in vigs and pay off at 2:1 ($38) instead of 9:5 (about $35).
- **Level 4**   Stay at that $19 level until one bet hits, then take down both of your bets.

So, in the first four basic levels you won $9 + $18 + $38 + $38, for a total of $103.

FACT

The 4 and 10 each roll three times in thirty-six rolls, or a total of six times, compared to six times for the 7. Combined, the 4 and 10 roll the same amount as the 7. This means you have a 1:1 chance of winning the 4 or 10 before the 7 rolls.

For the more advanced progression we will start at a $20 buy bet on both numbers. On buy bets you must pay a 5 percent vig, so on $20 that is $1 per number, and most casinos only charge that if the bet wins.

- **Level 1**   Buy the 4 and 10 for $20 each. If you win either number you get $40 (at 2:1) less $1 vig.
- **Level 2**   Keep $2 and increase your buy bets to $39 each. This way you should still only pay $1 in vig because 5 percent of $40 is $2, and you are only betting $39. This $39 bet will pay $78 at 2:1 if it wins.

- **Level 3** Keep $12 and increase your buy bets to $59 on each number. This way you'll only pay $2 each in vig because 5 percent of $60 is $3 and you are betting under that. If you win this $59 bet you will get $118.
- **Level 4** Stay at this $59 level for one more hit, then take down both bets.

So now you've won $39 + $78 + $118 + $118, for a total of $353!

Inside Bet Progression

The inside numbers are 5, 6, 8, and 9. They constitute the four most popular numbers you can place bet. The 5 and 9 pay 7:5 and the 6 and 8 pay 7:6. An inside bet is standard on most craps tables. If you say, "$22 inside," the dealer will know you want $5 each on the 5 and 9, and $6 each on the 6 and 8. A $44 inside bet means $10 each on the 5 and 9, and $12 each on the 6 and 8.

- **Level 1** Bet $22 inside. If any inside number rolls, you will win $7.
- **Level 2** If the 5/9 hits, increase both the 6 and 8 by 1 unit each. If the 6/8 hit, increase the 5/9 by 1 unit each. Now you will win $14 if any of the inside numbers hit. You will now have $10 on the 5 or 9 or $12 on the 6 or 8.
- **Level 3** Again, if the 5/9 hit, increase both the 6 and 8 by 1 unit each, to $18. If the 6/8 hit, increase the 5/9 by 1 unit each, to $15. If any inside number hits now, you will win $21.
- **Level 4** Stay at this $15 or $18 level for one more hit, and then take down all your bets.

So, in four levels you won $7 + $14 + $21 + $21, for a total of $63.

The combination of 5 (rolls four times), 6 (rolls five times), 8 (rolls five times), and 9 (rolls four times) rolls a total of eighteen times in thirty-six sample rolls, compared to six times for the 7. This means that you have an 18:6 (or 3 to 1) chance of winning any one place bet before the 7 rolls in this system.

For the advanced inside place method, we will start off with $44 inside. This means $10 each on the 5 and 9, and $12 each on the 6 and 8.

- **Level 1** Bet $44 inside. If you win any number now, you will win $14.
- **Level 2** If the 5/9 hit, increase both the 6 and 8 by 1 unit each. If the 6/8 hit, increase the 5/9 by 1 unit each. Now you will win $21 if any number hits. You will now have $15 on the 5 or 9 or $18 on the 6 or 8.
- **Level 3** Again, if the 5/9 hit, increase both the 6 and 8 by 1 unit each to $24. If the 6/8 hit, increase the 5/9 by 1 unit each to $20. If any number hits now you will win $28.
- **Level 4** Stay at this $20 or $24 level for one more hit, and then take down all four bets.

So, in four levels you've won $14 + $21 + $28 + 28, for a total of $81.

Outside Bet Progression

The outside numbers are 4, 5, 9, and 10. These four numbers have the highest payoffs of any place numbers. The 4 and 10 place pay 9:5, so if you bet $5 you get $9. The 5 and 9 place pay 7:5, so if you bet $5 you get $7. An outside bet is standard at most craps tables. If you say, "$20 outside," the dealer will place $5 each on the 4, 5, 9, and 10. A $40 outside bet means $10 each on the 4, 5, 9, and 10.

- **Level 1** Bet $20 outside. If you win, you'll get $9 on the 4 or 10, and $7 on the 5 or 9.

- **Level 2**   If the 5 or 9 hit, increase both the 4 and 10 by 1 unit each. You would now have $5 each on the 5 and 9 and $10 each on the 4 and 10. If the 4 or 10 hit, increase the 5 and 9 by 1 unit each. You now have $5 each on the 4 and 10, and $10 each on the 5 and 9. If the 4 or 10 hit, you will win $9. If the 5 or 9 hit, you would have won $7.
- **Level 3**   Again, if the 5 or 9 hit, increase both the 4 and 10 by 1 unit each. If the 4 or 10 hit, increase the 5 and 9 by 1 unit.
- **Level 4**   Stay at this same level for one more hit, and then take down all four bets.

If four 4/10 numbers hit, you will win $9 + $18 + $27 + $27, for a total of $81. If four 5/9 numbers hit, you will win $7 + $12 + $21 + $21, for a total of $61.

FACT

The 4/10 combination rolls six times in thirty-six sample rolls, while the 5/9 rolls eight times. Together they roll fourteen times compared to six times for the 7. So, you have a 14:6 (or 7 to 3) chance of winning any outside place bet.

For the advanced system, we will start with a $40 outside bet. This means you will have $10 each on the 4, 5, 9, and 10.

- **Level 1**   Bet $40 outside. If you win, you'll get $18 on the 4 or 10, and $14 on the 5 or 9.
- **Level 2**   If the 5/9 hit, increase both the 4 and 10 by 1 unit each. You now have $10 each on the 5 and 9 and $15 each on the 4 and 10. If the 4 or 10 hit, increase the 5 and 9 by 1 unit each. You now have $10 each on the 4 and 10, and $15 each on the 5 and 9. If the 4 or 10 hit, you will win $18. If the 5 or 9 hit, you will win $14.
- **Level 3**   Again, if the 5 or 9 hit, increase both the 4 and 10 by 1 unit each. If the 4 or 10 hit, increase the 5 and 9 by 1 unit each.
- **Level 4**   Stay at this same level for one more hit, and then take down all four bets.

If four 4/10 numbers hit, you will win $18 + $36 + $54 + $54, for a total of $162. If four 5/9 numbers hit, you will win $14 + $24 + $42 + $42, for a total of $122.

Progression-Regression

This system takes place mostly on the don't side. We are going to combine a don't come progression with a place bet regression. As the don't come bets go up in value, the place bets will go down. So we will start with high place bets at the beginning of the roll and end up with high don't come bets at the end of the roll.

This is a three-level system and we'll be placing the 6 and 8, starting off at $30 each ($60 total). The second level is $24 each ($48 total), and the third level is $12 ($24 total). On the don't come we will be making a three-bet progression of $10, $20, and $30.

After the point is established, we'll make a don't come bet for $10 and, at the same time, place the 6 and 8 for $30 each. If the 6 or 8 rolls now in this first level, you will win $35 and the don't come bet will move to that number.

Whenever the 6 or 8 rolls, you will regress both numbers down to the next level. On every roll you will make a don't come bet until three don't comes are established.

If three don't comes are established and the 6 or 8 has not rolled yet, wait until either rolls and then take down both of them and wait for the 7 to roll. You'll never make more than three don't come bets.

If the shooter throws a lot of 7s, you can protect your don't come bet by laying the 4 and 10 until a point is rolled. For example, if you have a $30 don't come, you can lay both the 4 and 10 for $30 each, so if the 7 rolls you won't lose much. If the 4 or 10 roll you lose just $30, but you now have a good don't bet you can add odds to and win later on when the 7 rolls!

Let's look at some examples.

The point is 5. You make a $10 don't come bet and place the 6 and 8 for $30 each. The first roll is 9, so your $10 don't come goes to the 9, and you make a $20 don't come bet. The second roll is an 8, so you win $35 and regress both place bets down to $24 each, and make your last don't come bet for $30. You now have $24 each on the 6 and 8, $10 on the don't 9, and $20 on the don't 8. Now the 6 rolls and you win $28. You made three don't come bets, so you take down your 6 and 8. You have a $10 don't 9, a $20 don't 8, and a $30 don't 6. If the 7 rolls now, you will win $60 plus $63 from the place bets, for a total of $123.

The basic Progression-Regression rules:

- Progress the don't come $10, $20, $30 on every roll.
- Regress the 6 and 8 $30, $24, $12 on each 6/8 hit.
- Remove place bets after third don't come.
- If no 6/8 hit after your third don't come bet, take down your place bets.

You will have the 6 and 8 place bets up for three rolls only, and then they come down as you wait for the 7. In reality this will be more than three rolls from the come-out, as the shooter may roll several numbers before the come-out point is established.

The only time that your regression series of three will match your progression series of three is if the three numbers rolled are all 6s and 8s. Let's see how this develops.

The point is 9, so you place $30 each on the 6 and 8, and make a $10 don't come bet. The next roll is an 8, so you win $35. Now you regress both bets down to $24 each and make a $20 don't come bet. The next roll is another 8, so you win $28 but lose your $10 don't come bet. You make a $30 don't come bet and regress your place bets down to $12. This time a 6 rolls, so you win $14 and take down both of your place bets. You are left with a $30 don't 6 and a $20 don't 8. If the 7 rolls, you'll win $50 from these two bets plus $53 ($63 − $10) from the place bets, for a total of $103.

Let's look at one last important example, this time if the point is 6. Even though 6 is the point, you still place the 6 and 8 for $30 each and make a don't come bet of $10. The next roll is 8, so you win $35, regress the place bets down to $24 each, and make a $20 don't come bet. Now however, the 6 point rolls. You win $28 on the 6 and your don't come bet moves to the 6. So, now you have a $20 don't 6, a $10 don't 8, and a $24 place bet on the 8.

You may or may not to be asked by the friendly dealer if you want your place bets on or off. Since the combination of 6 and 8 roll more than the 7 does, you should tell the dealer you want them on. However, if the shooter throws a come-out 8, you will win the place bet and lose the don't bet. So, you need to make a judgment call. If you think the shooter will throw a 7, remove the place bets. If you think he will throw a 6 or 8, remove the lay bet.

ALERT!

When you ask the dealer to have your place bets "on" (or working) during the come-out, make sure there is an "On" button on your bets. Also, when you lay a number it should have a "Lay" button placed on top of it. You don't want to lose any of your bets to a dealer error!

You should base this decision on how many 6s and 8s he rolled before, and what his pass line bet is. If he is betting big that he will roll a 7, you should assume that he will, and remove your place bets.

If he does roll a 7, you should take down your bets and start all over. If he rolls a point without any 7s, you should resume play (you were on level two) and regress the place bets one more time (to $12), and make one last don't come bet for $30.

The reason for this is that you always have to be mindful of the 7s, and the ratio of numbers to 7s. If a 7 is supposed to roll approximately once every six rolls, and the shooter has already rolled six times, makes his point, and establishes another point, then you might suspect that a 7 might be coming. You don't want to expose your place bets to a possible 7, but you do want to expose your established don't come bets to one!

Give this a try the next time you play—you'll be surprised how easy and profitable it is!

Chapter 13

Combination Systems

There are other ways to win that don't fit neatly into a certain category. These are combination type systems, which combine two different methods into one system. One of the most popular of these is hedge betting. Playing partners is becoming more popular, and you'll learn the advantages of team play. You'll also learn exactly how to "convert" a come bet, how to do a Hoyle Press, and how to bet before the come–out—both the basic and advanced methods!

Hedge Betting

A hedge is a bet that almost cancels out another bet, resulting in a small but positive profit. Even though you only make a few dollars each play, it is a consistent way to make money on a regular basis. And if you bet consistently in this manner, the comps you receive from the casino can add even more to your profits.

For example, if you have a don't come bet of $20 and it goes to the 6 or 8, you can place bet the same number for $18. Then if the 7 rolls, you win $20 and lose $18, giving you a $2 profit. If the 6 or 8 rolls, you win $21 and lose $20, giving you a $1 profit.

The next time you play, look at the bets that the other crapshooters are making and see if you can devise hedge bets for them. And when you are making bets yourself, always see if making a hedge bet would be profitable.

If you bet $25 on the pass line, you can hedge it from the 2, 3, and 12 by betting three-way craps.

You can also add place bets before the come-out and have them hedged by the pass line bet. For example, you can bet $22 inside ($5 each on the 5 and 9, and $6 each on the 6 and 8), along with your $25 pass line and $3 three-way. If one of the inside numbers hits, you win $4 ($7 – $3). If the 7 or 1 rolls you break even ($25 – $22 – $3). The 2/12 will give you a $5 profit ($30 – $22 – $3). Your only loss comes from the 3 ($15 – $25 – $2 = a loss of $12), but you can hedge that (if a lot of 3s are rolling) by betting $2 instead of $1 on the 3.

You can easily hedge a $25 don't come bet. Many times a don't bettor will see their $25 don't come go to the 6 or 8 and they will yell "no action." Instead they could place a hedge bet and be assured of a small profit. You can place either number for $24. If the 7 rolls, you win $1 ($25 – $24). If the 6 or 8 rolls, you win $3 ($28 – $25)—not much in either case, but certainly better than the nothing you would have received by removing your bets!

If you're on the don't come and the point is not a 6 or 8, the betting gets easier. If your $25 don't come goes to the 4 or 10, you can place $15 on that number. If the 7 rolls you win $10 ($25 – $15) and if the 4 or 10 rolls, you win $5 ($30 – $25).

The 5 or 9 also can give you a profit on $25 hedged don't come bets. Just bet $20 on the number. If the 7 rolls, you win $5 ($25 – $20). If the 5 or 9 hits, you also win $5 ($30 – $25).

As you can see, once you have a don't come point, you are assured of making a profit by using hedge bets. Not a large profit, but you will also get full comp credit for both of these bets at casinos that give comp credit for spread.

Playing Partners

Craps is the only casino game that gives you a significant advantage if you play with a partner. Not only can you win more money, but you'll get more comps as well.

The most common method of partner play is when one person bets on the pass line and the other on the don't pass. The pass line player will lose here on the 12, but that means only once in thirty-six rolls or so. You won't win any money doing this, but you'll get free room, food, and beverage for both of you, worth much more than the occasional loss on the 12.

FACT

The purpose of playing partners is to get double comps for bets that would normally cancel out and receive no comps. (See Chapter 20 for more on comps.) It also lets you bet primarily on the free odds, which have no casino advantage.

A better way of playing is to use the previous method, but take odds on favorable points and lay odds on unfavorable ones. For example, if the point is 5, 6, 8, or 9, the partner on the do side can take double odds on the pass line, while the don't side partner will only make the flat bet. On the other hand, if the point is a 4 or 10 the don't side partner can lay odds while the do side player only makes flat bets. Of course, when both of you are finished playing, you'll split the profits evenly, so you can take turns playing the do or the don't.

A third method of play is bypassing the come-out roll and one player betting come on every roll and the other don't come. If the 5, 6, 8, or 9 is the point, the come player will take odds, and if 4 or 10 is the point, the don't come player can lay odds. Again, you will get paid on the come's free odds only—with almost no house advantage.

These methods seem to work best if the players have different last names and play on opposite sides of a crowded table. Hand your comp cards to the pit boss separately and don't talk to each other. Play for an hour or so, for at least $10 per bet so you'll get the maximum comps. Have a silent signal to end each session and cash out separately.

Give partner playing a try—it's a great way to get the most out of every craps game!

Hoyle's Press

Hoyle's Press is in most craps systems books but hardly anyone uses it because it takes a little getting used to. In Hoyle's Press, your bets will have a simple progression, from 1× to 5× the starting bet. You will increase by 1 unit on a win, and decrease by 1 unit on a loss. At the same time, you will be switching from pass to don't pass (or vice versa) on wins and staying where you are on losses. Let's take a practical look at this system using $5 units.

You start with a $5 bet on the pass line. The shooter makes his point, so you win. You increase your bet and switch, so you now bet $10 on the don't pass. The shooter makes his point again, but this time you lose so you decrease your bet and stay there. You have $5 on the don't pass. Now the shooter 7s-out, so you win your bet. You won, so you increase your bet to $10 again and bet on the pass line.

The important thing to remember is to always increase your bets by 1 unit when winning and decrease your bets by 1 unit when losing. And when you win a bet, you switch to the other side. When you lose a bet, you stay where you are. When you are at the 5× level and win, the progression is over and you start from the beginning.

If the shooter is a qualified good shooter, you should start out with Hoyle's Press on the pass line. If you have any doubt about his abilities, you should start on the don't pass. If you are unsure about a shooter, don't make a bet—just wait for the next shooter.

Sample Roll

- You start on the pass line and lose $5, so you stay there and bet another $5.
- You win this second bet, so you are now at the $10 level and you switch to the don't pass.
- You win again, increase your bet to $15, and switch to the pass line.
- You lose on the pass line, stay there, and go down to the $10 level.
- You win, so now you bet $15 on the don't pass.
- You win $15 on the don't pass, so you switch to the pass with a $20 bet.
- You win there, and go back to the don't pass with a $25 bet. You win there, and the series is over.

You must mentally keep track of all of your bet levels. When you win, put the chips in your back rack and ignore them. You should be concentrating on your progression and bet level, and nothing else. Don't let anything distract you. The goal of this system is to win more money at higher levels and lose less money at lower levels.

Converting Come Bets

Most of us were taught to play the pass line with odds, and have two come bets up. Come bets are favored by many players because they represent the hot numbers. By betting the come many people believe that they can take advantage of a hot streak or a "monster roll." In addition, come bettors often take double (or more) odds, both on the pass and come lines, to maximize their wins.

The come bet, however, does have some disadvantages. Let's say you have a come bet on the 6 and 8, 9 is the point, and the point is made. You now have a 6 and 8 working on the come-out, with odds. If the 7 hits now, you would win your new pass line bet, but lose the flat portion of your left-over come bets. Another disadvantage is that the payoffs for come bets are not much higher, and in many cases they are lower, than equal place bets. For example, a $10 come bet on the 6 with $25 odds returns $30 for the odds plus $10 on the flat portion, a total of $40. However, if you bet $36 on the 6 as a place bet, you would win back $42. In addition, you can not take down a come bet. If you stay on the come line with every roll, eventually you'll lose all of the flat portions of your bets.

Craps pros know that a number has to hit twice for a come bet to win, compared to only once for a place bet. Plus you get to choose which place bet you want, while you may have to settle for a 4 or 10 with a come bet.

Instead of having your come bet poised to follow the trend of the table, it is easier and more profitable just to make what is called a converted come bet.

A converted come bet is a place bet that is made instead of the corresponding come bet. For example, if the first roll is a 4 and the next two rolls are 5 and 6, you might normally have come bets of $10 with odds on the 5 and 6—$20 odds on the 5 and $25 on the 6. So, you have a total of $65 in play—$30 on the 5 and $35 on the 6. If you win the come bets, you get $40 on the 5 and $40 on the 6, for a total of $80.

Instead of betting on the come, you could just place $30 on the 5 and $36 on the 6, giving you $66 in play. You would win $42 on the 5 and $42 on the 6, for a total of $84. Of course, you can then take down your bets so you don't have to worry about the come-out 7 (if the point was made), or the 2, 3, or 12 (while in the come box).

The next time you want to make a come bet, try a converted come bet instead!

Before the Come-Out—Basic

This method involves placing the 5, 6, 8, and 9 before the come-out along with a $25 pass line bet to protect you from the 7. You'll bet $25 on the pass line, place $5 each on the 5 and 9, and $6 each on the 6 and 8. Be sure to request that all of your bets be "on" for the come-out roll. The basic system results are:

- 4/10—no win/loss
- 5/9—win $7 (7:5 odds on $5)
- 6/8—win $7 (7:6 odds on $6)
- 7—win $3 ($25 pass line; $22 place bets)
- 11—win $25 ($25 pass line)
- 2/12—lose $25 ($25 pass line)
- 3—lose $25 ($25 pass line)

Thirty-six sample roll results:

- 4/10—no win/loss
- 5/9—win $56 ($7 × 8; the 5 and 9 roll four times each)
- 6/8—win $70 ($7 × 10; the 6 and 8 roll five times each)
- 7—win $18 ($3 × 6; the 7 rolls six times)
- 11—win $50 ($25 × 2; the 11 rolls two times)
- 2/12—lose $50 ($25 × 2; the 2 and 12 roll one time each)
- 3—lose $50 ($25 × 2; the 3 rolls two times)

This comes out to a $194 win (56 + 70 + 18 + 50) and a loss of $100 (50 – 50), resulting in a net profit of $94!

FACT

What this system really does is shift the primary burden of losing from the 7 (at 6:1 odds) to the 3 (at 18:1 odds), so you are three times more likely to win your bets using this system.

Remember, you will still have a $25 pass line bet that you can not remove. "Before the come-out" is for regular pass line players only, because it leaves you with a regular pass line bet. It is a terrific method for you, as a pass line bettor, to make some extra money before the come-out. After the come-out you're left with a pass line bet (you've already dealt with the craps numbers) and you can leave your place bets up for one more hit. You can also take odds on your pass line bet, like you would normally do.

If you're a pass line player anyway, you really should give this system a try before the come-out. You'll be surprised at how much you'll win and how easy it is to play!

Before the Come-Out—Advanced

A slight variation of the previous play is to make a $30 pass line bet instead of $25. This way the 7 will give you a bigger profit, but you'll lose even more on the craps numbers. You can also place $5 bets on both the 4 and 10, but this will require a $32 pass line bet to balance things out.

ALERT!

Besides generating more profits, the advanced system generates a lot more comps. You'll have about $80 on the table and more if you add odds to your pass line bet. Once you're a $100 bettor, you'll get a lot more attention from the pit! This translates into more shows, better food, and unlimited drinks—plus you make more money as well!

If you have the bankroll, you might try $40 pass line. This way, you can place the 4 and 10 for $5 each, and make $8 profit ($40 pass − $32 place) on the 7s, in addition to $9 for each of the 4s or 10s. Let's see what happens if you bet an extra $15 ($40 instead of $25) on the pass line. So you'll be betting $5 each on the 4, 5, 9, and 10, and $6 each on the 6 and 8, in addition to your $40 pass line bet. The advanced system results are:

- 4 or 10—win $9
- 5 or 9—win $7

- 6 or 8—win $7
- 7—win $8 ($40 – $32)
- 11—win $40
- 2 or 12—lose $40
- 3—lose $40

Thirty-six sample roll results:

- 4/10—win $54 (the 4 and 10 roll three times each)
- 5/9—win $56 (the 5 and 9 roll four times each)
- 6/8—win $70 (the 6 and 8 roll five times each)
- 7—win $48 (the 7 rolls six times)
- 11—win $80 (the 11 rolls twice)
- 2/12—lose $80 (the 2 and 12 roll one time each)
- 3—lose $80 (the 3 rolls twice)

This comes out to a $308 win and a $160 loss, for a profit of $148! This is $54 more than the previous system. You are left with a $40 pass line bet and all the place bets working. You can, of course, take the place bets down and/or add odds to your pass line bet after the come-out. Like the last system, this is for regular pass line players only. If you would not normally play the pass line at this level, then this system is not for you.

But if you do play the pass line, give this method a try. It's easy, it's fun, and—it's profitable.

Chapter 14

Other Methods and Systems

This is the last of the system chapters and contains five supersystems no expert crapshooter should do without! The Two-Level Doey-Don't has long been a favorite of old-timers who like switching back and forth. You'll also learn two regression systems, one for three levels and one for four. You'll see what "following the trend" really means in practical terms. And finally, you'll learn how the experts play the Don't Hop Hedge System.

Two-Level Doey-Don't

Sometimes when you play craps, you end up on a choppy table, and even with charting and qualifying, it still stays choppy. Wouldn't it be nice to bet on both sides at once and then, if a trend presents itself, just latch onto the table direction and rake in the profits?

This system is actually a combination of a two-level do, plus a two-level don't. You bet on the do side to start off and end up, after five or six rolls, mostly on the don't. Of course, if the shooter starts to look good you can stay on the do side and keep your bets up. The good thing about this system is that after the first two hits on the do side, it is all profit on the don't.

FACT

Before starting out on the do side with this system, wait for a 7 to roll and the new point to be established. If you start out on the don't side, wait for the point to be made before you start betting.

First, make a bet for $44 inside. That's $10 each on the 5 and 9, and $12 each on the 6 and 8. After any number hits, regress that bet by $5 for the 5 or 9, and $6 for the 6 or 8. After any two hits, keep your regular and regressed bets up and use your winnings to make two don't come bets.

Your first don't come bet is for $20 and the second is $10. Then, as each remaining place bet hits, you take them down and wait for the 7 to show.

Sample Roll

The shooter rolls a 10 point and, after you bet $44 inside, the shooter rolls a 5. You win $14 and regress the 5 down to $5. Now a 6 shows so you win another $14 and regress your 6 bet down to $6. So you now have $5 on the 5, $6 on the 6, $10 on the 9, and $12 on the 8.

Since you've won two bets, you place $20 on the don't come. The shooter rolls a 4. Your $20 don't come goes to the 4 and the 6 rolls again. You win and take the place 6 down, as the second don't come bet for $10 goes to the 6.

An 8 rolls, so you win and regress the place 8 to $6. Now, you have $5 on the 5, $10 on the 9, and $6 on the 8. You also have a $20 don't come bet on the 4 and a $10 don't come bet on the 6.

The shooter throws a 9, so you win and take it down. The shooter rolls a 7, so you lose $5 on the 5 and $6 on the 8. You won $14 (on the first 5), $14 (on the first 6), $7 (on the second 6), $14 (on the 8), $14 (on the 9), and $30 (on both don't comes). So, you won $93 and lost only $11.

The reason why you bet $20 on the first don't come and only $10 on the second is to afford you some protection against the 7. If it rolls with the $10 in the don't come box, you would still win $10 for your established don't come ($20 − $10) rather than just pushing. If the shooter rolled the point (in this case 10), you don't lose anything and all of your bets will stay up. When he finally rolls a 7, your two don't come bets should be more than any of your remaining place bets.

This is a terrific way to win on choppy tables, so give it a try the next time you find one!

Three-Level Regression

A regression play is one where you reduce your bets after a win to ensure a profit, even if you lose your next bet. In this regression, you will be starting out with a $12 bet on both the 6 and 8. When either one of these two bets hit, you will win $14 and tell the dealer to regress both bets down to $6.

So, now you have a $14 profit in your pocket and only $12 on the layout. If the 7 rolls now, you are still $2 ahead. If the 6 or 8 rolls, however, you are in even better shape. You won another $7, giving you a total win of $21. Now, leave the 6 and 8 up and give the dealer another $3 (to be added to your $7) to place the 5 and 9 for $5 each. Now you have $6 each on 6 and 8, and $5 each on 5 and 9. When any of these four numbers hit (paying you another $7), you take down all your bets and now have an easy $28 profit.

Here's how the Three-Level Regression works:

- Place the 6 and 8 for $12 each.
- Regress the 6 and 8 to $6 each.
- Add place bets to the 5 and 9 for $5 each.

The secret to winning the Three-Level Regression is to start betting only after a 7 shows. If the shooter makes the point, you should take down your bets until a 7 shows again.

FACT

When you play, you should have a 30 percent win goal and a 30 percent loss limit: If you buy in with $200 you should stop when you win or lose $60. If you buy in with $100, you should stop when you win or lose $30.

Sample Roll

The shooter's point is 6. You place the 6 and 8 for $12 each. It doesn't matter if either is the point. The very next roll is an 8, so you regress both bets down to $6. The shooter makes her point, so you win but you take all your bets down and wait until the next 7 shows, and then you start all over with $12 6 and 8. If the shooter had not made her point, then you would have added $5 place bets on the 5 and 9.

This three-level system is easy to play and once you get used to it, you can also use it on the don't side if the table turns.

Four-Level Regression

The Four-Level Regression is similar to the three level. First, you must wait until a shooter 7s out and you have a brand-new shooter. When he establishes his point, bet $18 each on 6 and 8. Since you have $36 on the table, you should have a bankroll of $360. You should quit when you win (or lose) approximately $100.

Even though you're betting at a higher level, you really need only one hit to show a profit. Plus, the amount of regression you achieve will determine your future profit.

Here's how the four-level system works:

- Place the 6 and 8 for $18 each.
- Regress both bets all the way down to $6 each.

- Bet $22 inside
- Press the 6 and 8 to $12 each.

Sample Roll

The new shooter throws a 5 as the point. You place $18 each on the 6 and 8, and the shooter rolls a 6. You win, and regress your bets all the way to $6 each. You won $21 on the 6, and only have $12 on the table, so nothing can hurt you.

This time you win on the 8, so you win another $7 for a total win of $28. Since you already have $12 on the layout, you toss the dealer another $10 and ask for $22 inside. He puts $5 on the 5 and 9, and you already have $6 each on the 6 and 8. Now, the 9 rolls and you win another $7. You add $5 to that and press your 6 and 8 up to $12. You now have $5 on the 5 and 9, and $12 each on the 6 and 8. When any one of these four numbers hit, you take everything down.

The secret to winning this system is that it should only start with a new shooter. If the current shooter makes his point, you do not start betting on the new come-out. You must wait until he 7s out and you have a new shooter. When this happens you start all over with an $18 bet on the 6 and 8.

Here's another example: After the first hit on the 6 or 8, you won $21 and only have $12 at risk on the table. Even if the 7 hits now, you are still ahead by $9. The second hit gives you another $7, and you add $3 to make place bets on the 5 and 9.

You still have the $6 profit plus the $22 inside bet, which means the shooter can't hurt you no matter what she does. On the third hit you get another $7. You give $12 to the dealer and press your 6 and 8 to $12 each.

Now, you have $12 bets on the 6 and 8, and $5 bets on the 5 and 9, and still have a $1 profit, which means that all of your bets are now "free." If any of the four bets win, you are now ahead by $35, and you were never in any danger of losing your buy-in.

Go over this again. It is a terrific system to try out on place bets if you have enough bankroll.

Following the Trend

"Following the trend" used to mean watching another player (especially a high roller) and doing what that player did. If someone bet $50 on the come and took maximum odds, so would you. Unfortunately, this does not always work out the way you want it to.

Most crapshooters are always in search of a long roll. This does not occur very often, but when it does, you should be prepared to bet in a manner that will give you the maximum returns with minimum risk. Conversely, you don't want to have a lot of money on the table when someone 7s out.

The best way to profit is to use the casino's money (your winnings) and take back a portion of those winnings so you will always show a profit. You can do this by following the trend of the table.

Let's say you have a $44 inside bet, which means you have $10 on both the 5 and 9, and $12 each on the 6 and 8. Your normal method of play is to leave your bets up until any two numbers hit, and then take them down. If the first two rolls are a 6 and 8, you would normally take everything down and wait for the next come-out. However, if you do this and the shooter keeps the dice for twenty rolls before she finally makes her point, you will miss out on most of the action.

When you won the 6 and 8, you had a $28 profit. You can take down your bets and place $22 inside, and still have a $6 win, even if the shooter 7s out. You now have $5 on the 5 and 9, and $6 on the 6 and 8.

But let's say he starts shooting numbers and rolls a 5 and 9. Now you have a total win of $28 from the 6 and 8, and $7 each from the 5 and 9, a total of $42 profit.

You can leave the $5 on the 5 and 9 and increase your bets to $12 on the 6 and 8. This leaves you with $34 on the table, and $8 in your pocket.

If the next roll is a 6, you have another $14. You could, for example, place the 4 and 10 (neither of which have rolled yet) for $5 each and put the extra $4 in your pocket. Now you have $5 on the 4, 5, 9, and 10, $12 on the 6 and 8, and, $12 in your pocket.

If the 10 rolls now you have another $9. You could increase your bet on the 4 to $10 and save the extra $4, giving you $16 even if the 7 rolls.

By now you get the idea—only increase your bets with your winnings, and bet so that you will always have a profit. The 7 will roll eventually and you don't want all of your money on the table. If the roll you're on turns into one of those "monster rolls" you've been hoping for, you'll be there, making a slow but steady profit. And, if the shooter 7s-out in 4 or 5 rolls, you'll still have some cash in your pocket, just waiting for the next time.

FACT

To really take advantage of a long roll, you must know your total profit, how much you have on the table, and how much you have in your pocket. You should never dip into the money in your pocket, so even when the 7 rolls, you will still be ahead.

But remember—keep track of your total winnings, the money on the table, and the money in your pocket. Increase your bets with some of your winnings and pocket the rest. Using this method, you'll be able to take advantage of a long, profitable roll, and make some money on a short roll as well.

Don't Hop Hedge

This system is based on the fact that casinos pay 30:1 on hopping hardways. So, if you bet $3 on a hard 4, for example, and it rolls, you will win $21 (at 7:1). However, if you bet $3 hop 2 and 2 and it rolls, you win $90 (at 30:1). In this method we will use the hard 4 hop, but you can use the hard 10 if you prefer. Some crapshooters wait until either the 4 or 10 rolls, and then use that same number for their hopping hardway hedge.

The concept is to have a bet on every number and win money, or at least not lose any money, on everything except the soft 4. If the soft 4 rolls you lose, but the 7 rolls six times (in thirty-six sample rolls) compared to the soft 4s only rolling once.

To start with, you lay the 4 for $70 and make a $3 hardway 2 and 2 hop bet. This means that if the 7 rolls, you win $35 on the lay bet and if the 2/2 rolls, you win $90 on the hop bet.

ALERT!

A hop bet is a one-roll bet. If it loses, you must put it back up. You can start a simple hop 2 and 2 progression when you get used to this system if you wish. You must remember to replace the losing hop bet, and if a small progression helps you remember to do so, you should use one.

Place $5 each on the 5, 9, and 10, and $6 each on the 6 and 8. Finally, you bet $1 C & E. You now have all the numbers covered and will win or push on everything except for the soft 4.

If the 2, 3, or 12 rolls, you win $7 and lose the hop bet, so you net $4. If the 11 rolls, you win $14 and lose the $3 hop bet, so you're ahead by $11. If the 6, 8, 5, or 9 rolls you win $7 but lose the hop and C & E bets for a net of $2. If the 10 rolls, you win $9 but lose the hop and C & E bets for a net of $4.

If the 7 rolls, you win $35 from the lay bet. You lose your place bets ($27) and your hop ($3) and C & E ($2) bets, so you end up winning $3.

If the soft 4 rolls, you lose the C & E, hop, and lay bets for a net loss of $75. If the hardway 4 rolls, you win $90 on the hop but lose the $70 lay bet and the $2 C & E for a net win of $18.

If you decide to hedge this system by betting soft 4 hopping, remember that this only pays 15:1, not 30:1 as does the hardway hop. So, if you bet $3 on a 1 and 3 hop, you will only win $45 instead of $90.

Sample Roll

You start out with a $70 no-4, a $3 2/2 hardway hop, a $2 C & E, place bets of $5 each on the 5, 9, and 10, and place bets of $6 each on the 6 and 8. That's a total of $102 on the table. Whenever a place bet hits, you take it down. You want a minimum of bets left when the 7 eventually hits.

1. 3—win $4 ($7 – $4), for a net win of $3
2. 8—win $2 ($7 – $5), for a net win of $5
3. 11—win $11 ($15 – $4), for a net win of $16
4. 5—win $2 ($7 – $5), for a net win of $18
5. 6—win $2 ($7 – $5), for a net win of $20
6. 4 (2/2)—win $55 ($90 – $35), for a net win of $75
7. 8—win $2 ($7 – $5), for a net win of $77
8. 10—win $4 ($9 – $5), for a net win of $81
9. 7—win $35, lose $10, for a net win of $106

Only one number (the 9) was left on the table when the 7 hit. Give this system a try—it's a lot of work but can provide you with a steady profit!

Chapter 15

Things You Need to Know

This chapter contains some things you really need to know when you play craps—not systems or rules, but ways to play. You'll learn an easy way to remember the odds on your pass or come bets. You'll see how to deal with CrapStress, and how "craps insurance" really works. You'll see how you will benefit by eating the right foods and giving the dealers tips. Finally, you'll learn about the "gambler's fallacy" and why it sometimes doesn't even apply to craps!

Remembering Pass/Come Odds

When you play craps, you probably know the payoffs for most numbers on place bets. For example, the odds on the 6 and 8 are 7:6 (bet $6, get $7), the odds on the 5 and 9 are 7:5 (bet $5, get $7), and the odds on the 4 and 10 are 9:5 (bet $5, get $9). But, when you want to add odds to your pass or come bets, the payoff is different. This is because they are true odds, which means that the casino has no advantage on these odds bets.

The true odds for the numbers 6 and 8 are the same, 6:5. The true odds for both the 5 and 9 are 3:2, and the true odds for the 4 and 10 are 2:1. If you just subtract one from the smaller of these numbers and relate it to six (the number of times a 7 rolls), you get the true odds.

To get the true odds for the 4 or 10, just subtract 1 from 4 (because 4 is smaller than 10) to get 3. So the true odds of the 4 or 10 are 6:3, or 2:1. To get the true odds for the 6 or 8, subtract 1 from 6 (because 6 is smaller than 8) to get 5. So the odds for the 6 or 8 are 6:5. Finally, to get the true odds for the 5 or 9, subtract 1 from 5 (because 5 is smaller than 9) to get 4. So the odds of the 5 or 9 are 6:4, or 3:2.

5 and 9 Example with Added Odds

If you have $10 on the come or pass line and your point is a 5 or 9, and you want to add some odds, just subtract 1 from 5 to get 4. The true odds are 6:4, or 3:2, so if you add $20 in odds, you'll win $30. For double odds you can add $20 odds to your $10 flat bet and win $10 from the flat portion and $30 from the odds portion, for a total of $40.

4 and 10 Example with Added Odds

If the point is 4 or 10, subtract 1 from 4 to get 3. The true odds are 6:3, or 2:1, so if you bet $20, you'll win $40. For double odds, you can add $20 to your flat $10 bet and win $10 on the flat portion and $40 to the odds portion, for a total of $50.

6 and 8 Example with Added Odds

The 6 and 8 are a little different. If you subtract 1 from 6 you get 5, which means the true odds are 6:5. If you have a flat bet of $10, you would be able to take $20 in odds, (on a 2× odds table). However, this would mean a $24 odds payout, which is awkward for most casinos. So, to even things up, most casinos let you place $25 in odds behind the 6 and 8, (which really gives you 2.5× odds instead 2×), giving you $10 for the flat portion and an even $30 for the odds portion, for a total win of $40.

This method works on don't come and don't pass bets as well, except the odds are reversed. This is because on the don't side you have the advantage rather than the house, so you have to bet more to get less.

Don't Side 5 and 9

If your don't pass or don't come flat bet is $10 and the point is 5 or 9, subtract 1 from 5 to get 4, giving you odds of 4:6 (instead of 6:4), or 2:3. This means you have to bet $30 (on a 2× table) in odds to get a $20 payout, winning you a total of $30 ($10 flat + $20 odds).

Don't Side 4 and 10

If your don't number is 4 or 10, subtract 1 from 4 to get 3. The odds are 3:6, or 1:2. You would have to bet $40 in odds to get a $20 payout, winning you a total of $30 ($10 flat + $20 odds).

Don't Side 6 and 8

For the don't 6 or 8, subtract 1 from 6 to get 5. The odds are 5:6. You would have to bet $24 in odds to get a $20 payout, winning you a total of $30 ($10 flat + $20 odds).

The next time you play craps, remember this simple method to calculate the true odds. This way, you'll know what odds to give the dealers, and what the correct payoff should be.

CrapStress

CrapStress is your stress level while playing craps in a casino. Many people's stress levels go way up when they play craps, even if they don't have a lot of money at risk. This is due to the fear of failure. If other people at the table make a lot of money on a roll and you don't, sometimes you feel like you have failed. But craps pros always look at craps as a learning experience—even if they lose. They are just climbing the ladder of success, and it takes more than one step to climb a ladder. They don't struggle—they learn.

To you, craps should always be a learning experience. You can always learn something from every game. A famous craps writer keeps a small notebook with her and jots down her thoughts every time she plays. She watches every player at the table and tries to figure out what their systems are and writes them down. Then, when her session is finished, she reviews everything that happened. Her CrapStress level is low, because she looks at playing craps as an information-producing class, not a gambling session. She is then able to change and perfect her own techniques to produce a better profit in her next session.

You probably have enough stress in your business and personal life, so you don't need any more when you gamble. Carry a notebook with you when you play and jot down your impressions of the way you play, and the way the other people at your table play. And the next time you have a losing session, don't get upset, but ask yourself the following five questions:

- How am I really feeling?
- Why did I play the way I did?
- What could I have done differently?
- What did I learn from this game?
- How will I play in my next session?

You should write these answers in your notebook so you'll have a record of what you did. This way you can refer to your "Class Notes" when you get home and prepare for your future class sessions! Remember—keep your CrapStress level low. You are constantly learning and progressing—going up the ladder of success one rung at a time!

Craps Insurance

One of the ratios you should always take into account when you bet is the bet's insurance factor. The insurance factor will give you a quick 7-to-wins ratio so you can see in an instant your chances of winning or losing a bet.

Although this section deals only with place numbers, you can easily figure out the insurance factor for all of your bets.

It is easy to do—just figure out the ratio of the success of the bet versus the failure of the bet. For example, if you place $6 on both the 6 and 8, you have a total bet of $12. The 7 can roll six times (out of thirty-six), the 6 and 8 roll five times each. So you have ten ways to win, and only six ways to lose. This gives you an insurance factor of 10:6, 5:3, or 1.7:1 This means that you are 1.7 times more likely to win than lose this bet.

Let's look at the 5 and 9. If you placed $5 on both numbers, you would have a total investment of $10. These numbers roll four times each for a total of eight times, compared to six times for the 7. So, you have eight ways to win and six ways to lose, or an insurance factor of 8:6, 4:3, or 1.3:1. This means you are 1.3 times more likely to win this bet than lose it.

FACT

If you increase the number of place bet wins and decrease the number of place bet losses, you could increase your insurance factor. And when your insurance factor increases, your profits will increase also!

You can also increase the insurance factor by increasing the number of place bet wins, while keeping the number of 7s the same. Instead of betting on just two numbers, you can bet on four of them—the 5, 6, 8, and 9.

One way of decreasing the number of 7s rolled is to remove all four of your place bets after only one win. Let's take a closer look at this and see just how it affects your insurance ratio, which was 1.7 on the 6 and 8.

The 6 and 8 roll five times each, and the 5 and 9 roll four times each. So, in thirty-six rolls, you win eighteen times and lose six times. This gives you an insurance factor of 18:6, or 3:1. This is almost twice as much as the insurance factor on the 6 and 8. A 3:1 ratio means that you are three times more likely to win than lose. It also means that it is three times more likely that a 5, 6, 8, or 9 will roll before the 7.

FACT

> The four inside place numbers are 5, 6, 8, and 9. If you bet $5 each on the 5 and 9, and $6 each on the 6 and 8, you'll have $22 in play. A quick way to bet this is to give the dealer the chips and say "$22 inside please."

The best way to make this $22 inside bet work is to take down all four of your bets as soon as any one hits. Then, you must wait for a 7-out (making the point does not count) before you put all four of your place bets back up again.

Remember, even if you don't use this inside place bet method, calculate the 7s-to-wins ratio. Find out exactly how much insurance you have before you make *any* bet!

Blood Type Betting

Have you ever wondered if what you ate the day before you played had any effect on your performance? Well, it might. The latest research indicates that what you eat might have a direct effect on the way you feel, how healthy you are, and whether your mind works at its peak capacity or not. The casino always gives players free alcoholic drinks, in order to lower their decision-making abilities. Although alcohol affects everyone, there are some foods that may only affect you—depending on your blood type!

In his landmark bestseller, *Eat Right 4 Your Type,* naturopathic doctor Peter D'Adamo shows that the food we eat should depend on what our various blood types are. Since there are four blood types, there are four totally different eating plans. Your own individual blood type determines the way you absorb nutrients and handle stress.

Athletes have tested this theory and found it to be a success, and some gamblers have as well. By eating properly (according to your blood type) a few days before you play, you too can maximize your body's efficiency, power, and stamina. If you think, feel, and react better, then you'll play better, too!

But, since everyone has a different blood type, we all must eat different foods to optimize our body's processes. There are only four main blood types—A, B, AB and O, and here are some very basic food suggestions for each of them.

- **Blood type O**—Eat meat (high protein, low carbohydrates); do not eat any grains (bread, pasta, most desserts).
- **Blood type A**—Eat vegetables (high carbohydrates, low fat); do not eat any red meat (beef, ham, liver, or pork).
- **Blood type B**—Eat a varied diet that includes vegetables, meat, and eggs; do not eat any corn, lentils, peanuts, or wheat products.
- **Blood type AB**—Eat soy products, seafood, dairy products, and green vegetables; do not eat any meat, beans, seeds, corn, or wheat.

You should consult your doctor before embarking upon a new diet for any length of time. But, if you try this diet for a week or two and you feel better, think better, lose a pound or so, and most important, win more money at craps, then you might want to make it permanent!

When you're playing at your peak, your mind will be operating at its peak also. You'll be able to think clearer, make faster decisions, and most importantly, make the right decisions at the right time!

Tipping the Dealers

You have probably read numerous articles about how little money the dealers make. Most of them make more in tips than salary. Well, you should tip the dealers, but not solely for their benefit. You should tip so that *you* can win more money!

We already looked at the concept of "pushing the house." Don't you think that a dealer would be more likely to allow you to make these bets if he knew in advance that you were tipping? A dealer would also take care of your bets, get used to your betting style, and do his best to help you win, so, in exchange, you'll tip him more.

Let's say you are betting $44 inside and taking all of your bets down after any two hits. Let's say the second hit comes, and you get distracted by a scantily clad drink server. (Ever wonder why the drink servers are dressed like that?) Your faithful dealer will interrupt your daydream and say, "Excuse me! Want your bets down?" You come to your senses and shake your head "yes," just before a 7 rolls. Your dealer just saved you $44.

When you tip, the dealers always announce it, so the floor people know about you. When they look at your rating card, they are liable to bump it up a few notches. Let's say they have you rated as a $25 player. A few tips and they might rate you at $30. Dealers want you to return to their casino, and they're certainly willing to bump up your comps just a little to keep your business and tips!

FACT

You can also give small gifts to the dealers, like pens, coffee mugs, or even ties. The dealers will appreciate them, and remember you for thinking of them.

You can tip the dealers in a number of ways. You can bet $5 pass line for them. When you put down your pass line bet, place $5 next to it, and tell the dealer, "for the dealers." He will announce "dealer on the line," and after a decision, both the dealer and stickperson will thank you, win or lose.

You can also make a hardway bet for the dealers, or a proposition bet. This way if it wins, you can parlay the bet, and the dealers can win a lot more. If you bet $5 hard 6 "for the dealers" and it wins, the payoff is $45. If they parlay it, your tip suddenly turns from a $5 tip into a possible $405 tip, the dealers will take notice of you—for sure!

So the next time you win a bet, think about investing some of it in a tip. It'll help you in the long run, the dealers will take better care of you, and you just might get some better comps—a good return on a small investment!

The Gambler's Fallacy

When you are playing craps and a random shooter holds the dice, you might come across an extraordinary occurrence. This random shooter may, for example, throw four passes in a row. There are some bettors who may then assume that the don't pass is now "due," and will begin betting the dark side.

In physics this process is called "maturity of chances," and can occur, for example, if someone flips a coin 1,000 times. According to the law of averages, it is assumed that approximately 500 tosses will be heads and approximately 500 tosses will be tails.

Sometimes, however, there might be 600 heads and only 300 tails after 900 tosses. Some people at that time might say that tails are now "due," so the remaining 100 tosses should be mostly tails.

If this were true, it would mean that the coin has some sort of innate intelligence and will determine its future behavior by what has happened in the past. Given a very, very long run of coins (or dice), it is probable that the heads and tails (or the pass and don't pass) will sort itself out. But this will be done by chance and circumstance, not by the determinate behavior of the coins or the dice.

If there is no way to deduce the outcome of a random roll of the dice, then why play craps at all? The gambler's fallacy applies to randomness, and is correct in stating that previous rolls of the dice have no effect on future rolls. However, there is a method in use today to help us predict the outcome of a nonrandom roll of the dice on a consistent basis.

FACT

There are two kinds of crapshooters—random rollers and rhythm rollers. Random rollers are susceptible to the gambler's fallacy, but rhythm rollers are not. It is up to you to decide who to bet on, and who to not bet on.

When you are playing craps and a rhythm roller holds the dice, you may also see four passes in a row. But these are not completely random occurrences. A rhythm roller sets the dice a certain way, grips them in a certain manner, and tosses them precisely so they land and bounce together. Due to various table conditions, this can't happen all the time, but even if the shooter controls the dice for only 1 to 2 percent of his throws, it is enough to overcome the house's slim edge on many bets—and produce a nonrandom occurrence.

Don't be surprised if a shooter rolls the same numbers (for example, 4s and 10s) every time she shoots. This is her own personal shooting "signature," and you should always be on the lookout for one! By observing a shooter's results, you may see a pattern develop, which you can use to latch onto a long roll. And the next time he shoots, be prepared to back him up with big bets! Mathematically, the shooter needs to affect the dice only one time out of forty rolls to turn the game from a negative expectation one (1 percent casino edge) to even odds (0 percent casino edge). This certainly is a skill well worth practicing!

Rhythm rollers are experts at what they do because of their knowledge, training, and experience. It is not easy to control the dice and not many people can do it. But it is possible, so you might want to move from table to table to find a good shooter. Once you find one, you should keep betting on him as long as he bets on himself. There is no gambler's fallacy to deal with because these are not random rolls, but trained rhythm rolls.

Chapter 16

E Craps Stats: Calculating the Edges

This section delves a little deeper into the math side of craps. You'll learn how craps odds and the casino advantage are calculated. You'll learn the difference a weighted pass line edge and an unweighted one. And finally, you'll learn how to find the edge to a two roll bet and a combined place bet.

How to Calculate Craps Odds

As you know, each die has six numbers on it. When you throw a pair of dice, two combinations of the six numbers appear on the craps table, so there are a total of thirty-six different combinations. To get the combinations for each number you need to look at both dice. Let's look at exactly how the craps odds are calculated.

The 7 can be made in the six different ways shown in **TABLE 16.1**.

TABLE 16.1 Combinations that make 7						
First Die	1	2	3	4	5	6
	+	+	+	+	+	+
Second Die	6	5	4	3	2	1
	7	7	7	7	7	7

This means that out of thirty-six rolls, it is probable that the 7 will roll six times, leaving thirty combinations for the rest of the numbers.

The 6 can be made five different ways (see **TABLE 16.2**).

TABLE 16.2 Combinations that make 6					
First Die	1	2	3	4	5
	+	+	+	+	+
Second Die	5	4	3	2	1
	6	6	6	6	6

The 8 can also be made in five different ways (see **TABLE 16.3**).

TABLE 16.3 Combinations that make 8					
First Die	2	3	4	5	6
	+	+	+	+	+
Second Die	6	5	4	3	2
	8	8	8	8	8

The 5 can be made in four different ways (see **TABLE 16.4**).

	TABLE 16.4	Combinations that make 5		
First Die	1	2	3	4
	+	+	+	+
Second Die	4	3	2	1
	5	5	5	5

The 9 can also be made in four different ways (see **TABLE 16.5**).

	TABLE 16.5	Combinations that make 9		
First Die	3	4	5	6
	+	+	+	+
Second Die	6	5	4	3
	9	9	9	9

The 4 can be made in three different ways (see **TABLE 16.6**).

	TABLE 16.6	Combinations that make 4	
First Die	1	2	3
	+	+	+
Second Die	3	2	1
	4	4	4

The 10 can also be made in three different ways (see **TABLE 16.7**).

	TABLE 16.7	Combinations that make 10	
First Die	4	5	6
	+	+	+
Second Die	6	5	4
	10	10	10

The 3 can be made in two different ways (see **TABLE 16.8**)

TABLE 16.8	Combinations that make 3	
First Die	1	2
	+	+
Second Die	2	1
	3	3

The 11 can also be made in two different ways (see **TABLE 16.9**).

TABLE 16.9	Combinations that make 11	
First die	5	6
	+	+
Second Die	6	5
	11	11

The 2 can only be made one way (see **TABLE 16.10**).

TABLE 16.10	Combination that makes 2
First Die	1
	+
Second Die	1
	2

The 12 also can only be made one way (see **TABLE 16.11**).

TABLE 16.11	Combination that makes 12
First Die	6
	+
Second Die	6
	12

So, when we're using a pair of dice, we can make the amount of combinations for the numbers that will roll as shown in **TABLE 16.12**.

TABLE 16.12 Combinations that make each number	
Number of roll	**Number of combinations**
7	6
6	5
8	5
5	4
9	4
10	3
4	3
3	2
11	2
2	1
12	1
Total number of combinations	*36*

The casino, of course, knows this chart well, and will offer you a much higher payoff if you bet on the 12 (the number that rolls the least) rather than the 7 (the number that rolls the most). The reason for this is that the 12's combination will roll only once compared to the 7's six times. So, in 36 sample rolls, the 7 might roll six times, while the 12 might roll only once.

For another example, let's look at the 4 (or 10) compared to the 7. In thirty-six sample rolls, the 4 should roll three times compared to six times for the 7. This means that for every one roll of the 4, you will see two rolls of the 7. So the true odds of the 4 (or 10) is 2:1.

Using the same method we can see that the true odds of the 5 or 9 (which rolls four times) compared to the 7 (rolling six times) is 6:4 or 3:2. So for every three rolls of the 7, you should see two rolls of the 5 or 9.

Finally, the 6 or 8 will roll five times compared to the 7's six times so the true odds are 6:5. For every six rolls of the 7, you should see five rolls of the 6 or 8.

Calculating the Casino Advantage

The casino's advantage on a place bet on the 6 or 8 is 1.52 percent. The casino pays 7:6 on this bet but the true odds are 6:5. What this really means is that in eleven decisions you will win five times and lose six times. So if you bet $12 you will win $70 ($14 × 5) and lose $72 ($12 × 6). This is a difference of $2. This $2 is divided by the total amount bet, or $132 ($12 × 11 decisions), and you get the casino edge of 1.52 percent.

Calculating the Weighted Pass Line Edge

To calculate the famous 1.4 percent casino edge for the pass line bet is a little more difficult, as you must take into account all of the available numbers, both before and after the come-out roll. The 1.4 percent result will be a weighted average of all the possible results, both before and after the come-out.

As you've seen, the 2 and 12 can roll one way, the 3 and 11 two ways, the 4 and 10 three ways, the 5 and 9 four ways, the 6 and 8 five ways, and the ubiquitous 7 can roll six ways.

On the pass line, you can win with the 7 or 11. The 7 can be rolled six ways, and the 11 two ways, so you will win 8 of 36 times on the pass line, or 2/9 of the time.

You will lose on the pass line with a 2, 3 (twice), or 12, so you lose 4 of 36 times, or 1/9 of the time.

This means that 1/3 of the time, the pass line bet is decided without a point, as 1/9 (losing) plus 2/9 (winning) equals 3/9 or 1/3.

The other 2/3 of the time a point is established. There are six points: the 4, 5, 6, 8, 9 and 10, with twenty-four possible point rolls.

If the point is 4 (or 10), as an example, there are 3 ways to roll a 4 (or 10) but 6 ways to roll a 7. Thus, a 4 (or 10), which rolls three times, compared to the seven, which rolls six times, will roll 3/9 (or 1/3) of the time a 7 does.

Similarly, with the 5 and 9, rolling four times, each is 4/10 (or 2/5) as likely to roll as the seven. The 6 and 8, rolling five times, is 5/11 as likely to roll as the 7.

The 1.4 percent Casino Edge

To get the winning percentage, then, we simply have to take how often you can possibly win with each point, and multiply it by how often each point occurs. The casino's edge is the losing percentage minus the winning percentage.

▶ After the come-out, there are six point numbers which can be rolled 24 possible ways (4 - three, 5 - four, 6 - five, 8 - five, 9 - four, and 10 - three).

The 4 or 10 will roll 3/24 (or 1/8) of the time. The 5 or 9 will roll 4/24 (or 1/6) of the time. And the 6 or 8 will roll 5/24 of the time.

The chance of winning the 4 or 10, then, is 1/3 of the time, but it only comes up 1/8 of the time. The chance of winning the 5 or 9 is 2/5 of the time, and comes up 1/6 of the time. And, the chance of winning the 6 or 8 is 5/11 of the time, and comes up 5/24 of the time.

So, for the 4 and 10, we multiply $1/3 \times 1/8 \times 2$. For the 5 and 9, we multiply $2/5 \times 1/6 \times 2$. And for the 6 and 8, we multiply $5/11 \times 5/24 \times 2$.

All this adds up to 67/165.

▶ However, we know from before that an actual point is established only 2/3 of the time. 1/3 of the time you will win or lose without the point being established. And, when no point is established, you'll win 2/3 of the time and lose 1/3 of the time.

So, we need to take 2/3 of 67/165 and add it to 1/3 of 2/3, which is 244/495, or the winning percentage (which is 49.3 percent, or .493). Since the winning percentage is 49.3 percent, the losing percentage is 50.7 percent (or .507).

We can now finally find the house edge, in percentage, by subtracting the winning percentage (49.3 percent) from the losing percentage (50.7 percent). This is 1.4 percent, the house edge for the pass line with no odds.

Now you might not remember all this, but at least you've read it and maybe even understood it. Remember, the more you know, the more confidence you'll have! And the more confidence you have, the more money you'll win!

Calculating the Two Roll Bet Edge

Now that you have some basic understanding of the math behind calculating the odds in a craps game, let's look at an illustrative example. If you are with some friends, they may talk to you about making some simple side bets. Since craps is a game of math, you should be able to figure out whether the bet is favorable or not, now that you know how to calculate odds.

For example, let's say that your friend wants to bet you that a five or nine will not be the next roll. You know that the five and nine together rolls eight times (four times each) compared to the seven's rolling six times, in 36 average rolls. This means that the probability of the five or nine rolling next will be 8/36. So, the very next roll has a 22 percent (8/36 = .222) chance of being a five or nine.

The probability then of both the five and nine not rolling next is 28/36 (36/36 − 8/36). This means that the very next roll has a 78 percent (28/36 = .78) chance of not being a five or a nine.

Average Number of Rolls

Let's say the same friend wants to bet you that a winning decision will be produced every six rolls. This seems about right to you, but before you reply, you take out a pen and paper and look at the math.

The Seven and Craps Numbers

The seven rolls six ways, and the eleven three ways, out of 36 average throws. The two, three and twelve roll once each. So, before the come-out, the seven, eleven, two, three and twelve can make a decision twelve times, or 1/3 (.333) of the time.

The Four and Ten

After the come-out, the four (or ten) rolls three times or 3/36 (.083) of the time. But a decision can also be made by the seven, which rolls six times. So a decision on the four (or ten) will be made nine times out of 36, or four rolls. Add the come-out and we have five rolls. The average number of rolls needed to make a decision is therefore 3/36 of five rolls, or .416. For both the four and ten, the total is .832 .

The Five and Nine

After the come-out, the five (or nine) rolls four times or 4/36 (.111) of the time. But a decision can also be made by the seven, which rolls six times. So a decision on the five (or nine) will be made ten times out of 36, or every 3.6 rolls. Add the come-out and we have 4.6 rolls. The average number of rolls needed to make a decision is therefore 4/36 of 4.6 rolls, or .511. For both the five and nine, the total is 1.022.

The Six and Eight

After the come-out, the six (or eight) roll five times or 5/36 (.138) of the time. But a decision can also be made with the seven, which rolls six times. So a decision on the six (or eight) will be made eleven times out of 36, or every 3.27 rolls. Add the come-out and we have 4.27 rolls. The average number of rolls needed to make a decision is therefore 5/36 of 4.27 rolls, or .593 . For both the six and eight, the total is 1.186 .

The decision maker

If we add the .333 for before the come-out, plus .832 for the four and ten, plus 1.022 for the five and nine, plus 1.186 for the six and eight, we get a grand total of 3.373 rolls. This means that a decision (win or lose) is made approximately every four rolls.

Calculating the Unweighted Pass Line Edge

Once the point is established, what do you think the casino edge is for your pass line bet? 1.4 percent?

Nope. It's higher. In fact, much higher. Let's look at the numbers. Over any time period, let's assume you are betting pass line on every new come-out.

▶ You will win twice as many times as you lose, due to winning on the 7/11 and losing on the 2, 3, and 12. So, in 1,980 come-outs, you will win 440 and lose 220 times, for a total of 660, which is one third of all numbers rolled. The other 1,320 (2/3 of all numbers rolled) do not reach a decision on the come-out and become points. Of these points, only 536 will win and 784 will lose. The resultant casino edge for the weighted calculation on the pass or come line is 1.414.

- Total of come-out losses 220 (twos, threes and twelves)
- Total of come-out wins 440 (sevens and elevens)
- Total of point number wins 536 (4, 10, 5, 9, 6, 8)
- Total of point number losses 784 (4, 10, 5, 9, 6, 8)
- Total come-out plus point losses 1004 (220 + 784)
- Total come-out plus point wins 976 (440 + 536)
- Total number of all wins and losses 1980 (1004 + 976)
- Total losses minus total wins 28 (1004 - 976)
- Casino come or pass line percentage 1.414 (28/1980)

▶ Now, let's look what happens after the point is established and you no longer have that 2:1 pass line come-out edge.

- Total number of pass line losses 784 (4, 10, 5, 9, 6, 8)
- Total number of pass line wins 536 (4, 10, 5, 9, 6, 8)
- Net point number losses 248 (784-536)
- Total number of points 1,320 (2/3 of 1980)
- Casino advantage 18.8 percent (248/1320)

As you can see, the advantage now really swings to the casino. According to the casino's 1,980 rolls table (which is fully reproduced in the appendix) there will be 1,320 point numbers (again, 2/3 of the decisions). Of these, 784 pass line decisions will fail, and only 536 will be successful. As you can see, we had only 28 net losses and a 1.4 percent edge with the come-out advantage included. But *after* the come-out point was established, we had 248 net losses and a huge, never-mentioned-by-the-casino 18.8 percent edge!

▶ If you take this one step further and figure out the casino edge for each of the individual point numbers *after* the point is established, you get:

- 4 or 10, 33.3 percent
- 5 or 9, 20.0 percent
- 6 or 8, 9.09 percent

Even when you add double odds, you still get a higher than expected casino edge:

- 4 or 10, 11.1 percent
- 5 or 9, 6.67 percent
- 6 or 8, 3.03 percent

Compare these numbers to the casino edge on place bets:

- 4 or 10, 6.67 percent
- 5 or 9, 4.00 percent
- 6 or 8, 1.51 percent

Calculating the One Roll Place Bet Edge

If you make a lot of place bets, you might wonder what the casino advantage is, compared to the pass line's 1.4 percent. If you think that it's more than 1.4 percent, you're correct. But what if you place more than one number at a time—how does that affect the casino edge?

▶ Let's look at one number first—the eight. As you know, there are five ways to win (2-6, 3-5, 4-4, 5-3, and 6-2) but six ways to lose (1-6, 2-5, 3-4, 4-3, 5-2, 6-1). The number of events equals the ways to win, plus the ways to lose, so we have a total of eleven possible events. When you win on the 8, you get back $7 ($6 at 7:6 odds) plus your bet of $6, for a total of $13.

If you bet $6 on the 8 eleven times, you have invested a total of $66. You will win five times for a total of $65 ($13 × 5) and lose $1 ($66 − $65). Divide loss (1) by investment (66) and you get the casino edge of 1.515. Not bad, but still higher than the 1.4 percent pass line. Now let's look at placing both the six and eight together for $6 each. There are now ten ways to win (5 on the six, and 5 on the eight) but still only six ways to lose (on the seven).

We will take both bets down after either number hits, so after a win we receive back $6 (from the six) + $6 (from the eight) + $7 (from the winner) for a total return of $19. The number of events now is 16 (ten plus six) and the total investment is $192 (16 × $12). You will win $190 (10 × $19) so your loss here is $2 (192-190). Loss (2) divided by investment (192) now plummets down to 1.042!

- Ways to win place bet 8 = 5
- Ways to win place bet 6 = 5
- Total ways to win = 10
- Ways to lose to seven = 6
- Total number of events = 16
- Investment (16 × $12) = $192
- Return (10 × $19) = $190
- Casino's win = $2
- Casino's advantage = 1.0417 percent

Placing the six and eight is clearly a more advantageous bet than just placing the six or the eight. In fact, the edge for the six or eight is 1.51 percent. If you figure out these percentages, you'll see that placing both numbers is 45 percent more profitable than placing either number!

Placing the six and eight (1.04 percent edge) is also a better bet than the pass line (1.4 percent edge).

Chapter 17

E Dice Control: The Set, Grip, and Throw

This chapter contains everything you need to know about rhythm rolling. Some crapshooters do not believe in this, but even if it has just some small chance of success, shouldn't you be knowledgeable about it? You'll learn all about setting, gripping, and throwing the dice. You'll also see how to "go away" from the table. And finally you'll learn how to possess both a controlled betting system and a controlled attitude—so that you win more money, whether you are the shooter or not!

Setting the Dice

It is possible to turn the game of craps from a negative expectation into a positive expectation game. In addition to setting, you must learn how to grip and throw the dice properly, which is covered in the next few sections.

First, imagine the two dice are rotating on a vertical axis at the same time. If they stay straight and continue rotating, the numbers on the right and left sides of each die will never show. If you set, grip, and throw them properly, you should only see the numbers that are on the vertical axis. If you get a pair of regulation dice right now it will be easier to follow along.

There are only six different dice sets available and we'll look at all six. The purpose of dice setting is to arrange the dice so that the 7s appear on the outside horizontal axis. If the dice are rolled smoothly, that one 7 on each die will never appear, thus decreasing the available 7s. A 7 can be rolled 1 and 6, 2 and 5 and 3 and 4. The first three dice sets will eliminate these first three 7 combinations.

ALERT!

Most boxpersons will complain if your set takes longer than 3 seconds. You really want to have the dealers on your side and not fighting you. Practice your sets at home, and bring some dice with you so you can practice in your hotel room until you get it right!

The 2, 3, 5, 4 Set—
Eliminating the 1 and 6 Combination

Set both dice identically so when you rotate them toward you, all you see are the 2, 3, 5, and 4 on the vertical axis. The totals showing would be all hardways—the hard 4, hard 6, hard 10, and hard 8. You will see that the 1s and 6s have been eliminated (on the horizontal axis), so in addition to fewer 7s, you would not be able to throw a 2, 3, 11, or 12 with this set. This set is great for hardways, place bets, and 6s and 8s. You can set this quickly just by placing the 1s and 6s on both horizontal axis (on the outside). Of course, you can also set the dice on vertical axis by keeping the

2, 3, 5, and 4 in sequence as you rotate the dice toward you. It doesn't matter which numbers are on top as long as you keep the 2, 3, 5, and 4 order maintained.

The 1, 3, 6, 4 Set—
Eliminating the 2 and 5 Combination

Both dice should be set on the vertical axis for 1, 3, 6, and 4. This set eliminates the 5s and 2s on the horizontal axis so it is impossible to roll a 3 or 11. It actually increases the frequency of 7s, so it is used only for don't bettors and the come-out. You can set this quickly just by placing the 5s and 2s on both horizontal axis (on the outside). You can set this vertically by keeping the 1, 3, 6, and 4 in sequence as you rotate the dice toward you. It doesn't matter which numbers are on top as long as the 1, 3, 6, and 4 order is maintained.

The 1, 2, 6, 5, Set—
Eliminating the 3 and 4 Combination

Another don't bettor set is the 1, 2, 6, and 5. You will have the 4s and 3s eliminated on the sides, so these numbers will not roll. This set will produce more 7s but no 5s or 9s, so if you see someone laying the 5s and 9s, he's probably using this set! You can set this quickly just by placing the 4s and 3s on both horizontal axis (on the outside). You can set this vertically by keeping the 1, 2, 6, and 5 in sequence as you rotate the dice toward you. It doesn't matter which numbers are on top as long as the 1, 2, 6, and 5 order is maintained.

Now that we know the three basic 7-eliminating sets, let's look at the three sets that combine the above methods to produce even better results!

The 1, 2, 6, 5/2, 3, 5, 4 Set

When you set the dice, each die can be set differently. For example, you set the first die as 1, 2, 6, 5 and the second die as 2, 3, 5, 4. Although this may take a little longer to set, it has terrific advantages—only two 7s, and two each of the 4, 5, 6, 8, 9, and 10. This set would be really good for place bettors after the come-out! You can set this quickly by placing the 4 and 3 on one horizontal die axis and the 1 and 6 on the other. You can set this vertically with a 1, 2, 6, 5 sequence on one die and a 2, 3, 5, 4 sequence on the other. It doesn't matter which numbers are on top as long as the correct orders are maintained.

The 1, 2, 6, 5/1, 3, 6, 4 Set

You can also set the first die to 1, 2, 6, 5 and the second to 2, 3, 5, 4. On the first die you are eliminating the 4 and 3. On the second die you are eliminating the 2 and 5. This combination gives you two of each of the 5, 6, 7, and 8. This is the famous "6-T" set, because if you place the two 6s together to form a *T*, you have this set in one quick motion. You can set this quickly by placing the 4 and 3 on one horizontal die axis and the 2 and 5 on the other. You can set this vertically with a 1, 2, 6, and 5 sequence on one die and a 1, 3, 6, and 4 sequence on the other. It doesn't matter which numbers are on top as long as the correct orders are maintained.

The 1, 3, 6, 4/2, 3, 5, 4 Set

This one is the most profitable. Set the first die to 1, 3, 6, 4 and the second to 2, 3, 5, 4. This set will produce only two 7s, but three each of the 6 and 8! There are also no 2s or 12s and one each of 3, 4, 10, and 11. You can set this quickly by placing the 5 and 2 on one horizontal die axis and the 1 and 6 on the other. You can set this vertically with a 1, 3, 6, and 4 sequence on one die and a 2, 3, 5, and 4 sequence on the other. It doesn't matter which numbers are on top as long as the correct orders are maintained.

When you use a set, it doesn't matter exactly where the numbers are located, as long as the proper ones are there. For example, in the 1, 3, 6, 4/2, 3, 5, 4, it is fine to set them 6, 4, 1, 3 on one and 4, 2, 3, 5 on the other. Please note that in this particular set you will be eliminating the 5 and 2 on one die and the 6 and 1 on the other die. As long as these numbers remain on the axis, it really doesn't matter where the other numbers end up.

The really good thing about dice setting is that it doesn't cost you anything to use, except for maybe a little practice. So, if you're going to shoot anyway, why not set the dice?

Now that you know how to physically set the dice, the next step is properly gripping them so they stay together when you toss them.

Gripping the Dice

Your dice gripping procedure should begin as soon as the stickperson begins to push the dice toward you. In order to produce the desired results, you need to hold the dice in a certain manner so they leave your hands properly and stay together. First, just look at the dice and notice which numbers are facing up. Then imagine, in your mind, exactly what to do to the dice to turn them so they land in the position you want them to end up.

If you are tipping the dealers, you can ask if they will return the dice to you "6s on top," or some other easy to manipulate position. You should buy a pair of dice (regulation size) and practice with them at home, so you can set them (after watching their return from the stickperson) in about two seconds, so you don't hold up the game.

When the current shooter 7s out, you should start watching what the stickperson does. He will return the used dice to the bowl and choose five dice and push all of them toward you. If, for example, you are looking for a hardway set, you should look for two dice with 2, 4, or 6 facing up so you can set them easier. Of course, after you establish a point you will have only one pair returned each time so you need to set them even quicker.

One easy method to set the dice quickly is to remember that opposite sides add up to 7. So if they are returned to you with 1s and 2s showing, you know that 6s and 5s are on their opposite sides. You need to remember to use one hand only, and if your other hand even remotely hovers near the dice you will really invite heat from the boxperson, and he might even take the dice away if he thinks you've touched them with both hands.

Once you can flip the dice quickly, you are ready to grip the dice properly in a firm manner to ensure that they travel together in parallel paths, at the same time.

In order for this to occur, your finger pressure must be equalized all over so the force is symmetrical. Depending on the size of your fingers, your grip might be different than mine or another shooter's. There are many grips and each has a name, like the three-finger top, four-finger diagonal, five-finger top, and several others.

The three-finger front grip is the easiest and most popular. After the dice are set, you place your second, third, and fourth fingers along the upper ridge of the front dice, and your thumb on the upper ridge in between the two back sides. Your pinky is tucked away and not used. You would make sure the dice are perfectly symmetrical and then toss them with a slight back spin, so they land and bounce once around the pass line and, still spinning, just glance off the rubber backboard and come to rest the way you want them to. The throw is covered in detail in the next section, just as setting the dice was covered in the last one.

Now that you know how to grip the dice, you need to toss them so they land in the same spot each time and produce the desired results!

The Expert Throw

There are three components of dice setting—the set, the grip, and the throw. In the two previous sections we looked at the set and the grip, and now we'll learn about maximizing the effects of the way you throw the dice, in order to attain the desired results.

In order to perfect your throw, you should establish yourself at the same table position whenever you play. There are two positions that will reduce the length of your throw to an absolute minimum—just to the left of the stickperson or just to the right of the stickperson. You should try both positions and choose the one that works the best for you.

After the dice have been set and you are gripping them properly, visualize the throw in your mind. See the dice leaving your hands, traveling together in a straight line without wobbling, and landing around the pass line. Then they bounce together, lightly glance off the backboard, and end up showing your desired results. This visualization is very important, so take the second or two it requires before you actually toss the dice.

When they are tossed they should be at an angle to minimize any energy gathered during their descent. Try to toss them low, not more than a 45-degree angle from the table. When they leave your hands they should match your visualization perfectly, and you should be seeing what happens now a second time, just as you did in your mind.

The dice will leave your hand at the same time, without wobbling or changing course. They should fly through the air together, side by side, spinning forward as they move. They should bounce once around the pass line and, still spinning, glance lightly off the backboard and come to rest without bouncing or hitting any chips.

FACT

There are usually chips present on the pass line, on the other end of the table. You can politely ask the bettors to move them to the side. They usually will, as they want to make money on your roll as much as you do.

Your throw will achieve more consistent results if you put your whole body into it, rather than just your wrist and arm. Shooting dice is very much like playing golf—you need to have your entire body participate in the experience. When the dice leave your hand, your hip and upper body is contributing to the velocity of the dice, not just your arm. Your body should move with the dice as they are released.

After the dice are set and gripped, just turn toward the stickperson and imagine your throw and its result. Bend your fingers on the dice back a bit to increase their spin, and then turn your body in front of and past the stickperson to release them. After a little practice, this will become one fluid motion, and should become almost second nature to you after you've done it a few times.

Here is a trick that may work for you. When you shoot, imagine a cereal bowl sitting on the pass line. It is your job to just toss the dice so they land in the cereal bowl. For some people it is easier to imagine this happening than it is aiming for the pass line. You might try some different things you are more familiar with, like a shoebox, a hatbox, or even a cigar box. Do whatever it takes for you to succeed!

When you are shooting, you'll see a lot of distractions from fellow players, the stickperson, the dealers, drink servers, and assorted casino noises. Wouldn't you shoot better if you could tune all these things out of your mind and concentrate on the important stuff—like making money?

Going Away from the Table

When you know how to set the dice, have developed your own personal professional grip, and have perfected the expert throw, you could still find a problem at certain tables. The boxperson or the dealers may talk to you to disturb your rhythm. Suddenly there are beautiful drink servers all around you. A floor person may start talking to you, asking if you want a free buffet. All of these things are done on purpose by the casino. They are all meant to distract you, to throw off your rhythm, and encourage you to 7-out and pass the dice to the next shooter.

When you are distracted at the table, you need to block out everything that does not contribute to your efficient shooting. You need to focus all of your energies toward obtaining the results you want from the dice in your hand. The easiest way to do this is to let your subconscious mind take over and "go away" from the table.

ESSENTIAL

Gripping, setting, and throwing takes quite a bit of practice, and you need to practice before you play, perhaps on a low-limit table or even in your hotel room. But it's worth it. Once you learn how, you'll possess a real money-making skill that you will always use whenever you play!

To "go away," you need a calming spot. This is place to go on a temporary vacation. Pick a favorite spot—the perfect beach, a beautiful mountaintop, or perhaps even an undersea grotto. This is a place for you to relax and leave the cares and worries of the world behind. To accomplish this, you must see your calming place out of your eyes, as though you are actually there. You must not see your body in a beach chair, as though you are watching yourself. You must see, out of your eyes, all the things around you, and feel the sun upon you, and the gentle breezes blowing.

You must not be looking at the other end of the craps table, but at the ocean, or the mountain, or the trees. You should not be smelling cigarette smoke or stale drinks, but flowers or trees or the salty ocean. And finally, you should not be hearing the drink girls, or the drunk players, or the floor people. You should be hearing seagulls, gentle waves, or wind rustling the leaves. You can practice this all at home, of course. And when you do, have a trigger point so you can easily retreat to your calming spot. You can touch a certain spot on your arm, for example, or you can recite a phrase, or whistle a tune. When your calming spot is triggered, you should be able to retreat there instantly, and let its sights, smells, and sounds take over in your mind.

When you are about to shoot at the craps table, perform your trigger and go away. Your subconscious mind will take over and remember how to set, grip, and throw the dice. You will not worry about the hassles or anything else. When you finally do 7-out, you will probably be awakened by the sound of applause, and you will leave your calming spot and be relaxed and invigorated—and have lots more chips than you did before!

Now that you have controlled your mind, how about controlling your betting? Even if you shoot expertly you need to know how to make bets that make money!

Controlled Betting

If you are playing at a table and the new shooter is a dice controller, you might want to bet a little differently than you normally would. Many dice controllers hold the dice for ten or twenty rolls compared to the normal five to nine rolls for an average shooter.

Over time, an expert shooter develops what is referred to as a signature roll. The easiest way to discover this is to notice what the shooter is betting on. He will probably make a pass line bet and then also place some numbers, like maybe the 4 and 10. He has to make a pass line bet to shoot, but the 4 and 10 place bet is somewhat unusual, so he might have a signature. It would be best if you followed his lead and bet the same way he did.

Obviously, though, he will throw a 7 eventually and you can't leave all of your money up forever. You need to have a good regression system. The easiest one to use is to start out at your highest bet, and buy the same two numbers the shooter does. Then, just regress the numbers down by 1 unit after each win until you are at the table minimum.

FACT

If you are an expert shooter yourself, you can bring your spouse or friend along. The casino will let them take care of your bets while you are concentrating on shooting. This way you can give your full attention to your set, grip, and throw!

You can also try pushing the house to get a better deal. For example, if you buy the 4 and 10 for $50, you would have to pay $2.50 vig on each number. Sometimes this is rounded up to $3. Ask if you can pay $2. If they say yes (and they should), ask if you can buy the 4 and 10 for $58 each and still only pay the $2 (5 percent of $58 is $2.90) vig.

Now let's say the 4 hits and you win $116. Leave the $58 on the 10 and regress the 4 down to $38, and ask if you can buy it for $38 and only pay $1 vig (5 percent of $38 is $1.90). If the 4 hits again, you win $76. Leave it at $38—you can't pay less than $1 vig on a buy bet and if they keep on letting you buy the 4 (and 10) for $38 and only pay $1, then keep on doing it.

Soon, if the 10 starts hitting you will have both the 4 and 10 regressed down to $38. Leave both bets up unless the shooter takes his bets down, or something unusual happens to ruin the shooter's concentration. By regressing your buy bets, you will always have something on the table during a hot roll, and after the first win, everything else is pure profit

Now that you are betting properly if you're the shooter, how about when someone else is shooting—do you have the right attitude?

Controlled Attitude

You might be tipping the dealers, calling them by name, and be close friends with your casino host. You are doing very well, and starting to win a lot of money. But suddenly the dealers turn against you, and start a campaign of harassment that ends in either you throwing a 7-out, or worse, them taking the dice from you and giving them to another shooter.

When you play craps, you should remember that the table personnel are people with their own problems and desires. Sometimes, casino management looks at their employees just as revenue sources. And sometimes, some crews make more money than other crews. If, for example, one boxperson had the misfortune to be at several tables that have lost money, she might be considered to be unlucky even though it is certainly not her fault. And if this particular boxperson ends up at your table, you will not do as well as you would at another table with a different boxperson.

The boxperson may talk to you and have the other dealers talk to you before and during your shoot. You might see the stickperson hit the dice with her stick, by accident. A drink server could spill a drink on you, also by accident. These things don't happen very often, but they do happen. And these aren't the worst things that can happen. The boxperson has the power to simply take the dice from you and not let you shoot at all, because you are slowing down the game. The thing to remember is that this is just one person out of hundreds of casino employees who has had a bad experience in the past, and she is letting this experience control her attitude toward your shooting.

The most important attitude here, however, is not the boxperson's, but yours. If you are to continue playing at another table, you can not let a casino employee rattle you. You don't want to end up giving your hard-won money back to the casino. You need to go to your calming place and relax. Then go back to your room and remember the good times you had in this casino, and all the comps you received over the last several years. Take a break. Read a magazine. Calm down. You can not let the boxperson's attitude take control of yours!

You are the only person who should control you. Whether it takes one hour or one day, you should not play again until your attitude is controlled, and you are sure you can perform to the best of your abilities.

When the incident is totally forgotten, it is time to attack the tables again. When your attitude is controlled by you and not the casino, you will win, and not the casino.

Chapter 18

Money Management: How to Keep What You've Won

It's great to win at craps, but how do you know when to stop playing? We'll look at win goals, loss limits, and how to qualify a shooter. You'll learn how to maximize your bets by using casino credit, and how to use discipline to increase your winnings. And finally, you'll see how to achieve real personal success as a crapshooter.

Win Goals and Loss Limits

Many of the people who play craps today will walk up to a table and just keep on playing until they lose all of their money. It doesn't matter if they are $100 ahead or even $500 ahead—they just keep on playing. These people have no win goal.

Both your win goal and your loss limit should be 30 percent of your buy-in. This means that if you start with $100, you should stop when you've won or lost $30. If you buy in with $600, you should stop when you've won or lost $200.

The reason you need a win goal is because tables fluctuate. You can be $100 up one moment and $100 down the next. How do you know when to stop and still leave with a profit? Your win goal should be based on your individual session money, and should be 30 percent of your buy-in. For example, if you buy in with $100 and are $30 ahead, you should quit. Leave the table and go to your room or have lunch. Then an hour or so later, buy in with your $130 and quit when you've won $39. Be precise. Be disciplined. Follow the plan. Set a win goal and stick to it!

ALERT!

If you keep on playing until you lose all of your money, you will do exactly that. When you play craps you need a definite, unchangeable win goal—something you can "shoot" for. You can't just play haphazardly and hope to win thousands from a $5 bet on a monster roll.

The opposite of a win goal is a loss limit, and it's also 30 percent—very easy to remember. If you buy in for $100, you leave when you win or lose $30. If you buy in for $500, you leave when you win or lose $150. You need a loss limit, because if your play is based on the thought that you brought $100 so the most you can lose is $100, then you certainly will lose it all. A lot of people bring $500 to a casino expecting to lose. It doesn't bother them because it was "extra" money that they could afford to spend on entertainment. So they break it up into five sessions of $100 each and just keep on playing until it's all gone.

You need a loss limit, and you need to stick to it. This section is one of the easiest to read, but the hardest one to use. It goes against the grain of every crapshooter, hoping for that huge roll where you can turn $5 into $50,000. But really, how often does that happen? You might have a buddy who knows someone who held the dice for three hours and the casino went broke. Everyone knows someone who knows someone who did this. But we're talking your own money here, the same money you use for rent, food, and your children's shoes. It is not a disgrace to come home after a weekend and only win $150. Or even $50. You can always lie to your friends about it. But when it comes to your own hard-earned cash, you've got to protect it.

One of the cardinal rules of craps is to increase your bets while winning but decrease them while losing. But when many people start losing, they keep on playing as if nothing has changed. Remember—it's better to come home with some money than no money!

Go into a session expecting to win "only" $30 on a $100 buy-in. Stop when you reach it. If you're losing, quit when you lose $30. In five $100 sessions the most you can lose is $150. You can, however, win more than $150, because your win dollar limit increases on each winning session, even though you have the same 30 percent win limit! So, stick to your guns. Set a win goal and a loss limit. Over the long run, you'll win more and lose less.

Casino Credit

When you're playing at a craps table you might see someone hand his comp card to a dealer and ask for "a thousand." The dealer gives the card to one of the floor people and the new player gets his money.

The credit procedure itself is fairly simple. You call the casino cage and ask for a credit application. They can even fax it to you right away. You fill it out and fax or mail it back. The casino will send you a letter a few weeks later informing you how much credit you have. What the casino does in those few weeks is check your credit with a credit-reporting agency. If you have good credit, they will then call your bank and ask for your current average balance. The higher this is, the more credit you'll get.

Let's say you have a large tax refund that you plan on using to pay off some bills. You put off the bills for a few weeks so you have almost $5,000 in your account. This is when you should apply for casino credit—when your bank account is at its highest. If you have $5,000 in your account, you could get a $5,000 line at most casinos, especially if you're a rated player.

Having a credit line tells the casino that you're really serious about gambling. They will be happy to loan you $5,000 every month or so—interest free. At the casino, when the dealer gives you your money, you need to sign a "marker," which is like a personal check. If you don't pay back the money by the time you leave the casino, they'll send you a bill in a month or so. If you don't pay this bill, the casino will use your marker to collect from your bank. Never borrow money from the casino that you can't pay back in a timely manner.

The big advantage to casino credit is that you don't have to bring any money with you when you gamble. The casinos like it, because they figure that you'll bet more this way—but don't.

ALERT!

The casinos are happy to lend you money because they think it will increase your bet amounts. Do not do this. Stick to your regular betting pattern, and be sure to pay strict attention to your established win goal and loss limit.

You don't need to use the entire credit amount at once. If you received $2,000 from the casino and break it up into five sessions, you'll have $400 per session. Your total bets per shooter should be $40. If you win $120 (30 percent of $400), you should leave the table. If you lose $120 (also 30 percent of $400), you should also leave the table.

This means, obviously, that you never play with all of the casino's money. If you win all five sessions you'll have $600 (not bad!). Even if you lose all five sessions, you'll lose only $600 (and not the entire $2,000), which should be about the value of your comps for three days—so you haven't lost much at all.

Another big advantage of casino credit is that it increases your comps. When you buy in, the dealer records your buy-in, your first bet, and your average bet. If your session money was to be $400, you could buy in with $1,000, and put six black chips in your pocket. Only play with the original $400. Never touch the black chips in your pocket! Never go past your win goal or loss limit!

If you buy in with $1,000 you'll get more comps than if you bought in with $400, even though in both cases you're only playing with $400. The extra $600 comes from the casino, not you. The casino is paying for your extra comps.

The casinos, of course, don't mind this at all. They figure that most people have no win goals or loss limits. They figure that if you have $1,000 burning a hole in your pocket, you'll just keep playing until you spend it all. But don't. You've got to beat them at their own game.

Playing with casino credit, if managed properly, will give you higher comps and a more convenient way to play.

QUESTION?

Should I ask for minor comps from the boxperson or get reimbursed for everything later when I check out?
Ask for everything you can before you check out. Ask for meals and even shows when you are finished playing your sessions. Try to leave just your room for your host to pick up. The more items you get comped for now, the less you have to worry about later!

Qualifying a Shooter

When you're playing craps, do you ever walk up to a table and put your money on the layout in the middle of a roll? After all, dice have no memory, so what difference could it make? Well, it makes a big difference.

First of all, craps pros will approach a table and look at the chips in the player's racks to see how they are all doing. They also may wait one or two points to see which way the table is going and if there are any profitable don't players betting. They think carefully and qualify the shooter before they start betting.

You should always walk around first, and then pick the most profitable table. Look at the players and see how they're doing. If you're a don't bettor, you should be looking for a different table than if you're betting on the do side! Some people think that the shooter makes no difference in the outcome of the dice. If it doesn't make any difference, it couldn't hurt to qualify the shooter, and it just might substantially increase your profits at the tables!

You should be looking for shooters that bet big on themselves while they have the dice. Sometimes, these shooters will only bet $5 pass line while someone else is shooting, but $25 or $50 while they have the dice themselves. Who knows, maybe they have a craps table at home and have perfected some method of rolling numbers, or perhaps they are accomplished rhythm rollers, and have been doing it for years. At any rate, if they have confidence in themselves as shooters, you should always be ready to back them up with a big bet.

The dealers know when one of these players comes along. They will try to talk to him, break his rhythm, maybe even send a cocktail server over, just to break his concentration. When you see this happen, try not to distract him yourself—don't smoke, talk to him, or distract him in any way. These "rhythm rollers" should be left alone.

ALERT!

No one really cares if you win or lose at craps—except yourself. You can lie to your friends and family, but don't lie to yourself. Remember, you are not playing for fun, you are playing with your rent money. This is investing, and you should treat it as such.

You might see one of these players, and watch her as she keeps rolling number after number. She arranges the dice in a certain way, and throws them so they always land in approximately the same spot in the far corner of the table.

After three points in a row, you might see the pit boss ask the player about his rating, but the shooter ignores him. The dealers keep talking to him, and he ignores them, too.

Then, the pit boss brings in some new racks of chips and starts to replenish his supply, still trying to stop this guy. Nothing works—he keeps on shooting numbers. After the fifth point, people begin crowding the tables, and the dice are examined. "Same dice" he calls, and the dealers finish their examination and reluctantly return the dice to him.

Then, a slightly tipsy man comes to the table and squeezes in right next to the shooter. He actually pushes himself in and buys in for a whole $10. He begins to talk loudly to the shooter, who clearly doesn't like him there.

If something like this happens, you should take down your bets, even if the shooter leaves his up. He doesn't know it, but the casino has finally succeeded in ruining his concentration. You really have to watch for things like this, and take down your bets if anything unusual or out-of-the-ordinary occurs. Needless to say, the next roll was a 7, and the shooter colored out and left. So did the "drunk," who had pushed himself in for just one roll for some strange reason and then went elsewhere.

The lesson here is simply to keep your eyes open and be aware of all the other players, and especially the shooter. If he is throwing numbers, it doesn't matter if he sets the dice, says a prayer, blows on them, or has his "niece" shoot for him. The only thing that matters is results. Once the dice go around the table, you should be able to determine the good and bad shooters by their previous performance. If someone looks confident of his abilities, he could be a good shooter. And if he shoots a lot of numbers while he bets big on himself, you should bet along with him. Hopefully your bets will stay up along with his for a very long—and profitable—roll!

Using Discipline to Increase Winnings

Let's say you have a heart attack. You go to your doctor and she says you need to cut down on your cholesterol and exercise more or you'll have another one. You ignore her advice and you have another one. You know what you should do, but you don't have the discipline to carry it through. When you have discipline you are making a promise to yourself to accomplish a certain goal. In your other business and personal agreements, your own integrity keeps that promise, even if it is an unwritten one. Why not keep your agreements with yourself when you play craps?

Now, let's say you are at a craps table, and know all there is to know about money management and setting win/loss goals. You buy in for $500 and have a $150 loss limit. You hit it, but keep on playing anyway. You lose all your money because you have the knowledge but no discipline. This goes for winning also. If you have a $150 win goal, reach it, but keep on playing anyway, you just might lose it all if the table turns.

Besides the obvious advantage of profiting more by using proven techniques when you play, you'll also have increased self-esteem and confidence because you kept your commitment. You'll make more money and feel better at the same time. Why then, do most players disregard their money management knowledge and win/loss goals? It is because we are greedy and want more winnings. Whether we're $200 ahead or $2,000 ahead, we still want more.

You should have as much discipline and integrity in a craps game as you do in an important business deal. In business you are not working for fun, and you are not playing for fun in craps—you are playing for money!

The real beginning of modern gambling started back in the early 1900s when a smart salesman was in a bar having a drink. He noticed a young woman playing one of the mechanical slot machines that were in nearly every establishment in those days. After a few pulls of the handle she won $200, which was a real fortune back then.

Everyone gathered around her and praised her playing. She was exhilarated when she was paid off! The salesman speculated how she would spend her newfound riches when she stuffed the 200 gleaming silver dollars into her purse.

After all the commotion died down he wondered why the woman was still in the bar, instead of at home sharing her small fortune with her family. A few minutes later he watched her walk back to her slot machine and put just one of the dollars back in. Then another. She got a chair and sat down, and soon fed every single one of her new silver dollars back into the machine. That salesman went off to start a slot machine marketing company. That woman went home broke, feeling terrible. It wasn't her fault—she just wanted more, just like most people do. She was greedy. She had no discipline.

The next time you play, make an agreement with yourself regarding your win/loss limits. You can write this down or memorize it, but keep this agreement! This way, you'll have discipline and increase your confidence so you'll make more money!

Achieving Personal Success

If you want to be happy and productive in your gambling, you must feel that you are learning and progressing in what you are doing. If you learn something from every game you play, you'll be able to use that knowledge in future games to play differently, increase your confidence, and most importantly, make more money!

CRAPS can very well mean that you get:

- Consistent
- Results
- Applying
- Personal
- Success

Your personal success is achieved by winning more or losing less. You learn how to do this by studying, practicing at home, and applying your wisdom to the game in a disciplined fashion.

Successful crapshooters know that if they fail to plan, they plan to fail, so they go into each game with a definitive system. They know exactly how they'll bet in advance, and never deviate from their plan. Not only do they win more money, but their increased personal success gives them increased self-confidence as well!

For example, you might like hedge bets. Perhaps you plan to bet don't come and then hedge each bet with a corresponding place bet. But when a hot-looking shooter appears, you forget about your plan and bet on the pass line. And the come. And the hardways. Your plan just went by the wayside. You had the knowledge but lacked the discipline, which resulted in inconsistent results.

The only way you can get consistent results is to apply wisdom to your game. Wisdom is knowledge applied. If you know what to do but don't do it, you are courting disaster. If you don't have a plan, read some of the many books on craps and get one. If you do have a plan, stick to it and then don't make any other bets. Learn from your results and then apply your learning to the next game you play until you achieve consistent results.

Chapter 19

Tournaments: Basic and Advanced Theory

Many people look at tournaments as ways to make money and win prizes, but it is also a way to make friends and new contacts. We'll first look at basic tournaments and then progress to the first phase in advanced tournaments—starting out. Then we'll look at the middle game, the end game, and, of course, the last shooter.

Basic Tournament Play

If you are a regular crapshooter, you might want to enter a craps tournament some day. Some of these contests are free to enter, some cost a few hundred dollars, and a few cost quite a bit more, depending on the prize money. Several casinos also have weekly craps tournaments with no entry fee and a low $50 buy-in, just to bring people in the door.

In a tournament you make different bets than you would in a normal craps game. You are no longer playing against the house, but against all of your fellow contestants. Your goal is to have the most money at the end of a certain number of rolls (like 100), or a certain amount of time (like thirty minutes). This means you need to keep an eagle eye on the chips in the racks of your fellow players and be aware of their bets.

Let's say you have $300 and your closest competitor has $200. She bets $90 on the 6 and 8. You need to aware of the consequences of the 6 or 8 rolling. In this case, she'll jump ahead by $5 (enough to win). Your strategy might be to match her bets to stay ahead.

Or, what if you're in second place with $200 and the number-one player has $300? You've placed the 6 and 8 for $90 each and he matched you. Maybe you might bet hardways or prop bets. You must do something different in order to overtake the front-runner.

FACT

Some players who are close to last place resort to bets not normally made—like betting a large amount on the 2 or 12. In the last few rolls of the game, they realize it's the only way they can win.

When you begin play, you'll see that there are conservative players, playing pass or come with maximum odds, and aggressive players who bet hardways and proposition bets. If these aggressive players continue, they'll usually (but not always) lose their money before the final round. If you're in the group playing pass/come, you need some way of breaking out of the pack—like waiting for two consecutive points to be made and then jumping to the don't. You have to start doing something the other players are not doing in order to win.

Let's say the leader has $100 on the pass line and the point is 4. He takes $200 odds. You could then lay the 4 for $200. If a 7 rolls, he would lose $300 and you would win $100. You've got to try things, be inventive, and make bets that the other players wouldn't think of making.

For example, in the last few rolls of the game, you must become super-aggressive if you're behind. Sometimes this means betting all of your bank-roll on one number. Say 8 is the point and the leader is $300 ahead and has $100 on the pass line with double odds. You're in third place, and all you have left is $300. You might place the whole $300 on the 6, take it down after it hits once, and then pray that a 7 rolls before the 8 does!

Tournaments are not for everyone, but they're fun to play, especially the inexpensive or free ones. Give them a try. You're sure to learn a lot, make some friends, and maybe some good money as well! Now, let's get down to the technical aspects of how to win a craps tournament. There are three sections to explore, the beginning, the middle of the contest, and the end game.

Starting out in an Advanced Craps Tournament

When you play in an advanced craps tournament, it means the entry fee is higher than a basic tournament—over $500 usually. When you play with more money than the basic tournament described in the last chapter, there are more precise methods required to stay ahead of your fellow players.

When you first start playing, you need to be aware of three things and keep these three things in mind the entire time you play. These three items are player advancement, player bankroll, and player threats.

If there are twelve people at your table and only three people advance to the next round, you need to be one of the top three. If you are number four at the end of the game, your tournament is over. Your goal, from your first bet, is to ensure you are ahead of at least nine of your fellow players. Once you achieve this goal, you must make bets to ensure that you stay there!

Finally, you must know exactly where you are, compared to your competitors. You will actually be basing the size of your bets on what your closest challengers do. If someone has more chips than you do, you must catch up and surpass him. You also should know how many chips the top three players will have after either the point is made or a 7 rolls. This way you will know where you stand no matter what the shooter does.

Finally, you need to be aware of threats from other players. If you are in the top three, the other players will know this (by counting your chips) and try to catch up. If you are in third place and the player in fourth makes a big bet, you need to know what will happen if he wins or loses his bet, and make every effort to counteract it.

ALERT!

Players in advanced tournaments must have all of their chips displayed in their racks, but a common strategy is to mix them up, making them harder to count. Before the tournament, become very familiar with the chip colors so that you can accurately count everyone's chips.

When the game starts, you will see that most people bet identically—one pass and a come bet or two. Those that make crazy bets (like prop bets) may win in the beginning but usually end up losing everything. If you keep pace with the other players, you'll see that several will fall behind, leaving maybe five or six out in front. When this happens, it's your chance to break out of the pack and become one of the top three.

Next stop—the middle game.

The Middle Game

When you are in the middle of an advanced craps tournament and see that some players are falling behind, it is time to make your move to catapult yourself into the top three.

Let's say you are fifteen minutes into an hour tournament and you've kept pace with the leaders. You count everyone's chips and find you are in fifth place. Not bad, but not good enough to advance into the next round. It's time to move out of the pack! If everyone has been betting pass and come, you might starting making moderate place bets and taking them down after they hit. You are at the stage now where place bets are best because they are flexible. You can put them up and take them down as the need arises. By now you will have gotten used to the shooters, so you know who is good and who isn't. With controlled shooters you might leave your place bets up, while with others, you will take them down after only one hit.

ESSENTIAL

You must remember to keep track of everyone's chips as you inch your way to the top, a little at a time. If you find yourself falling behind, you must make a major bet to catch up, like betting don't come or laying the 4 and 10 when everyone else is betting right (that is, on the do side). Now is not the time for hardways or prop bets. You want to regain your lead slowly with little or no risk.

Think outside the box. If you reach the table limit, you can also bet on the big 6 and 8. You can also combine a pass line bet on, say, the 9 point, with both a place bet and a field bet. You've got to get ahead, and stay ahead.

Once you are in the top three, the other players may try to distract you by talking to you, especially if they think you are counting their chips. If you pick some of your chips up from your rack and are a little slow putting them on the table, your opponent can protest and accuse you of hiding chips in your hand. These are just some of the things that your competitors will do to make you lose your concentration, and you must be prepared for them. When people realize you are a major competitor, they will base their bets on what you do.

Once you are in the top three you need to stay there in both the end game and most importantly, the final roll. Next stop—the end game!

ALERT!

One way to shake off your competition is to make stealth bets. Make your bets the normal way and when the other players are distracted or making bets themselves, you can place bets directly on the field or the big 6 and 8. The dealers will see this, of course, but your major competitor may not and if you win you will surge ahead!

The End Game

Once you are one of the top three players in a craps tournament you need to stay there through the end game, and on to the last roll. If the tournament you are in is more than half over and you are in the top three, you need to stay there by matching the other players' bets and taking few chances. You want to stay right where you are until the game ends. However, if you are not where you want to be, you need to catch up fast.

Start thinking about combining your bets to get the best results. One combined bet is to place bet the 6 and 8 for the maximum and also bet the big 6 and 8 for the maximum. You can also buy and place the same number. If you're on the don't side, you can bet don't come and then lay the same number. If you're on the pass (or don't pass) you can buy (or lay) the point you're on.

If you need to make some large bets to get to the top, now is the time to do it. You should be ready to invest all of your chips and either hit the top or go down in flames—there is no middle ground.

If you get to where you want to be, you need to single out your most serious opponent. Once you do, you need to match her bets in such a manner that you stay ahead. For example, if you bet a slightly smaller amount than she does, you will still be ahead if you both win, and still be ahead if you both lose.

ALERT!

You need to be aware of the table maximums. If your opponent can bet a maximum of $600 on the 6 and 8, she will win $700. You should figure out what you will have to bet along with her bet in order to stay ahead.

Once you are ahead you must stay there—at all costs—until the very last roll, because that last roll is where everyone will try desperate measures to overtake you—and you must survive! And now for the last shooter—your very last chance to win!

The Last Shooter

In every craps tournament the last shooter may hold the dice for a few minutes or an hour. He may make or break the other players, but however he shoots, you should never allow him to have the final say on whether you win or lose.

By the time the last shooter gets the dice, you should be in the top three, ready to go on to the next tournament session. If there are four or five of you, all with approximately the same bankroll, you need to take a chance and break free of the pack. One way to do this is to lay the point for the table maximum. This way you will either win everything or lose everything. Remember, there is no middle ground—only the top two or three go on to the next round. If this is not you, you need to risk everything to win. If everyone is on the do side, you could lay all the numbers. If everyone is on the don't you could buy all the numbers. The very worst thing you can do is keep all of your chips in your rack. Bet them all—this is your last chance!

If you are in the top three you need to match your closest competitor's bets—exactly—so you stay ahead. Whatever he does, you do. You also must continue to count your closest opponent's chips and know in advance how many he will have if a 7 or the point rolls. You can not afford to just sit back and wait for the last shooter to decide your fate! It is not enough to have the most chips in your rack—you must have the most chips if a 7 or the point rolls—and you have to bet accordingly.

If you can match your opponent's bets, do it. If you can make a bet that will lock the tournament (like betting the 6 and 8 with your excess chips), do it. Watch out for people making last-second bets on the field or the big 6 or 8—it always happens.

Instead of taking bets down, some people call them off, so the bets are still on the layout but not working. Make sure you know who these bets belong to and add them to your totals.

If you are in fourth place in a three-place tournament, look at what the player in third place is doing and bet the opposite on the remaining rolls. Finally, when the last shooter is shooting, you should always consider each bet as if the next roll is a 7 or the point and determine what would happen if either rolls. If everyone else is on the 6 and 8, maybe you should try the outside numbers, or maybe even a big field bet. And after every roll recount all the chips and make a new assessment, and a new bet.

You won't see many contract bets these last few rolls because everyone will be watching their opponent's chips and changing their bets. You need to be totally aware of everything that is going on at the table—how everyone else is betting and what your standing is—right then, and what happens to your standing if any number is thrown.

Tournaments are fun to participate in. Sometimes the casino will give you free gifts just for entering, and in many casinos there are often minor tournaments that are free to enter!

Memorizing Tournament Dice Rolls

One way you can increase your chances of winning a tournament is to keep track of all the numbers that are rolled. Since you are not allowed to use a pad, paper, or computer in most tournaments, you must remember all of the numbers in your mind. This gives you an advantage in a tournament based on the law of averages that the casino uses to calculate its odds. For example, the 7 will roll six times in thirty-six ideal rolls, the 6 and 8 will roll five times, etc.

If you are at a table where the 8 has rolled, say five times, and the 6 only three times, some people will place the 6 for $30 rather than $12 on both numbers. If a proposition number (such as 11) hasn't rolled in a long time, some people will begin making progressive bets on it.

This method is not that hard to learn, and once you know how, you'll remember it forever. You can walk up to any craps game anywhere and you'll soon know how many 6s, 8s, 7s, or other numbers have rolled in a long series. You can memorize dice rolls by utilizing common memory pegs. It's not difficult and there are many other uses (besides craps tournaments) for using memory pegs. You can use the rhyming memory pegs shown in **TABLE 18.1**, or you can make up your own.

TABLE 18.1 Memory Peg Chart

Number	Peg	Explanation
One	bun	a large bun or muffin with a creamy topping
Two	shoe	a pair of shoes with really long shoelaces
Three	tree	a large bushy tree with lots of empty branches
Four	door	a door opening up to reveal something
Five	hive	a large beehive with lots of bees flying around
Six	sticks	a bunch of wooden sticks lying in a pattern
Seven	heaven	nice fluffy clouds you can put things in
Eight	gate	wooden gate that opens to a yard full of stuff
Nine	wine	a big bottle with a large descriptive label
Ten	den	a large cave filled to the brim with stuff
Eleven	leaven	as in bread, a large loaf, stuffed with things
Twelve	shelves	bookshelves you can store items on

As you can see these pegs are not too hard to memorize, and we'll use the same pegs for both the numbers rolled and the amount of times the numbers rolled. The first image in your mind should be the actual number rolled and the second image would be the amount of times that number has appeared since you started counting.

For example, if the first roll is a 4, you can visualize a door (4) with a bun (1) behind it. If the second roll is also a 4, you can see a door (4) with a shoe (2) behind it. Let's say the first series of rolls is 4, 4, 8, 9, 10, 7. You could see the following after the 7 is rolled:

- A door (4) with a shoe (2) behind it:
  4 rolled two times
- A gate (8) with a bun (1) behind it:
  8 rolled one time
- Some wine (9) with a bun (1) on its label:
  9 rolled once

- A den (10) with a bun (1) inside:
  10 rolled one time
- Heavenly clouds (7) with a large bun (1) sitting on top:
  7 rolled one time

All you have to do is keep the pegs for the numbers 1 through 12 in your head, and your imagination will take care of the rest. Try to think of some ridiculously funny associations, and you'll remember them better. For example, say the next twelve rolls after the previous seven are: 5, 7, 6, 6, 7, 6, 9, 10, 7, 4, 6, 7. You can visualize the following exaggerated scenes to represent the totals for all nineteen rolls.

- A giant wooden door (4) opens to reveal a giant redwood tree (3) behind it:
  4 rolled 3 times
- A hive (5) of bees is gathered around a bun (1) soaked with honey:
  5 rolled 1 time
- A bunch of large arrows (sticks) (6) resting up against a door (4) of a castle:
  6 rolled 4 times
- A large heavenly (7) cloud swirling around a bee hive (5):
  7 rolled 5 times
- A gate (8) opens up to reveal a baking pan filled with a giant fresh bun (1):
  8 rolled 1 time
- A wine (9) bottle with a pair of shoes (2) on its label:
  9 rolled twice
- A bear in his den (10) putting on his cowboy boots (2):
  10 rolled twice

Now, what does this tell us? There have been no rolls of the 2 or 3, 11 or 12. Now might be a good time to bet the horn or C & E. The 5 rolled once but the 9 rolled twice. Maybe we should bet on the 5 rather than the 9. The 6 rolled four times compared to the 8 rolling one time. Placing the 8 now looks like a terrific bet! And, the 7 rolled five times in eighteen rolls—a good sign for things to come. It should have rolled only three times, so it might be wise to press your bets or cover any inside numbers you don't have bets on.

FACT

You can add "hero" for zero to get a total of twelve memory pegs. You can use these to memorize phone numbers or zip codes. For example, the zip code for the Las Vegas strip, 89109, could be a large iron gate (8) hiding a bottle of wine (9) and a loaf of bread (bun—1). A hero (0) is standing behind those items, drinking another bottle of wine (9).

Give this memory peg system a try—you'll be able to memorize twelve rolls of all eleven numbers (2 through 12) with it—you'll always know whether a 7 (or any other number) is "due." You'll also know if it's better to bet on the 6 or 8, and, the 5 or 9.

And remember—the more you know, the luckier you get!

Chapter 20

Complimentaries: Maximizing Your Winnings

Comps are much more important than most people realize. It is not uncommon for a $25 player to get $1,000 worth of comps in a single weekend. This means that even if you play badly and lose $500, you can still come out $500 ahead. We'll look at choosing the most profitable casino, and how to get the most comps possible. Finally, we'll look at exactly what you should do before that "monster roll" finally arrives!

Choosing a Profitable Casino

A casino that will maximize both your profits and your entertainment expectations is extremely important. Many people end up at casinos due to the proliferation of "fun books" that are mailed or given out at tourist bureaus. These coupons will give you free hot dogs, drinks, or coffee cups. But is this really the best method to choose a casino?

If you play craps for profit, you need to carefully choose a resort that will maximize your comps while offering favorable playing conditions. For example, some casinos offer 100× odds, while others offer only 2× odds. And, some casinos offer comp credit for your spread rather than for individual bets. Both of these are terrific advantages for the craps player.

However, after you have finished playing for the required amount of time and get your "free" meal or show, you might find that this is not exactly what you wanted. For example, say you visit a particular casino that offers 100× odds but they have standard rooms, no major show, and there is only one mediocre restaurant. Even though this casino offers superior playing conditions, you're bound to get tired of going there several times a year.

Another casino offers only 2× odds, but they offer a superior show, five different restaurants, and a Jacuzzi suite. Although this casino's craps policies are less favorable than the first one, you might end up getting more value for your money in the long run.

FACT

All casinos calculate comps as part of their expenses. If you don't ask for them, you are giving up a part of your benefits for visiting that casino. Why should someone else get free services while you have to pay for them? You should always ask for comps—it's your right in any casino!

Before you gamble, you should call a casino on their toll-free number and ask to speak to a casino host. Ask about the different restaurants, shows, and rooms the casino offers. Ask if they base comps on individual bet or spread. Ask about the minimum bets and play required to get a free room. Write down the answers and call the other casinos you're interested in, so you can make an accurate comparison. The ideal casino is different for every crapshooter.

One crapshooter might smoke cigars and so he chooses his casino by the brands of cigars that are offered as comps. Someone else might only want to stay in a hotel that offers a Jacuzzi, or an adjustable bed. Perhaps you would like a casino that has several different room floor plans, or one that has two shows instead of just one. One resort might have a terrific Chinese restaurant, while another might have a good Italian one.

In many casinos the high odds being offered do not compensate for the inferior quality of comps. Quite often, a casino offering 2× odds might be a better deal than one offering 100× odds. So, choose your casino with care and make sure it is the best one—for you!

Playing to Your Best Advantage

When you play craps, there are several things to take into account even before you start playing. For example, you should have a player's, or "comp" card. But what else can you do to maximize your profits—even before you start playing?

You should be a rated player and if the casino has a separate card for slot play, get one of those, too. This way, whenever they have promotions of any kind you will get mailings from them for free offers. Sometimes it is even possible to combine the promotions of the slot and table games offers.

You should apply for credit. You can call the casino cage (on their toll-free line) and ask how to do this. Your potential credit is based on your checking account balance, so the higher your balance, the higher your credit. Not only is casino credit more convenient, but you can sometimes withdraw your credit and then use it free for thirty days as well. You'll also have a higher comp rating and be an established player in the eyes of the casino.

You should get as many player's cards as you can, but try to limit your credit applications to one or two casinos. If you apply to more, your credit rating may suffer and, as a result, you will not get as large a credit draw.

When you begin playing, just give the friendly dealer your comp card and ask for your buy-in. He will check your rating and give the money to you in a few minutes. For example, you might say "a thousand please," and he might say, "in blacks or greens." He will then count out your chips on the table and set them aside while they check their computer.

Once you have the chips, you can play with the full amount, or not. For example, you can play with $500 worth and put the other $500 in your pocket and use it later or cash it in and use it in another casino if you like. When you leave the table, you may be asked if you want to pay off your marker. Don't be intimidated by this request. Just say no. Most casinos require that you pay back your markers in thirty days or it will adversely affect your credit with them in the future.

It is to your benefit to buy in with a larger amount than you will play with. Your comps are calculated by three criteria—(1) your buy-in, (2) your first bet, and (3) your average bet. So, if your buy-in and first bet are larger than normal, your comps will be bumped up a little.

Something else you can do to increase your comps is to tip the dealers. Tipping will also get the dealers on your side, so you can set the dice easier. The dealers will also notice your playing patterns and help you however they can—including bumping up your comps. The dealers would rather have you, a good tipper, back in their casino, than an inexperienced player who doesn't tip.

FACT

Notice the dealers' nametags, and call them by name. Be friendly with them. If they remember your first name and use it when you leave the table, you've done a good job—and they'll be doing everything they can to get you back!

Saving Money with Comps

Many people discount the extra value added to craps games that can be achieved with comps. They say it is too much trouble, not enough return, and too difficult to manage. But once you get used to it, you will find that you can make a lot more in comps than winnings! There are four major components to maximizing your comps at the tables:

- **Choice:** Choosing the best casino for your own individual needs
- **Odds:** Maximizing the odds, or benefits at your chosen casino
- **Money:** Increasing your comps by using credit and money management
- **Play:** Utilizing the casino personnel to make more money

These four components, in combination, produce a hefty savings for the average crapshooter! For example, if you play four hours each day for three days, the casino will usually give you two free nights lodging, eighteen meals, and two shows! Let's take a closer look at these free, added benefits that you receive just by playing the way you normally would.

Two weekend nights at a nice hotel can cost $150 per night, or a total of $300. But if you play a little more you can request a Jacuzzi room or a two-bedroom suite worth $200 per night. Eighteen meals at $10 each (buffet or coffee shop only) is $180. This includes three meals per day for two people. But if you play a little more you can eat in one of the casino's gourmet restaurants, which is worth triple what the buffet or coffee shop costs.

Finally, you get two show tickets worth $50 each, or a total of $100. If you play a little more, you can get four, better show tickets in a different casino. These four tickets could be worth $400, which is $300 more than your original tickets.

Let's say you are a $25 player and play four hours a day. You could receive $300 in hotel benefits, $180 in restaurant benefits, and $100 in shows. This is a total of $580 you didn't have before! This means that even if you break even playing, you are really $580 ahead.

Now let's say you are a $70 player and play for the same four hours. You could receive $400 in hotel benefits, $500 in restaurant benefits, and $400 in shows—a grand total of $1,300. This means that if you just broke even while playing, you really made a profit of $1,300!

Achieving this $70 level is not difficult if you and your partner (who occupy the same hotel room) both play. In this case you would both only have to be $35 players (only $10 more than the $25 player) to make $1,300 extra in three days. Just ask the boxperson to combine your play. The pit might even bump you both up a little, as they really want good players to return to their casinos. They know that by giving you more comps, you'll be encouraged to return—and bring your friends with you.

FACT

It always pays to bring a spouse or friend along. You can buy in together, combine your play, and double your comps. Even if your partner does not bet as much as you do, you will still get a lot more comps than you would have by yourself. The casino always encourages their players to bring their friends along.

Getting Free Junkets and Trips

Junkets, along with comps, provide a lot of free services to the crapshooter! For example, you can get RFB (room, food, and beverages) from both junkets and comps. Further, once you establish yourself as a steady gambler you will be invited back, and in doing so, the casino will offer you more free rooms, free food, and free beverages in return for your continued gambling. The difference between "full RFB" and RFB is that full RFB includes unlimited alcohol, including rare wines and champagnes. Full RFB is often worth double that of regular RFB—especially if you know your wines and liquors!

Junkets first started on the East Coast, as a means to lure seasoned gamblers away from Las Vegas and into Atlantic City. Now, Las Vegas casinos do the same thing, in order to lure people away from the East Coast and into their own golden coffers.

A junket always involves travel, and usually involves a group. The junket operator (hired by the casino) will charter an airline to take eighty or so gamblers from one coast to the other. They will all receive RFB, and have run of the casino. In return, they all pay the junket operator a certain amount of money (usually between $5,000 and $10,000) up front. When they get to the casino they can use this money to gamble with. Sometimes they get casino credit, and sometimes the operator gives them the full amount back in non-negotiable chips. Either way, you always pay your junket expenses in advance of your travel and your gambling sessions.

Comps, on the other hand, are given to you after you gamble. Although airline reimbursement is possible, it will not happen until after you play and meet a certain minimum playing criteria, like over $100 average bets for four hours a day. Comps are also available to players who bet as little as $5, but junkets are available only to higher rollers.

There is a third way to get some free casino services, which is a combination of the junket and comps. This is called a "turnaround," and is a day trip to the casino, either by bus, train, or local airline. Like the junket you need to pay in advance, but it is only $100 or so, and you will usually receive non-negotiable chips for this. In return they transport you to your favorite casino early in the morning, and then will bring you back to your starting point very late at night.

They will usually throw in a meal or two as well. Turnarounds are very popular with Indian casinos and local resorts that cater to low rollers.

If you're interested in these types of trips, just call your favorite casino and ask them for information. If your gambling budget is $5,000 to $10,000, ask about junkets. If you gamble with $500 to $5,000, ask what kind of comps you can get. And if you gamble with $100 or so, ask if they have any turnaround trips.

Increased Odds Casinos

Many crapshooters believe that betting at a table offering 10× odds is more advantageous than betting at a table offering 2× odds. If this is true, why is it that many casinos are now offering "true" (3×, 4×, and 5×) odds? Are they really trying to help the player?

Let's see what is really happening with craps odds. You are probably aware that a pair of dice has thirty-six combinations. The 2 and 12 can roll one way, the 3 and 11 two ways, the 4 and 10 three ways, the 5 and 9 four ways, the 6 and 8 five ways, and the ubiquitous 7 can roll six ways. On the pass line, you can win with the 7 or 11, without a point being established. The 7 can be rolled six ways, and the 11 two ways, so you will win eight out of thirty-six times on the pass line, or 2/9 of the time. You will lose on the pass line with a 2, 3 (twice), or 12, so you lose four out of thirty-six times, or 1/9 of the time. This means that 1/3 of the time, the bet is decided without a point, as 1/9 (losing) plus 2/9 (winning) equals 3/9, or 1/3. The other 2/3 of the time a point is rolled (4, 5, 6, 8, 9, or 10). Therefore, when you place odds after the point is established, you will do so in only 2/3 of the rolls. You, of course, have a choice of placing 1× odds or 2× odds in most casinos, after the point is established. Single odds does really decrease the house edge, from 1.4 percent down to .85 percent. And double odds reduce the edge further, down to .61 percent.

Now let's look at three different players. Player one makes 100 bets at $10 on the pass line with no odds. Player two makes 100 bets at $10 with single odds. Player three makes 100 bets at $10 with double odds. Who will come out ahead?

Let's look at the math. Player one (betting no odds when a point is established) puts $1,000 in action and her expected loss rate is 1.4 percent, or a total of $14, over a course of 100 rolls.

Player two has single odds on all points (which, remember, occur 2/3 of the time). So he bets $1,000 (1/3 of the time no point is established), plus 2/3 of $1,000 odds when the point is established ($666), or a total of $1,666. The house edge on a pass line bet with single odds is .85 percent, multiplied by $1,666, which is, surprisingly, $14.

Player three places double odds on each point (2/3 of the time). So he had $1,000, plus 2/3 of $2,000, a total of $2,333 bet. The house edge on a pass line bet with double odds is .61 percent, multiplied by $2,333, which is—surprise again—$14.

ALERT!

The lesson here is to always bet the minimum flat bet with the maximum odds, but only if you can afford them. Betting $5 with $50 odds does you little good if your bankroll is only $100. Be careful, and work the numbers out in advance, before you play.

When you bet higher odds, you will reduce the house edge, but it will also increase your total money in play. Your expected total loss (and the casino's gain) remains exactly the same. If you do bet double odds and win, of course, you will win more than if you bet single odds, or no odds at all. So when you choose a casino, look at some other things it has besides high odds—a nicer pool, better restaurants, classier shows. But don't choose a casino solely because of its craps odds—no matter how high they are!

Preparing for a Monster Roll

Let's say you are playing craps and the "monster roll" finally arrives, and you are in the middle of it. You start with a $10 pass line bet, two $10 come bets with maximum odds, and then keep increasing your bets by 1 unit when you win. You plan to decrease your bets when you lose, but that never happens—the shooter keeps rolling numbers. Finally, after he makes his eighth point, he 7s-out, and then another shooter does the same thing. Your red chips turn to green and your green chips to black. At the end of two hours, you count your chips and find that you have $3,500! You're on the top of the world! Think of what you can do with the money! $3,500, tax free! Or is it?

You are, of course, technically required to report any gambling wins as income to the IRS. All casinos have a policy paper on taxes, which is available free of charge at the casino cage. If you do opt to report a big win as income in exchange for not having to worry about it for the next seven years, there is an easy way to minimize your taxes.

The first thing is that you have to start preparing for your big win now. You have to keep accurate records of all of your play and all of your losses.

If you played several times this year and lost, say $2,500, you can deduct that from your previously mentioned $3,500 win and only pay taxes on $1,000. If you are in the 20 percent tax bracket, you would have paid $700 in taxes on your $3,500 win. On $1,000 you only have to pay $200 (20 percent of $1,000 is $200). This means that by keeping accurate records you've saved at least $500 ($700 – $200) this one time alone.

The IRS does not care if you lose money year after year. If you have just one winning year, you have to pay taxes on the win. To balance your wins with your losses, you need to keep an accurate diary. Your total losses on blackjack, slot machines, and roulette can balance out one big win on craps. If you get audited, you need to have records to support your diary—

markers, withdrawal receipts, bank statements, travel documents, and anything else you think will help support your claims. A consistent detailed journal is your best substantiation. You can always fib to your friends, but be truthful to yourself, and to your journal.

QUESTION?

I know I am supposed to pay taxes on my winnings, but what about all the rooms, food, and beverages the casino gives me as comps? Your comps are classified, in most cases, as gifts from the casino and therefore are not taxable. So, some comps could be more valuable than cash, if you would purchase the same items anyway. But remember, you should never play for comps. You should always play to win and follow a strict win/loss goal for every session!

One way of looking at it is exchanging a little bit of extra work (keeping journals) and money (owed taxes, if any) for not having to worry about tax penalties for the next seven years. This might seem like a great deal of trouble, but if you really expect to win big when you gamble, you should be prepared for it. Keep accurate records and you'll also keep more of your winnings in your pocket, so when that monster roll finally does come along, you'll really be ready for it!

Chapter 21
Other Dice Games

There are several other competitive dice games (besides regular craps). The most famous game is "crapless craps," which means you can't lose on the come-out to a craps number. Sic Bo is a very popular, flashy game with lots of bells and whistles. Electronic craps is played on an interface similar to a slot machine. Internet craps is played on a computer, and California craps is played, well, in California. Finally, we'll look at both Klondike and Hazard, both of which are coming back as slot machine games.

Crapless Craps

Many casinos have this game now, and it looks promising. You can't lose on the come-out to a 2, 3, or 12, and yet you still win on the 7! Sounds good, but if it's such a great deal, why are the regular tables so much more crowded than the crapless craps ones?

ALERT!

When you play crapless craps, remember to give the dealer your player's card. Not only will it get you more comps, but it will show them that you are a steady, experienced player as well—so they will pay attention to you even if you want to make some unusual bets.

One reason people don't play crapless craps is the casino advantage. The slight come-out advantage is offset by the fact that all of the other numbers besides the 7 can become the point. So, on a pass line bet you can now end up with a point of 2, 3, 11, or 12. This actually increases the pass line casino edge from 1.4 percent to 5.3 percent! One of the worst bets on the layout is now the pass line bet (5.3 percent casino edge), so this should be avoided at all costs. The standard 6 and 8 place bets are still there, just as in a regular craps game. A lot of people just play that and get along fine.

Plus, there are no don't come, don't pass, or lay bets, so a regular game offers more of an advantage to the player than does a crapless game. But, what if you *really* wanted to play crapless craps?

Sample Roll

After a seven rolls, just place both the 6 and 8 for $30 each, and when either one hits, take them both down and then wait for another 7 before betting again.

But there is a way to make some unique bets on this layout if you don't mind getting a little adventurous.

Outside Numbers

The outside numbers in this game are the craps numbers in the regular game—2, 3, 11, and 12. When you place the 2/12 you get 11:2 odds. When you place the 3/11 you get 11:4 odds. However, when you *buy* the same numbers (and pay a 5 percent vig), you get 6:1 on the 2/12, and 3:1 on the 3/11. Your job is to ask the friendly dealer to give you a better deal than the table advertises. You do this by pushing the house to decrease the vig charged.

If you buy the 2, 3, 11, or 12 for $20 (the minimum buy bet) you pay 5 percent, or $1. If you buy it for $40, you pay $2 vig. Ask the friendly dealer if you can buy the 2, 3, 11, or 12 for $36 and still only pay $1 vig. If the dealer says yes, ask if you can split up your bet and instead of betting $36 on one number, see if you can bet $9 each on all four numbers and still pay $1 vig for everything. If the answer is yes (you do tip the dealers, don't you?) then you've got a super deal and should stay with this dealer as long as possible.

With a $9 bet on the 2 and 12 you win $54 (at 6:1) and on the 3/11 you win $27. If your dealer is really, really friendly (look for a smiling dealer on a fairly empty table), you can make this bet and take everything down after one hit and then wait for another 7 before putting them all back up again.

If the dealer resists your offer, just come back later and try it with someone else, or bet the 6 and 8 method described previously. But you should try to push the house whenever possible! It's lots of fun to do—and very profitable!

Sic Bo

The term *Sic Bo* means "dice pair," even though this game is played with three dice. A lavishly lit Sic Bo table can be found in most casinos that have Asian Game rooms. There are many bets, all of which are explained on the colorful table. Each number from 4 to 17 is a point and after all the bets are made, the dealer "shakes" the dice container. No one in this game actually touches the dice themselves, and each game begins on a new shake after the bets are placed.

In Sic Bo you have fourteen point numbers (4 to 17). Besides betting on the three dice totals that form the points, you can also bet the following:

- Three of a kind—like 6, 6, 6 (must specify which number)
- Two of a kind—like 6, 6 (must specify numbers)
- Duo—two different numbers, like 4, 5 (must specify numbers)
- Any three—like 5, 5, 5 (will win on any three of a kind)
- Small—the sum is 10 or less (excludes any three of a kind)
- Big—the sum is 11 or more (excludes any three of a kind)
- One—any specified number that appears on 1, 2, or 3 dice

These seven basic bets plus the seventeen point numbers and more are all graphically illustrated on the beautifully lit Sic Bo table. When a decision is reached, the dealer lights up the winning combinations, removes the losing chips and pays the winners at the house odds. Unfortunately the house odds are not standardized and may be slightly different from casino to casino.

The two bets with the lowest casino advantage are the "big" bet and the "small" bet. These both provide a 2.7 percent house edge, which is the best you'll get in Sic Bo.

ALERT!

Many Sic Bo games are called in English, especially in larger casinos. But if the dealer speaks Chinese, just ask him to translate for you. Dealers (and most of the players) speak English and they would be more than happy to help you learn "their" dice game!

Also you must exchange your chips or money for Sic Bo chips, which are similar to roulette chips. The table minimums and maximums are posted. Most people play flat bet systems on the big and small numbers. Although the odds are better in craps, Sic Bo is a fun game to play—if you can find it.

Electronic Craps

There are a lot of new electronic craps games in casinos. These are espe-cially popular in places where real craps is illegal—like in some Indian casi-nos. Technically these games are slot machines, the casinos say, not illegal dice games. If you happen to find yourself staring at a craps slot machine, there may be ways to increase your chances of winning. The first thing you should do is look at the playing area. You will probably see no hardways, no don't come, and no don't pass. You also need to read the instructions on the side of the machine, as there are two basic machine types.

The first type of these "slot" machines is like a normal craps game— You win on the 7/11 come-out and lose if a 2, 3, or 12 is rolled. The second basic type is a "crapless" machine—You win only on the 7 come-out, there are no craps numbers, and any other number (2, 3, 4, 5, 6, 8, 9, 10, 11, or 12) becomes the point. This crapless craps is very bad for the player, as the casino edge is higher than the regular game. See the section on crapless craps at the beginning of this chapter for more details on this manner of playing.

In either case, find the chart depicting the payoffs for all the numbers. You may be surprised to find totally different odds than you are used to. In addition, the machine only pays off even dollars.

ALERT!

Look for electronic games with a card slot. Sometimes these are not labeled, but they will accept your player's card. Before you play, make sure that you have both a slot card and a table games card, just in case the machine takes one and not the other.

Sample Play

Let's say you normally bet $6 each on the 6 and 8, and for this bet you get 7:6 odds, or $7, when you win. You look at the chart and it says that 6 and 8 place bets pay 2.15 for 1. You may think this pays more than a regular craps bet. But 2.15 for 1 means 1.15 to 1, so if you bet $1 you get $1.15. Plus, you usually get paid in even dollars, so if the payoff is $1.50 or less, you get $1. If you bet $6 you will get $7 (rounded up from $6.90), but if you bet $3 you win $3 (rounded down from $3.45). This 1.15 to 1 casino odds turns out to be a 2.3 percent casino advantage, compared to a 1.5 percent one in normal craps. Make sure that you always bet the right amount so the machine rounds up your win instead of rounding it down.

One advantage to playing electronic craps lies in the minimum bet—it's usually only 25 cents. And most machines have a $25 maximum bet, so you can test your craps systems very inexpensively. For example, let's look at a simple double, as you would use in a Martingale-type system. In a normal seven-level $5 minimum game ($5, $10, $20, $40, $80, $160, $320) you can lose up to $635. But now you can test at the same seven levels (.25, .50, $1, $2, $4, $8, $16) and lose only a maximum of $31.75!

The other advantage to electronic craps is that the machines usually have a place for your comp card. Your comps are counted as slot credit, not table games. You can also use slot coupons and special slot promotions to play electronic craps.

Internet Craps

You can find anything on the Internet these days. There are a lot of craps games there, too, in over 1,000 different gambling sites. Depending on current laws, it may be illegal to gamble online, so you should find out before you try. If you search for "casino match play" in any search engine, you'll find plenty of online casinos with free money for you! Some may require an additional nonrefundable deposit, so be sure to read the fine print before you open an account.

If you're hundreds of miles from a casino and can only play craps on the Internet, there is a way to do it. Since there are literally thousands of online casinos, many use special promotions to entice you to play on their tables. Some will actually give you money in the form of match play credit. This means that if you deposit $50 or $100 into your online account, they will match it with $50 or $100 of their money. The only catch is that you must actually bet with this money and cannot cash out until all of it is wagered. This is really a terrific deal, and your job is to use up all this money in a successful manner and then move on to another online casino—and do it all over again.

What are the disadvantages of playing craps on the Internet?
Since there is a computer shooting the dice, you can not make any judgments about whether the shooter is a good one or a bad one. There can be no dice setting, table charting, or pushing the house.

There are many profitable systems in this book that you can use online. With the extra money the casino is giving you, you can try several and pick out your favorites. And when the free money or match play is gone, just move on to another site. Some Internet casinos offer special rewards, comps, or money back for frequent betters or high rollers. For some good online starting points, be sure to see the Internet part of the "Resources" section in the back of this book.

Finally, most online casinos have a "free play" option where you don't have to deposit any money to try them out. Give your favorite systems a try in these free casinos. When you see how easy it is, just deposit some money, get some match play, and watch your profits grow!

California Craps

California Craps is played similar to regular craps in that it uses the same layout, a pair of dice, and the same odds for payoffs. However, the dice in California Craps cannot be used directly to determine a number as there are laws to prevent "dice" games in certain states (like California). So, the dice are used to determine the value of playing cards used in the game, which are in turn used to determine numbers. This somehow makes it a "card game" instead of a "dice game." There are six different numbers on the cards, so you get a total of thirty-six combinations ($6 \times 6 = 36$). This is the same thing that would happen with the six faces of the dice, so the odds are the same.

When the shooter gets the dice and shoots, the dealers will notice the results, like, for example, 4 and 5. Then, everyone looks at the cards on the layout and at the fourth and fifth cards. Whatever value those cards signify is the value of the numbers used in the game. If, for example, the six cards are in the order 4, 5, 6, 1, 2, 3, then the numbers used would be 1 and 2, which is 3, or craps, so the pass line loses. The dealer calls out "three," not nine, so no point is established yet. The shooter shoots again (with the same card layout) and tosses a 1 and 5. Looking at the cards again, that is 4 and 2, so 6 becomes the point.

Sample Roll

The stickman pushes three or four pairs of dice to the shooter. The shooter picks up any two of the dice and tosses them to the far wall. His first roll is a 1 and 6, so you must look at the cards on the layout. Let's say they are in this order—6, 4, 5, 1, 2, 3. In California Craps, this would be $6(1) + 3(6) = 9$, so 9 becomes the point. Now, he must repeat the 9 in order to win. This means he must throw a 1 and 6 $(6 + 3 = 9)$, or a 2 and 3 $(4 + 5 = 9)$ to make his point.

ALERT!

Many dealers are not experienced and frown on deviation from what they are taught in dealer school. Some will not allow pushing the house, put bets, hop bets, or other out-of-the-ordinary bets. If you want to make even a slightly unusual bet, ask the dealer first to see if it will be allowed. If it's not, just go to another table and try again.

When you play, no one keeps track of the card order and how the numbers "translate." That is the job of the dealers, so after the roll, the dealers usually call out the translated number, not the number thrown by the shooter. So, for the shooters first roll of 1 and 6, the dealer will call out "nine." No one pays any attention to what the shooter tosses, and everyone waits for the dealer to call out the "real" number.

Klondike

Klondike used to be a real dice game, played with bankers, five dice, and, of course, the players. It was a combination of present-day baccarat and craps. Today, it has been converted into an electronic game similar to a slot machine (still called Klondike), and that is what we will look at now.

The electronic game Klondike is played with two plastic cups, each containing five dice. There are only three buttons on the machine for each player, labeled WIN, LOSE, and 2 ACES. You win your WIN bet if your total is higher than the machine's. You win your LOSE bet if your total is lower than the machine's. You win your 2 ACES bet if the machine throws at least two pair. The machine wins all ties.

To play, all the bettors make their wagers by depositing quarters and using the buttons in the side. After the betting is closed, the electronic banker throws the dice to establish the point number. Then each player tosses the five dice by pressing his or her individual roll buttons.

On the WIN and LOSE bets, the advantage is with the machine, with its win in ties. This comes out to be 5.2 percent. On the 2 ACES it is double that, at 11.1 percent.

This is a fun game to play, but the house advantage is always positive, and much worse than an electronic craps game. If you must play, stick to the WIN and LOSE bets only. And be sure to use your slots comp card—even if you just play for a few minutes, any comps are better than none!

Hazard

You might not ever see a Hazard game, but it was around before craps was. It is played with three dice and has myriad bets. The one big draw to this game is that it boasts several bets that pay off at the staggering odds of 180 to 1! In Hazard, you place your bet and the three dice are thrown. There is no real point to establish, as every time the dice are thrown, the point number is paid off. If, for example, you place your money on the 17 point and the 16 is thrown, you lose your bet. All of the bets in Hazard are one-roll bets that either win or lose.

You can recognize a Hazard layout because it has bets for raffles. Raffles are similar to hardways, but all three dice must be identical to win raffles. So you can bet $10 raffles 6 and if 2/2/2 show on the next roll, you will win 180 times your bet, or $1,800! There are six different raffles bets—3 (all 1s), 6 (all 2s), 9 (all 3s), 12 (all 4s), 15 (all 5s) and 18 (all 6s). All pay 180:1 and the true odds are 215:1, giving the house a very profitable 17 percent!

In the middle of the Hazard layout are four boxes labeled High, Low, Odd, and Even. These four bets pay 1:1, so if you bet $10 you win $10. The house edge here (almost 3 percent) is derived from the fact that you lose on any of these four bets if the shooter throws a raffle. If you bet high, you are betting on a total of 11 or more. Low means 10 or less. These four bets are the only bets you should make when you play Hazard.

The partner numbers (like the 6/8 in craps) are different here, because of the three dice being used. For example, the 4 and 17 both pay 60:1 (with a 16 percent house edge). The 10 and 11 are the most common numbers and pay only 6:1 (with a 13 percent house edge).

Even though the raffles bets are among the worst on the layout, they certainly are exciting to play—but leave them to the other players. Stick to the high/low and odd/even bets and you'll minimize your losses—until you can play craps again!

Chapter 22

Playing to Win: The Nontechnical Game

In this chapter we will look at important craps superstitions, how to "Imagineer" a craps game, and how to win more money using a "knowledge card." We'll also learn how to both chart and plan a table! Finally, we'll see just what it takes to become a really successful crapshooter!

Craps Superstitions

When dice are thrown off the table, do you think a 7 will show on the next roll? Do you think that when someone shoots for the very first time (a "virgin shooter"), you should bet on him because he will throw a long string of profitable numbers?

This is all based on superstition, not fact. But some dice superstitions are based on fact, and you should pay attention to them.

How often have you seen someone set the dice and roll numbers? How often have you seen a high roller have his female friend shoot for him and rake in the chips? And have you ever taken your bets down when the dice leave the table? Most craps players have.

There are some people who believe that the collective energy at a table can produce very positive results. For example, the high roller and his friend believe strongly that numbers will follow, and so do some of the other players—so numbers will somehow roll.

Unbelievable? Illogical? Well, maybe. But if it works, does it really matter how it works, especially if you make a lot of money from the shooter?

Let's say you are normally a don't bettor and the next shooter sets the dice meticulously and bets $50 on the pass line. He obviously thinks he knows something that no one else does, so it just might be time for you to switch to the do side and make a pass line bet with some place or come bets. The shooter will see your bets backing him up and somehow, very unscientifically, shoot more numbers. And, if he happens to throw the dice off the table and then calls his bets off, you would do well to follow him.

Many people consider it an honor and privilege to be a shooter and really do practice at it. Even if they see success in 1 or 2 percent more rolls than other shooters, that's enough to overcome the slim house edge.

You might normally be a don't bettor, but you should never bet against someone who carefully sets and throws the dice. Just follow his lead, and put your bets up like he does, and take them down like he does. You're probably not superstitious, but you should give him every advantage you can. Maybe he has a craps table at home and practices shooting. Maybe he's a psychic. Who cares, just as long as he shoots numbers.

When you see a shooter set the dice, back her up with a bet. Show her you have confidence in her shooting by following her actions. You'll see— the more people who bet along with the shooter, the better she'll do. Give it a try next time you play!

Imagineering Your Craps Game

Most people's imagination is stronger than their willpower. Before they play, it is easier to imagine themselves placing the proper hedge bets, or taking their bets down when they win. Sometimes, though, when the actual game starts, it is difficult to follow through. Some craps pros actually imagine the table to behave exactly the way they want. This is what is called "imagineering"—and you can imagineer yourself to greater profits if you use this tool in your craps play!

Mary used to have a lot of trouble with her win goal. Even when she was way ahead she would keep on playing, until everything was lost. When she decided to start imagineering, she imagined what would happen if a point rolled, a 7, a craps, or any other number—and what she would do in response. She would go over this many, many times in her mind, so when the event actually happened, she was totally prepared for it, and her mind made her do what she was supposed to do.

For example, if she bought in for $200, Mary gave herself a $60 win limit. This means that if she won $60 she would leave the table and go do something else for a while. So let's say she bet $12 on the 6 and $12 on the 8, and imagineered the results. If the 6 or 8 hit, she would see the dealer taking *both* bets down and not pressing the winning number.

Mary would actually imagine the 6 hitting and telling the dealer, "Both bets down, please." She did this many times until the shooter actually threw the dice, which was a 5. She went through the both bets down imagineering some more. Then, finally, when an 8 hit, her mind was conditioned enough to actually perform the deed.

"Both bets down," she would say.

The dealer looked surprised. "But Mary, don't you want to press the 8 like you normally do?"

"No, both bets down."

This was not easy for Mary to do. But remember her $60 win limit? She was expert at ignoring that. She'd get up to $100 and keep going. She used to keep on playing until she lost every cent she had.

Now, though, if Mary won $42 and she had another $12 bet on the 6 and 8 riding on the shooter, she would again imagineer the scene. The shooter throws a 6 (or 8), and the dealer pushes $14 in chips to her. She will say "both bets down" and then color out. She gives the dealer her chips, cashes out, and walks away from the table with a $56 profit.

Mary did not say any actual words out loud, but imagineered the whole scene happening over and over again, until it really did happen. Her mind was conditioned and ready, so she took down both bets, colored out, and walked away.

You can imagineer your way to profits, too! Just envision a plan for playing every time you gamble, and imagine that plan over and over in your mind until it eventually occurs. Your mind will be ready then to see it through. And when you actually do what you want to do, you'll have more self-confidence—and more profits!

Remember—just picture what the end result of your play will be. See it happening many, many times in your mind's eye. Then, when it really does happen, your mind will be conditioned enough to instruct your body. You'll be playing confidently, profitably, and joyfully—you'll be imagineering your way to success!

Planning a Table

One of the hardest things for a crapshooter to do is to leave the table. This is because he is really motivated to stay! If he's winning, he wants to stay and make more money. If he's losing, he wants to stay and recoup his losses.

This, unfortunately, ends up being a player's way of donating a lot of money back to the casino.

If you want to make money, you need to plan your table. You need to set things up in advance and stick to your plan. Craps is fun, but if you keep on losing every time you play, it won't be fun for long. You need to have a table plan every time you play. For example, if your buy-in is $1,000 and you are a $50 bettor, you can plan to leave when you've won or lost $200. However, if your buy in is $50 and you're a $5 bettor, a $200 goal is unrealistic—$10 is more like it. Further, you need to plan exactly what kind of betting you're about to do—even before you color in.

Something that has always helped crapshooters is to carry a small pad and pen at all times. Before approaching the table, you should formulate and actually write down what you're going to do. For example, before you actually go to the table, you might write down these three things:

- Buy-in—$500
- Win/loss limit—$100
- $10 pass line w/2× odds and place 6 and 8 for $12 each

Later, you should note the results so there are actually four things on the page:

- Placed money (your buy-in)
- Limits of your betting (win/loss goals)
- Assign yourself a system to use
- Noted results

To simplify things, you should write:

- P—$500 (placed money)
- L—$100 (limit win/loss)
- A—pass line w/odds + 6 and 8 (assigned system)
- N—+$30 in 40 minutes (noted results)

You should always leave the pad on your chip rack so it reminds you not to be greedy when you're winning. Give it a try the next time you play!

Charting a Table

When you play craps, the best method to avoid those financially destructive 7s is to use charting. But how can you chart the tables accurately and with a minimum of hassle? All you need is a small pad of paper and a pen to keep track of the rolls. There are two different ways to chart tables—mega- and supercharting.

Supercharting is maintaining a running total of 7s as compared to all the other numbers. Theoretically, 1/6 of all numbers rolled will be 7s.

Megacharting is keeping a running total of the inside numbers (5, 6, 8, and 9) and comparing this with all the other numbers. Theoretically, one half of all numbers rolled will be inside numbers. This means that in thirty-six sample rolls, eighteen of them will be the inside place numbers.

Megacharting really succeeds when guided by super charting. If a normal rate of 7s (1/6 ratio) exists, then the ratio of inside numbers (5, 6, 8, and 9) is the prevailing factor—if this is less than half, it's time to bet inside. However, when the inside number ratio is more than half, you should not be betting inside. And if the total of 7s is less than normal, you should be wagering don't pass or don't come.

In thirty-six sample rolls, eighteen of them should be inside place numbers, and only six of them should be 7s. If you count thirty-six rolls, and only twelve 5, 6, 8, or 9s appear, (with the normal amount of 7s), it's time to loosen your wallet! But if you see sixteen inside places, you should wait a while, make some other bets, or change tables.

And remember, this is dependent on the amount of 7s. Hopefully if you see 7 roll six or seven times (in thirty-six sample rolls), the above should hold true. But if fewer 7s appear, you might want to hold your bets back. And if there are more 7s, you might want to place larger place bets than you would normally.

FACT

By using charting you will be able to minimize your loss periods and maximize your win periods. Charting a table is extremely important to consistently make profits at the craps table. Write it on a napkin if you must, but chart your table the next time you play!

Winning with Knowledge

If you are a craps expert, you should know all the craps odds, and how much every bet pays off. You should know the difference between the place, buy, and come odds, all the prop and hardway odds, and exactly how much to place behind a pass line bet at a 2×, 5×, or 10× odds casino. If you know all this you really are an expert. But does all this knowledge you have guarantee that you will win most of the time you play? And if it doesn't, what can you do with this knowledge to increase your win percentages?

If your doctor tells you to eat only bland foods, but you continue to eat steak, you have the knowledge but lack the discipline to follow through on your plans. Likewise, if you know the field is a bad bet, but you have a hunch so you bet it anyway—you also have knowledge but no discipline.

When Sally had her first heart attack, her doctor told her to cut down on red meat and fried foods, but it was really hard for her to do, especially with all those great casino buffets! Plus she got a lot of those meals comped so, of course, she would rather eat a big juicy steak than a salad with no dressing. She had the knowledge but no discipline.

But Sally knew she would end up back at the doctor's if she didn't change her ways. So, Sally made a written and signed agreement with herself to eat only healthy foods. She kept a little card in her purse, and whenever she ate out, she took it out and read it. The card reminded her to actually apply the knowledge she had about eating so she would eat better and live longer. Then she got an idea. Why not make a little card for her own craps game? Her new card states that she will only make craps bets that have a vig of under 2 percent, and she will adhere to a 30 percent loss limit, and a 30 percent win limit. Sally signed it, laminated it, and whenever she plays craps she takes it out to reaffirm her written agreement with herself.

You should make a craps card for yourself, and before you make any bet you should have a look at the card. If the point is 6 and everyone else bets on the hard 6 because it is due, you should take out your card first, read it, and then not make the bet. No more hardways, field bets, prop bets, C & E bets, or even Yos (craps slang for 11s) on the come-out!

After you use it for a while, you'll see that your winning sessions have increased dramatically. It certainly is a simple method to ensure that your own personal craps knowledge is applied to what you are doing by re-enforcing your own discipline.

Your card could be different than someone else's, because everyone has different win/loss limits and other playing requirements. But once you come up with one, take it with you when you play, and stick to it! Why don't you make yourself a "knowledge card" right now, before you forget?

The Successful Crapshooter

The successful crapshooter is willing to do that which the unsuccessful crapshooter is not willing to do. The actual rolls of the dice, or whether the table is hot or cold, does not matter to the successful crapshooter. He knows how to adapt to conditions and is experienced enough to know how to switch his bets or take them down.

The successful crapshooter becomes profitable through her experiences and her learned knowledge. She has read dozen of books on craps, subscribes to gambling newsletters and magazines, and makes it her business to learn the latest systems and ideas when they pertain to her gambling. The successful crapshooter has wisdom and knows how to bet on any roll of the dice. She actually applies this wisdom to the game, and knows in advance exactly what she will win or lose with every throw of the dice.

The Successful Crapshooter is always evaluating his play and ensuring that the methods he uses are truly the most advantageous. He is a happy, excited, powerful player, and he receives his power from confidence. Confidence comes from a never-ending quest for knowledge, which is constantly adapting to the changing conditions of both the table and casino.

The successful crapshooter does not make bets that are unprofitable, but makes bets that give little, if any, advantage to the house. He knows how to chart the table and choose the best shooter. He is confident that his own shooting will produce a profit, as he practices at home. He plays at the one casino that gives him the best playing conditions and comps. And he knows the exact payoff of any number, be it place, come, lay or buy.

Becoming a consistently successful crapshooter is not easy. It takes years of study and learning the fine points of the game and the casino's policies. There is no one magic pill you can take or super book you can read that will make you a consistent winner. To be a successful crapshooter, you have to make a conscious decision to do everything you can to be a success, no matter how long it takes.

The successful crapshooter values the time she spends playing and studying to improve her game. She places a higher value on learning and progressing than on actual playing. In other words, she does what she really has to do—study—and she puts a high priority on it. She values learning enough to know that it will produce a consistent profit if that learning is properly applied.

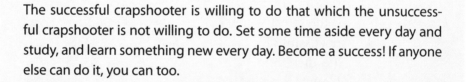

The successful crapshooter is willing to do that which the unsuccessful crapshooter is not willing to do. Set some time aside every day and study, and learn something new every day. Become a success! If anyone else can do it, you can too.

Congratulations! You've read through most of the book! You might want to go back and read some sections again, and maybe make some notes in the margins. Plus, you still have the appendixes and the resources section to look at. Finally, don't stop learning. Take some advanced craps classes. Read some more books. Subscribe to the *Crapshooter Newsletter.* Craps is a wonderful, fun game that not only makes you friends, but money as well!

Appendices

Appendix A

Glossary

Action
Money being wagered

Any craps
Single bet for the numbers 2, 3, or 12

Any 7
One-roll bet that the next roll is a 7

Back line
Another term for the don't pass area

Bankroll
Money set aside for this gambling session

Bet
A wager placed on a number

Betting limits
The minimum and maximum you can wager

Big red
Slang expression for the number 7

Big 6 and 8
Even money bets on the 6 and/or 8

Black chip
A gaming chip worth $100

Boat
The bowl the dice are kept in by the boxperson

Boxcars
Slang expression for the number 12

Boxperson
A seated casino employee who supervises the craps game

Buy bets
Paying commission to get true odds

Buy-in
When you start playing and buy chips

Cashier's cage
The area where players redeem chips

Casino rate
Special room rate for preferred players

C & E bet
Any craps number plus 1, one-time bet

Call bet
A verbal wager by experienced, known players

Chips
Tokens that are used instead of cash

Cold dice
Dice that rarely make the point

Color out
To exchange chips for money

Come bet
Your own personal point bet

Come-out roll
The first roll before a point has been established

Comps
Free room, food, and beverages for qualified gamblers

Craps
When the dice total 2, 3, or 12

Crossroader
Slang expression for a crook or cheater

Devil
Slang term for the 7

Die
Singular of dice

Dimes
Slang term for $10 in chips

Don't come bet
A separate bet against a point passing

Down
To take money off a bet

Drop box
Repository in the table where the dealers place money collected

Easy
A number not made with two identical numbers

Eighter from Decatur
Slang term for the number eight

Even money
A bet that pays off 1:1

Field bet
The numbers 2, 3, 4, 9, 10, 11, 12

Floorperson
Pit supervisor in charge of games

Free odds
Odds portion of bet that has
no house advantage

Fun book
Free coupon book available
at some cashier cages

George
Slang term for a player who is a good tipper

Green chip
A chip worth $25

Hardway
A number made with two identical numbers

Hedge bet
Wagering on both sides of a bet

High roller
A gambler who bets more than $100 per hand

Hop bet
An oral one-roll bet for a specific number

Horn bet
A one-roll bet on the 2, 3, 11, and 12

Hot dice
Dice that usually make the point

House edge
The amount the casino keeps from wagers

Inside bet
The numbers 5, 6, 8, and 9

Jimmy sticks
Slang term for the number 6

Juice
Slang term for vigorish

Junket
RFB (room, food, and board) plus
travel for experienced gamblers

Lay bet
A bet that the 7 will roll before
a specific number

Little Joe from Kokomo
Slang term for the number 4

Limits
Posted table maximum and minimum bets

Line bet
A wager usually on the pass line

Lumpy
Slang term for a brand-new dealer

Marker
An IOU check signed by a player

Natural
Rolling 7 or 11 on the come-out

Nickels
Slang term for $5 chips

Odds
Probability of a certain bet winning or losing

Off
An oral request to have bets not working

Off and on
Being paid for a bet while leaving the same bet up

Outside bet
The numbers 4, 5, 9, and 10

Parlay
When the entire win is added to the bet

Pass
A winner for the shooter

Pass the dice
Term used by someone who does not wish to shoot

Pips
The spots on the dice

Pit
Area in the casino where the table games are located

Pit boss
High-level casino employee in charge of games

Place bet
Any of the numbers 4, 5, 6, 8, 9, or 10

Point
The number 4, 5, 6, 8, 9, or 10 when rolled on the come-out

Press
To increase the bet

Progression
To increase your bets in an orderly fashion

Proposition bets
Center spread table bets

Push
A tie between the casino and bettor

Pushing the house
Getting better than advertised odds on a bet

Quarters
Slang term for $25 chips

RFB
Complimentary room, food, and beverages

Rack
Area on table for organizing your chips

Red
Slang term for $5 chips

Regression
To decrease your bets in an orderly fashion

Right bettor
Wagering with the shooter, against the 7

Set
A certain manner to arrange the dice

7-out
Pass line loses, wrong bettors win

Shill
A person secretly employed by the casino

Shooter
The player who rolls the dice

Snake eyes
Slang term for the number 2

Stickperson
The dealer in charge of the dice
and carrying the stick

Toke
A tip for the dealer

Two-way bet
One bet for yourself, and one for the dealer

Unit
A fixed betting amount, usually the initial bet

Vigorish
A commission paid to the house for certain bets

White
Slang for $1 chips

Working
To have bets "on" during the come-out

World Bet
Any craps bet plus 7

Wrong bettor
Bettor betting that shooter does
not make his or her point

Yo
Slang term for the number 11

Appendix B

Additional Resources

The Top Ten Craps Books

1. *Beat the Craps Out of the Casino,* by Frank Scoblete
   Learn all about the five count, the captain, and his crew.

2. *Advanced Craps,* by John Patrick
   Learn over fifty advanced systems and money management methods.

3. *Make Your Living Playing Craps,* by Larry Edell
   Comps, right/wrong, attitude, presetting, and systems.

4. *Pre-Setting the Dice,* by Zeke Feinberg
   Everything about presetting the dice.

5. *Tina Trapp's Guide to Craps,* by Tina Trapp
   A novel method of learning and winning at craps.

6. *Scarne on Dice,* by John Scarne
   Craps gimmicks, cheats, and some very interesting stories.

7. *Get the Edge at Craps,* by "Sharpshooter"
   How to get a measurable advantage in the game of craps.

8. *The Dice Doctor,* by Sam Grafstein
   How successful crapshooters make profitable plays.

9. *Cutting the Crap out of Craps,* by Zeke Feinberg
   How craps losers can transform themselves into craps winners.

10. *Craps: A Winning Strategy,* by David Medansky
    The Medansky Strategy and all of its permutations.

The Top Ten Gambling Books

1. *Casino Gambling,* by Jerry Patterson
   How to beat the odds by using player advantage systems.

2. *American Casino Guide,* by Steve Bourie
   How to save hundreds of dollars in hundreds of casinos.

3. *The Everything Casino Gambling Book,* by Meg Schneider
   Everything you need to know about gambling.

4. *Gambling's Greatest Secrets Revealed,* by Ben Berry
   Advanced systems for craps, roulette, and blackjack.

5. *The Best of the Best,* by Henry Tamburin
   How you can make the best bets in the best games.

6. *Scarne's New Complete Guide to Gambling,* by John Scarne
   Almost 900 pages of everything you need to know to win.

7. *Guerrilla Gambling,* by Frank Scoblete
   How you can beat the casinos at their own games!

8. *Smart Casino Gambling,* by Olaf Vancura
   A highly educational and entertaining tour of casino gaming.

9. *How to Win at Casino Gambling,* by Roger Gros
   Wonderful illustrations, plain language, easy to follow.

10. *How to Win at Gambling,* by Avery Cardoza
    An expert's look at all the casino games.

The Top Ten Craps Web Sites

1. *www.thecrapshooter.com*
   Free newsletters, craps games, advanced systems, book excerpts.

2. *http://www.casino.com/craps*
   Hundreds of free articles, "Ask the Pro," and system archives.

3. *http://goldentouchcraps.com*
   Precision shooting, dice control, and the Craps Club.

4. *www.sharpshootercraps.com*
   Home study courses for precision shooting and dice control.

5. *www.dicecoach.com*
   Personal craps training sessions in Las Vegas.

6. *http://casinocity.com*
   Includes over 500 articles on how to win at craps!

7. *http://casino.com*
   Popular portal includes craps, blackjack, and roulette.

8. *www.cgtv.com*
   Craps tournaments and news of the casino world.

9. *www.crapspit.org*
   General craps site with lots of good information.

10. *www.bj21.com*
    Stanford Wong's site on beatable casino games.

The Top Ten Craps Related Internet Newsgroups

1. *rec.gambling.craps*
   Analysis and strategies of craps games everywhere in the world.

2. *rec.gambling*
   Everything about gambling, many posts about many different games.

3. *rec.gambling.misc*
   Items not covered specifically in other groups.

4. *rec.gambling.craps.faq*
   The Craps Frequently Asked Questions Newsgroup.

5. *alt.gambling*
   General information about gambling.

6. *alt.las-vegas.gambling*
   Gambling information specific to Las Vegas casinos.

7. *alt.vacation.las-vegas*
   Information specific to vacationing in Las Vegas.

8. *rec.gambling.faq*
   The Frequently Asked Questions group about general gambling.

9. *rec.gambling.blackjack*
   There are a lot of blackjack players who also play craps.

10. *rec.gambling.roulette*
    There are a lot of roulette players who also play craps.

The Top Ten Craps-Related Publications

1. *The Crapshooter*   ✍*www.thecrapshooter.com*
   Quarterly newsletter exclusively devoted to craps.
   The Crapshooter, PO Box 421440, San Diego, CA 92142

2. *Casino Player*   ✍*www.casinoplayer.com*
   Bestselling monthly casino magazine.
   Casino Player, 5240 S. Eastern Ave., Las Vegas, NV 89119

3. *GamingToday*   ✍*www.gamingtoday.com*
   All the news you can bet on. Weekly newspaper.
   Gaming Today, PO Box 93116, Las Vegas, NV 89193

4. *Midwest Players*   ✍*www.mwplayers.com*
   Your guide to gaming in the Midwest.
   Midwest Players, PO Box 296, Big Lake, MN, 55309

5. *Las Vegas Advisor*   ✍*www.lasvegasadvisor.com*
   The best deals for the best prices in Las Vegas.
   Las Vegas Advisor, 3687 S. Procyon Ave., Las Vegas, NV 89103

6. *Las Vegas Insider*   ✍*www.lsvegasinsider.com*
   How to get rooms, shows, tours, dining, and more at discount prices.
   Las Vegas Insider, PO Box 1185, Chino Valley, AZ 86323

7. *Play Savvy Magazine*   ✍*www.playsavvy.com*
   All about craps, poker, blackjack, and sports betting.
   Play Savvy, PMB 205, 8917 Hypoluxo Road, Lake Worth, FL 33467

8. *Player*   ✍*www.cardozaplayer.com*
   Men's magazine with large gambling section.
   The Player, 857 Broadway, Third Floor, New York, NY 10003

9. *What's On*   ✍*www.ilovevegas.com*
   Las Vegas magazine with casino ads and gambling columns.
   What's On, 4425 Industrial Road, Las Vegas, NV 89103

10. *Gambling Online Magazine*   ✍*www.gamblingonlinemagazine.com*
    Magazine about Internet and electronic gambling.
    G.O.M., 1925 Vaughn Road, Kennesaw, GA 30144

The Top Ten Craps-Related Free Catalogs

1. Leaf Press
   Craps books, newsletters, videos, audios, and more—all at discount prices.
   1-877-244-1814

2. Gamblers Book Club
   The largest selection of gambling material in the world.
   1-800-522-1777

3. Gamblers General Store
   The largest gambling store in the world.
   1-800-322-2447

4. Golden Touch Craps
   Dice control class and Frank Scoblete's products.
   1-866-SET-DICE

5. Casino Gambling Edge
   Jerry Patterson's Advantage Gaming products.
   1-775-265-9224

6. Great Stuff for Gamblers
   Anthony Curtis's Las Vegas books and other products.
   1-702-252-0655

7. Cardoza Publishing
   Avery Cardoza's books, magazines, and software.
   1-212-255-6661

8. Blackjack 21 Store
   Books and other material from Stanford Wong.
   Send email to *orders@bj21.com*

9. ConJelCo
   Interesting gambling newsletter and catalog.
   Send email to *weinstock@conjelco.com*

10. Smart Gaming
    Books and other material from Henry Tamburin.
    Send email to *htamburin@aol.com*

The Top Ten Craps-Related Software Titles

1. WinCraps   *www.cloudcitysoftware.com*
   Auto-betting, customized sounds, highly configurable.

2. SimCraps   *www.simcraps.com*
   Terrific craps game, simulator, and tutorial.

3. Avery Cardoza's Casino   *www.Cardozapub.com*
   Interesting 3D casino and characters.

4. Jackpot Games   *www.encoresoftware.com*
   Craps and twenty-six more games, all customizable, all 3D.

5. Leisure Suit Larry's Casino   *www.sierraplanet.com*
   The funniest casino game you'll ever play!

6. Casino Master   *www.centronsoftware.com*
   Learn eleven games, taught by John Patrick.

7. Casino Games   *www.masque.com*
   Combination gambling CDs with lots of features.

8. Smart Craps   *www.deepnettech.com*
   Specific craps software for dice controllers.

9. Accidental Craps   *www.accidental.com*
   Cute animated craps game.

10. Six Different Craps Games   *www.doublegames.com*
    Erotic, Egyptian, Island, Prehistoric, Classic, and Japanese.

The Top Ten Craps-Related Movies

1. *Casino* (1995)
   Robert DeNiro, Sharon Stone, and Joe Pesci
   Offers real insight into the "old time" values of Las Vegas.

2. *Guys and Dolls* (1955)
   Frank Sinatra, Marlon Brando, and Jean Simmons
   A comedy/musical/romance—all about craps!

3. *The Cooler* (2003)
   William H. Macy and Jeff Bridges
   A professional "cooler" is someone who "cools down" hot tables.

4. *Oceans 11* (1960)
   Frank Sinatra, Dean Martin, Sammy Davis, Jr.
   Comedy/musical about robbing five Vegas casinos simultaneously!

5. *Viva Las Vegas* (1964)
   Elvis Presley, Ann Margaret
   Can a poor, lonely racecar driver/waiter win the gal of his dreams?

6. *Casino Royale* (1967)
   David Niven, Peter Sellers, Orson Welles, and Woody Allen
   Niven as Bond, with lots of guest stars, gags, and strange happenings.

7. *Showgirls* (1995)
   Elizabeth Berkley, Gina Gershon, and Kyle MacLachlan
   The trials and tribulations of a Las Vegas dancer.

8. *The Gambler* (1974)
   James Caan, Paul Sorvino, and Lauren Hutton
   An excellent portrait of a very compulsive gambler.

9. *Buck Privates* (1941)
   Bud Abbott and Lou Costello, with the Andrews Sisters
   Watch Abbott and Costello do their craps routine in the army.

10. *Atlantic City* (1980)
    Burt Lancaster, Susan Sarandon, and Kate Reid
    The story of the new Atlantic City, when gambling was legalized.

The Top Ten Craps-Related Instruction Videos and Audios

1. *Supercraps*
   Videotape by John Patrick
   The best advanced video course on craps.

2. *Craps, Blackjack, and Slots*
   DVD by Frank Scoblete, starring James Coburn
   This three-in-one set teaches the best of all three games.

3. *Craps—Rolling to Win*
   Videotape by Henry Tamburin
   Ninety minutes of winning tips and strategies.

4. *Sharpshooter Craps*
   Audiotape by Frank Scoblete
   How to use the five-count, control the dice, and more.

5. *Advanced Craps*
   Videotape by John Patrick
   Everything from Patrick's 41 no-10 to the famous Patrick System.

6. *Play to Win Combo*
   DVD by David Wilhite
   Get craps, blackjack, and slots on one DVD.

7. *Action Craps*
   Videotape by Dr. Richard McCall
   Use "Warrior Trader" craps to reduce the house edge!

8. *How to Get Comps at a Casino*
   Audio tape by Jean Scott
   How and when you should ask for comps.

9. *Power of Positive Playing*
   Audiotape by Frank Scoblete
   Learn the Players three-tier strategy, comps, myths, and lots more.

10. *Intermediate Craps*
    Videotape by Jimmy Scot Jordan
    Entertaining, accurate, and interesting craps instruction.

The Top Twelve Stick Calls of All Time

12. All the spots, all the dots!

11. Yo Field Yo Come, Both Gonna Get You Some!

10. Ten's the point in this gambling joint!

9. Who shot Jesse? A 45 I guessee!

8. Ozzie and Harriet (the square pair)

7. Front Line Winner, Back Line Skinner!

6. The Lumber Number (2×4)

5. Thirty Two Scadoo!

4. Baskin Robbins (3-1 Flavors)

3. Acey Deucy On The Loosey

2. You Got Aces in Both Places

(no roll) In the Sequoias, Can't Call it For Ya's!

Appendix C

Best and Worst Bets

The Ten Best Craps Bets

1. Taking over or buying player don't bets
   If someone calls off their don't come six or eight, ask if you can take it over.

2. The oddsman's bet
   If a bettor doesn't add maximum odds to a bet, ask if you can add your odds to it.

3. Don't pass with odds or don't come with odds
   Always make a minimum flat bet and add maximum table odds to it.

4. Pass with odds or Come with odds
   Always make a minimum flat bet and add maximum table odds to it.

5. Place the six and eight to win
   Place them both for $12 each and when either hits, take them both down.

6. Lay both the four and ten
   Lay $20 each and win $20 when the seven rolls.

7. Buy the Four and Ten
   Buy them both for $20 each and when either hits, take them both down.

8. Place the five and nine
   Place them both for $20 each and when either hits, take them both down.

9. Place $22 inside for one roll only
   This is $5 on the five and nine and, $6 on the six and eight, for one roll only.

10. The Field (if it pays triple on either the 2 or 12)
    If the field only pays double on the 2 or 12 then it becomes a bad bet.

The Ten Worst Craps Bets

1. Any seven
   The worst bet on the table—a 16.7 percent casino edge.

2. Two or twelve
   The second worst bet with a 14 percent edge.

3. Three or eleven
   People betting Yo (eleven) on the come out get a minus Yo (11) percent edge.

4. Any Craps
   Also has an 11 percent edge. Pass line bets are better off without it.

5. Hard 4 or Hard 10
   The true odds of either bet are 8:1, but you only get 7:1 so the casino
   gets to keep 11 percent if you win and 100 percent if you lose.

6. Hard 6 or Hard 8
   The true odds of either bet are 10:1, but you only get 9:1 so the casino
   gets to keep 9 percent if you win or 100 percent if you lose.

7. Big 6 or Big 8
   This is a flat (1:1) bet. Make a 6 or 8 place bet instead, you'll win more.

8. Place 4 or Place 10
   These are bets you pay 6.7 percent for, since the true
   odds are 2:1 but the casino only pays 9:5.

9. The field
   It's a bad bet, with about a 5 percent edge for the
   casino, assuming the 2 or 12 only pays 2×.

10. Placing the Five or Nine
    You lose 4 percent on this. You're better off betting them together.

Appendix D

Charts and Tables

TABLE 1 Odds Chart				
Number	**True Buy Odds**	**Place Pay Odds**	**Hardway True Odds**	**Hardway Pay Odds**
4	2:1	9:5	8:1	7:1
5	3:2	7:5	n/a	n/a
6	6:5	7:6	10:1	9:1
8	6:5	7:6	10:1	9:1
9	3:2	7:5	n/a	n/a
10	2:1	9:5	8:1	7:1

TABLE 2 House Edge Chart			
Number	**True Odds**	**Pay Odds**	**House Edge**
2	35:1	30:1	13.1
3	17:1	15:1	11.1
7	5:1	4:1	16.7
11	17:1	15:1	11.1
12	35:1	30:1	13.9
Any Craps	8:1	7:1	11.1

TABLE 3   Setting the Dice

Horizontal Numbers	Results
3 & 4 (both)	no 5 or 9
1 & 6 (both)	no 2 &3, no 11 & 12
2 & 5 (both)	no 3 & 11
3 & 4 + 2&5	(4) sevens, (4) sixes, (4) eights
1 & 6 + 2&5	(4) sevens, (6) sixes, (6) eights
1 & 6 + 3&4	(4) sevens, (4) sixes, (4) eights

TABLE 4   Odds Payoff Chart

Type	4	5	6	8	9	10
True Odds	2:1	3:2	6:5	6:5	3:2	2:1
Pass/Come	1:1	1:1	1:1	1:1	1:1	1:1
Don't Pass/Come	1:1	1:1	1:1	1:1	1:1	1:1
Pass/Come Odds	2:1	3:2	6:5	6:5	3:2	2:1
Don't Pass/Come Odds	1:2	2:3	5:6	5:6	2:3	1:2
Place Bets	9:5	7:5	7:6	7:6	7:5	9:5
Buy (minus vig)	2:1	3:2	6:5	6:5	3:2	2:1
Lay (minus vig)	1:2	2:3	5:6	5:6	2:3	1:2

TABLE 5 $30 Flat Bet Payoff Chart

Bet	4	5	6	8	9	10
Pass/Come Flat	30	30	30	30	30	30
Don't Bets Flat	30	30	30	30	30	30
Pass/Come Odds	60	45	36	36	45	60
Don't Bets Odds	15	20	25	25	20	15
Place Bets	54	42	35	35	42	54
Buy (minus vig)	60	45	36	36	45	60
Lay (minus vig)	15	20	25	25	20	15

TABLE 6   Casino Advantage on All Bets

Bet	Casino Advantage	Bet	Casino Advantage
Don't Pass with 2× odds	.459	Place Bet on Ten	6.67
Pass Line with 2× odds	.606	Big Six	9.09
Don't Pass with 1× odds	.691	Big Eight	9.09
Don't Come with 1× odds	.691	Hardway Six	9.09
Pass Line with 1× odds	.848	Hardway Eight	9.09
Come Bet with 1× odds	.848	Hardway Four	11.11
Don't Come with no odds	1.403	Hardway Ten	11.11
Don't Pass with no odds	1.403	Any Craps	11.11
Pass Line with no odds	1.414	Eleven (16 for 1)	11.11
Come Bet with no odds	1.414	Three (16 for 1)	11.11
Place Bet on Six	1.515	Two (31 for 1)	13.89
Place Bet on Eight	1.515	Twelve (31 for 1)	13.89
Field (2×-2, 3×-12)	2.78	Eleven (15 for 1)	16.67
Place Bet on Five	4.00	Three (15 for 1)	16.67
Place Bet on Nine	4.00	Two (30 for 1)	16.67
Field (2×-2, 2×-12)	5.56	Twelve (30 for 1)	16.67
Place Bet on Four	6.67	Any Seven (5 for 1)	16.67

TABLE 7 Pass Line Bets, Before the Come Out, With No Odds	
Point	Weighted Casino Advantage
4	1.414
5	1.414
6	1.414
8	1.414
9	1.414
10	1.414

TABLE 9 Pass Line Bets, At the Come Out, with 2X Odds	
Point	Weighted Casino Advantage
4	.606
5	.606
6	.606
8	.606
9	.606
10	.606

TABLE 8 Pass Line Bets, After the Come Out, with No Odds	
Point	Actual Casino Advantage
4	33.3
5	20.0
6	9.09
8	9.09
9	20.0
10	33.3

TABLE 10 Pass Line Bets, At the Come Out, with 2X Odds	
Point	Actual Casino Advantage
4	11.11
5	6.67
6	3.03
8	3.03
9	6.67
10	11.11

TABLE 11 Casino Wins on $5 Hardway Bets				
Bet	Payoff	True Odds	Casino Advantage	Casino Win ($)
Hard Four	7 to 1	8:1	11 percent	.56
Hard Ten	7 to 1	8:1	11 percent	.56
Hard Six	9 to 1	10:1	9 percent	.45
Hard Eight	9 to 1	10:1	9 percent	.45
Hard Four	7 for 1	8:1	22 percent	1.11
Hard Ten	7 for 1	8:1	22 percent	1.11
Hard Six	9 for 1	10:1	18 percent	.91
Hard Eight	9 for 1	10:1	18 percent	.91

TABLE 12	Right Bettors Casino Probability Table for 1980 Rolls	
Come-Out Rolls	**Winners**	**Losers**
Eleven	110	—
Seven	330	—
Two	—	55
Three	—	110
Twelve	—	55
Totals	**440 winners** +	**220 losers** = **660 rolls**
Four	55	110
Ten	55	110
Five	88	132
Nine	88	132
Six	125	150
Eight	125	150
Totals	**536 winners** +	**784 losers** = **1,320 rolls**

Total Wins = 440 + 536 = 976

Total Losses = 220 + 784 = 1004

Total Rolls = 660 + 1320 = 1980

Excess Losses = 1004-976 = 28

Casino Edge = 28/1980 = 1.414 percent for pass/come

TABLE 13   Wrong Bettors Casino Probability Table for 1980 Rolls

Come Out Rolls	Winners	Losers
Eleven	-	110
Seven	-	330
Two	55	-
Three	110	-
Twelve	(55)	(55)
Total	**165 winners** +	**440 losers + 55 pushes** = 660
Four	110	55
Ten	110	55
Five	132	88
Nine	132	88
Six	150	125
Eight	150	125
Total	**784 winners** +	**536 losers** = 1,320

Total losses = 440 + 536 = 976

Total wins = 165 + 784 = 949

Excess losses = 976 – 949 = 27

Total rolls = 1980 – 55 pushes = 1925

Casino Edge = 27/1925 = 1.402 percent for don't pass/come

	TABLE 14	Sample Casino Comp Criteria
Average Bet	**Hours per Day**	**Complimentaries Extended**
$25	4	Room Only
$50	4	Room Plus Limited Food/Beverage
$75	4	Full Room Food and Beverage
$100	4	Full RFB plus $150 airline reimbursement
$125	4	Full RFB plus $250 airline reimbursement
$150	4	Full RFB plus $400 airline reimbursement
$175	4	Full RFB plus $575 airline reimbursement
$200	4	Full RFB plus $750 airline reimbursement

Index

THE EVERYTHING SERIES!

BUSINESS & PERSONAL FINANCE

Everything® Budgeting Book
Everything® Business Planning Book
Everything® Coaching and Mentoring Book
Everything® Fundraising Book
Everything® Get Out of Debt Book
Everything® Grant Writing Book
Everything® Home-Based Business Book
Everything® Homebuying Book, 2nd Ed.
Everything® Homeselling Book, 2nd Ed.
Everything® Investing Book, 2nd Ed.
Everything® Landlording Book
Everything® Leadership Book
Everything® Managing People Book
Everything® Negotiating Book
Everything® Online Business Book
Everything® Personal Finance Book
Everything® Personal Finance in Your 20s
  and 30s Book
Everything® Project Management Book
Everything® Real Estate Investing Book
Everything® Robert's Rules Book, $7.95
Everything® Selling Book
Everything® Start Your Own Business Book
Everything® Wills & Estate Planning Book

COOKING

Everything® Barbecue Cookbook
Everything® Bartender's Book, $9.95
Everything® Chinese Cookbook
Everything® Cocktail Parties and Drinks
  Book
Everything® College Cookbook
Everything® Cookbook
Everything® Cooking for Two Cookbook
Everything® Diabetes Cookbook
Everything® Easy Gourmet Cookbook
Everything® Fondue Cookbook
Everything® Gluten-Free Cookbook

Everything® Grilling Cookbook
Everything® Healthy Meals in Minutes
  Cookbook
Everything® Holiday Cookbook
Everything® Indian Cookbook
Everything® Italian Cookbook
Everything® Low-Carb Cookbook
Everything® Low-Fat High-Flavor Cookbook
Everything® Low-Salt Cookbook
Everything® Meals for a Month Cookbook
Everything® Mediterranean Cookbook
Everything® Mexican Cookbook
Everything® One-Pot Cookbook
Everything® Pasta Cookbook
Everything® Quick Meals Cookbook
Everything® Slow Cooker Cookbook
Everything® Slow Cooking for a Crowd
  Cookbook
Everything® Soup Cookbook
Everything® Thai Cookbook
Everything® Vegetarian Cookbook
Everything® Wine Book, 2nd Ed.

CRAFT SERIES

Everything® Crafts—Baby Scrapbooking
Everything® Crafts—Bead Your Own Jewelry
Everything® Crafts—Create Your Own
  Greeting Cards
Everything® Crafts—Easy Projects
Everything® Crafts—Polymer Clay for
  Beginners
Everything® Crafts—Rubber Stamping
  Made Easy
Everything® Crafts—Wedding Decorations
  and Keepsakes

HEALTH

Everything® Alzheimer's Book
Everything® Diabetes Book
Everything® Health Guide to Controlling
  Anxiety

Everything® Hypnosis Book
Everything® Low Cholesterol Book
Everything® Massage Book
Everything® Menopause Book
Everything® Nutrition Book
Everything® Reflexology Book
Everything® Stress Management Book

HISTORY

Everything® American Government Book
Everything® American History Book
Everything® Civil War Book
Everything® Irish History & Heritage Book
Everything® Middle East Book

HOBBIES & GAMES

Everything® Blackjack Strategy Book
Everything® Brain Strain Book, $9.95
Everything® Bridge Book
Everything® Candlemaking Book
Everything® Card Games Book
Everything® Card Tricks Book, $9.95
Everything® Cartooning Book
Everything® Casino Gambling Book, 2nd Ed.
Everything® Chess Basics Book
Everything® Craps Strategy Book
Everything® Crossword and Puzzle Book
Everything® Crossword Challenge Book
Everything® Cryptograms Book, $9.95
Everything® Digital Photography Book
Everything® Drawing Book
Everything® Easy Crosswords Book
Everything® Family Tree Book, 2nd Ed.
Everything® Games Book, 2nd Ed.
Everything® Knitting Book
Everything® Knots Book
Everything® Photography Book
Everything® Poker Strategy Book
Everything® Pool & Billiards Book
Everything® Quilting Book
Everything® Scrapbooking Book

All Everything® books are priced at $12.95 or $14.95, unless otherwise stated. Prices subject to change without notice.

Everything® Sewing Book
Everything® Test Your IQ Book, $9.95
Everything® Travel Crosswords Book, $9.95
Everything® Woodworking Book
Everything® Word Games Challenge Book
Everything® Word Search Book

HOME IMPROVEMENT

Everything® Feng Shui Book
Everything® Feng Shui Decluttering Book,
  $9.95
Everything® Fix-It Book
Everything® Homebuilding Book
Everything® Lawn Care Book
Everything® Organize Your Home Book

EVERYTHING® *KIDS' BOOKS*

All titles are $6.95
Everything® Kids' Animal Puzzle & Activity
  Book
Everything® Kids' Baseball Book, 3rd Ed.
Everything® Kids' Bible Trivia Book
Everything® Kids' Bugs Book
Everything® Kids' Christmas Puzzle
  & Activity Book
Everything® Kids' Cookbook
Everything® Kids' Crazy Puzzles Book
Everything® Kids' Dinosaurs Book
Everything® Kids' Gross Jokes Book
Everything® Kids' Gross Puzzle and
  Activity Book
Everything® Kids' Halloween Puzzle
  & Activity Book
Everything® Kids' Hidden Pictures Book
Everything® Kids' Joke Book
Everything® Kids' Knock Knock Book
Everything® Kids' Math Puzzles Book
Everything® Kids' Mazes Book
Everything® Kids' Money Book
Everything® Kids' Nature Book
Everything® Kids' Puzzle Book
Everything® Kids' Riddles & Brain Teasers Book
Everything® Kids' Science Experiments Book
Everything® Kids' Sharks Book
Everything® Kids' Soccer Book
Everything® Kids' Travel Activity Book

KIDS' STORY BOOKS

Everything® Fairy Tales Book

LANGUAGE

Everything® Conversational Japanese Book
  (with CD), $19.95
Everything® French Phrase Book, $9.95
Everything® French Verb Book, $9.95
Everything® Inglés Book
Everything® Learning French Book
Everything® Learning German Book
Everything® Learning Italian Book
Everything® Learning Latin Book
Everything® Learning Spanish Book
Everything® Sign Language Book
Everything® Spanish Grammar Book
Everything® Spanish Practice Book
  (with CD), $19.95
Everything® Spanish Phrase Book, $9.95
Everything® Spanish Verb Book, $9.95

MUSIC

Everything® Drums Book (with CD), $19.95
Everything® Guitar Book
Everything® Home Recording Book
Everything® Playing Piano and Keyboards
  Book
Everything® Reading Music Book (with CD),
  $19.95
Everything® Rock & Blues Guitar Book
  (with CD), $19.95
Everything® Songwriting Book

NEW AGE

Everything® Astrology Book, 2nd Ed.
Everything® Dreams Book, 2nd Ed.
Everything® Ghost Book
Everything® Love Signs Book, $9.95
Everything® Numerology Book
Everything® Paganism Book
Everything® Palmistry Book
Everything® Psychic Book
Everything® Reiki Book
Everything® Tarot Book
Everything® Wicca and Witchcraft Book

PARENTING

Everything® Baby Names Book
Everything® Baby Shower Book
Everything® Baby's First Food Book
Everything® Baby's First Year Book
Everything® Birthing Book
Everything® Breastfeeding Book
Everything® Father-to-Be Book
Everything® Father's First Year Book
Everything® Get Ready for Baby Book
Everything® Get Your Baby to Sleep Book,
  $9.95
Everything® Getting Pregnant Book
Everything® Homeschooling Book
Everything® Mother's First Year Book
Everything® Parent's Guide to Children
  and Divorce
Everything® Parent's Guide to Children
  with ADD/ADHD
Everything® Parent's Guide to Children
  with Asperger's Syndrome
Everything® Parent's Guide to Children
  with Autism
Everything® Parent's Guide to Children with
  Bipolar Disorder
Everything® Parent's Guide to Children
  with Dyslexia
Everything® Parent's Guide to Positive
  Discipline
Everything® Parent's Guide to Raising a
  Successful Child
Everything® Parent's Guide to Tantrums
Everything® Parent's Guide to the Overweight
  Child
Everything® Parent's Guide to the Strong-
  Willed Child
Everything® Parenting a Teenager Book
Everything® Potty Training Book, $9.95
Everything® Pregnancy Book, 2nd Ed.
Everything® Pregnancy Fitness Book
Everything® Pregnancy Nutrition Book
Everything® Pregnancy Organizer, $15.00
Everything® Toddler Book
Everything® Tween Book
Everything® Twins, Triplets, and More Book

All Everything® books are priced at $12.95 or $14.95, unless otherwise stated. Prices subject to change without notice.

PETS

Everything® Cat Book
Everything® Dachshund Book
Everything® Dog Book
Everything® Dog Health Book
Everything® Dog Training and Tricks Book
Everything® German Shepherd Book
Everything® Golden Retriever Book
Everything® Horse Book
Everything® Horseback Riding Book
Everything® Labrador Retriever Book
Everything® Poodle Book
Everything® Pug Book
Everything® Puppy Book
Everything® Rottweiler Book
Everything® Small Dogs Book
Everything® Tropical Fish Book
Everything® Yorkshire Terrier Book

REFERENCE

Everything® Car Care Book
Everything® Classical Mythology Book
Everything® Computer Book
Everything® Divorce Book
Everything® Einstein Book
Everything® Etiquette Book, 2nd Ed.
Everything® Inventions and Patents Book
Everything® Mafia Book
Everything® Philosophy Book
Everything® Psychology Book
Everything® Shakespeare Book

RELIGION

Everything® Angels Book
Everything® Bible Book
Everything® Buddhism Book
Everything® Catholicism Book
Everything® Christianity Book
Everything® Jewish History & Heritage Book
Everything® Judaism Book
Everything® Koran Book
Everything® Prayer Book
Everything® Saints Book

Everything® Torah Book
Everything® Understanding Islam Book
Everything® World's Religions Book
Everything® Zen Book

SCHOOL & CAREERS

Everything® Alternative Careers Book
Everything® College Survival Book, 2nd Ed.
Everything® Cover Letter Book, 2nd Ed.
Everything® Get-a-Job Book
Everything® Guide to Starting and Running
    a Restaurant
Everything® Job Interview Book
Everything® New Teacher Book
Everything® Online Job Search Book
Everything® Paying for College Book
Everything® Practice Interview Book
Everything® Resume Book, 2nd Ed.
Everything® Study Book

SELF-HELP

Everything® Dating Book, 2nd Ed.
Everything® Great Sex Book
Everything® Kama Sutra Book
Everything® Self-Esteem Book

SPORTS & FITNESS

Everything® Fishing Book
Everything® Golf Instruction Book
Everything® Pilates Book
Everything® Running Book
Everything® Total Fitness Book
Everything® Weight Training Book
Everything® Yoga Book

TRAVEL

Everything® Family Guide to Hawaii
Everything® Family Guide to Las Vegas,
    2nd Ed.
Everything® Family Guide to New York City,
    2nd Ed.
Everything® Family Guide to RV Travel &
    Campgrounds

Everything® Family Guide to the Walt Disney
    World Resort®, Universal Studios®,
    and Greater Orlando, 4th Ed.
Everything® Family Guide to Cruise Vacations
Everything® Family Guide to the Caribbean
Everything® Family Guide to Washington
    D.C., 2nd Ed.
Everything® Guide to New England
Everything® Travel Guide to the Disneyland
    Resort®, California Adventure®,
    Universal Studios®, and the
    Anaheim Area

WEDDINGS

Everything® Bachelorette Party Book, $9.95
Everything® Bridesmaid Book, $9.95
Everything® Elopement Book, $9.95
Everything® Father of the Bride Book, $9.95
Everything® Groom Book, $9.95
Everything® Mother of the Bride Book, $9.95
Everything® Outdoor Wedding Book
Everything® Wedding Book, 3rd Ed.
Everything® Wedding Checklist, $9.95
Everything® Wedding Etiquette Book, $9.95
Everything® Wedding Organizer, $15.00
Everything® Wedding Shower Book, $9.95
Everything® Wedding Vows Book, $9.95
Everything® Weddings on a Budget Book,
    $9.95

WRITING

Everything® Creative Writing Book
Everything® Get Published Book
Everything® Grammar and Style Book
Everything® Guide to Writing a Book Proposal
Everything® Guide to Writing a Novel
Everything® Guide to Writing Children's Books
Everything® Guide to Writing Research Papers
Everything® Screenwriting Book
Everything® Writing Poetry Book
Everything® Writing Well Book